SUSTAINABLE COMMUNITY DEVELOPMENT SERIES

VISION and LEADERSHIP
in Sustainable Development

Chris Maser

Lewis Publishers

Boca Raton   Boston   London   New York   Washington, D.C.

Library of Congress Cataloging-in-Publication Data

Catalog information may be obtained from the Library of Congress.

This book contains information obtained from authentic and highly regarded sources. Reprinted material is quoted with permission, and sources are indicated. A wide variety of references are listed. Reasonable efforts have been made to publish reliable data and information, but the author and the publisher cannot assume responsibility for the validity of all materials or for the consequences of their use.

Neither this book nor any part may be reproduced or transmitted in any form or by any means, electronic or mechanical, including photocopying, microfilming, and recording, or by any information storage and retrieval system, without prior permission in writing from the publisher.

The consent of CRC Press LLC does not extend to copying for general distribution, for promotion, for creating new works, or for resale. Specific permission must be obtained in writing from CRC Press LLC for such copying.

Direct all inquiries to CRC Press LLC, 2000 Corporate Blvd., N.W., Boca Raton, Florida 33431.

Trademark Notice: Product or corporate names may be trademarks or registered trademarks, and are used only for identification and explanation, without intent to infringe.

© 1999 by CRC Press LLC
Lewis Publishers is an imprint of CRC Press LLC

No claim to original U.S. Government works
International Standard Book Number 1-57444-188-4
Printed in the United States of America 1 2 3 4 5 6 7 8 9 0
Printed on acid-free paper

SUSTAINABLE COMMUNITY DEVELOPMENT SERIES

Chris Maser, Editor

We are on the watershed between a dying civilization based on individualism, once arrogant, now abject, and a collective civilization yet to be formed in which the free development of each will be the condition for the free development of all. We are thus in the passage from an epoch of individual despairs to one of a shared hope in an ever richer material and spiritual life.

Thomas Merton

To the memory of Diana, Princess of Wales, who exemplified for me the essential qualities of a compassionate, courageous, and authentic person—all qualities of true leadership. As a very young woman thrust on the global stage at 19, her personal vulnerability and frailty as a human being was sorely tested. As she matured into psychological adulthood, her immense inner struggles to conquer herself were in no small way shared with the world, which simultaneously loved and despised her, applauded and crucified her.

Through it all, Princess Diana remained accessible and dared to live her truth even in the face of tremendous pressures for mindless conformity from those who represent a consciously aloof, privileged, and waning era. In so doing, she touched people in every walk of life and every social station therein. She showed us all that true leadership begins with personal authenticity and the courage to live one's truth and grow within it. It is my fervent hope that those who accept the helm of society, whether locally, nationally, or internationally, can find within themselves the foresight, courage, truth, and selflessness to follow her lead.

TABLE OF CONTENTS

EDITOR'S NOTE

The book you are holding is part of a series on the various aspects of sustainable community development, where "community" focuses on the primacy and quality of relationships among people sharing a particular place and between people and their environment. "Development" means personal and social transformation to a higher level of consciousness and a greater responsibility to be one another's keepers, and "sustainability" is the act whereby one generation saves options by passing them to the next generation, which saves options by passing them to the next, and so on.

This series came about because, during the 25 years I was in scientific research, I discovered disturbing patterns of human thought and behavior that continually squelch sustainable community development. They are as follows:

1. While physicists have found a greater voice for the spiritual underpinnings of physics, the biological sciences have all but lost their spiritual foundation, casting us adrift on a sea of arrogance and increasing spiritual, emotional, and intellectual isolation.
2. There is a continuing attempt to force specialization into ever-narrowing mental boxes, thereby so fragmenting our view of the world that we are continually disarticulating the very processes that produce and maintain the viability of the ecosystems on which we, as individuals and societies, depend for survival.
3. People point outside themselves to the cause of environmental problems without understanding that all such problems arise within ourselves, with our thinking. Before we can heal the environment, we must learn to heal ourselves emotionally and spiritually.

4. We are asking science to answer questions concerning social values, which science is not designed to do. Social questions require social answers.
5. One who has the courage to ask questions outside the accepted norm of scientific inquiry is ostracized because, as English philosopher John Locke said, "New opinions are always suspected, and usually opposed, without any other reason...[than] they are not already common."

This series of books on the various facets of sustainable community development is thus a forum in which those who dare to seek harmony and wholeness can struggle to integrate disciplines and balance the material world with the spiritual, the scientific with the social, and in so doing expose their vulnerabilities, human frailties, and hope, as well as their visions for a sustainable future.

The first four books in this series, of which the present book is the fourth, form the hub of sustainable community development and of necessity have various amounts of overlap because sustainable community development is a subject without discrete boundaries. But now, with the hub complete, future books in this series will be like the spokes of a wheel and bring new ideas into the hub to strengthen it, but with little or no overlap.

Chris Maser
Series Editor

FOREWORD

I tend to be a linear thinker, as do many engineers. When I have been involved with systems behavior, and the parts of the system interact as they always do, the conclusions reached are often too vague to implement. Since I'm always trying to solve problems and I am driven to find a solution, I tend to revert to the linear approach. Show me a mountain, and I'll move it, but don't make me worry too much about anything more than that.

It is people like me Chris Maser is trying to reach with this book. And there are many of us. We focus on the here and now and the immediate future. But we also frequently wonder, in our quiet moments, where all the things we do are leading us and whether we should choose a more sensible course if we are to act truly responsibly. Lily Tomlin once said, "The trouble with the rat race is that even if you win, you're still a rat." Her observation gives us cause to think about our actions and the impacts they may have in the future. Chris would have us act on those thoughts.

In his many years as a research scientist, Chris has personally witnessed the extensive alteration and degradation of our natural environment through the effects of shortsighted human activity. His experiences in forest, shrub steppe, subarctic, desert, coastal, agricultural, and urban settings have caused him to think deeply about human behavior in relationship to the environment and what this relationship means to future generations.

Currently an author, lecturer, and consultant who facilitates the resolution of environmental disputes and issues surrounding sustainable community development, Chris has focused his observations on the local community, urging us to consciously assume responsibility for that which we can control. He urges us to act at the local level, understanding that widespread individual attention to sustainability can and will improve the quality of life now and enhance what seems to be an increasingly uncertain future for our children and grandchildren. This is important because Chris has concluded over the years that humankind can only avert an increasingly miserable existence and the ultimate demise of society as we know it, and perhaps even the demise of humanity itself, by adhering to a recipe for sustainability that he calls *The Prime Directive.*

With *The Prime Directive* in mind, we learn Maser's approach to the process of creating a shared vision within a community and the essentials of leadership necessary to help ensure the vision is meaningful to a sustainable future. He gives the reader tools that can be used to bring others of diverse backgrounds along the path toward a shared vision based on the notions contained in *The Prime Directive,* which he tells us up front, based on his research and experience, is the only way he believes we can "fix" the world if we really seek sustainability. And he then gives us tools to help us find solutions to the problems while simultaneously inspiring others to join us.

One of the powerful tools Maser provides for use in the visioning process involves rephrasing negatives into positives. I've tried it, and it works. He urges us to concentrate on what we want to happen, not on what we want to prevent from happening.

In my own experience with visioning exercises, they often lead to a statement of vision but no plan to implement the vision. In addition, the time frame for a vision's fruition is often our life span or less. But if we are to have a good vision of real social/environmental sustainability, we need to understand that we may not experience the benefits of the vision we create. We are but a blip in geologic time, yet we need to create a vision that recognizes our own inability to see the future clearly. It is a sobering thought that we are required to take actions that may never benefit us materially as individuals.

Because cultures, like species, evolve, creating a vision with the intent to consciously and rapidly change a culture can be inherently fruitless. People resist change, even if they understand that it may be good in the long term, in order to pursue temporal pleasures. Even if we are willing to change, often the best we can do is speed up the rate of cultural evolution. A fundamental problem is that by simply existing, we change the rate of evolution exponentially as our human population expands geometrically. There are too many of us now, and we are inherently selfish.

This self-centeredness makes planning a better future, in which we will not personally benefit, difficult in the best of times, even for the sake of our children and grandchildren, and in the bad times, our fear of personal material loss makes such planning seem all but impossible. Nevertheless, Maser asks us to face these issues head on.

For a vision to have any real value, it must be implemented, which requires monitoring to evaluate the behavioral changes that result from implementing the vision. When one observes (monitors) and plans to make adjustments based on those observations (target corrections), the best solutions always provide several preplanned actions (i.e., if A happens, I will do B; and if C happens, I will do D; and so on). Otherwise, we monitor only outcomes and hope that, if they are not desirable, a solution or corrective action can and will be available.

An example might be the assumption that placing fish ladders in dams would sustain salmon migrations and hence perpetuate migrant populations. Over time, however, it has been learned that the reservoirs created by the dams (in addition to a host of other human activities) also impact the survival of salmon. Monitoring a single variable, such as counting salmon, has done nothing to clarify the issue or save the fish, which was the objective of the ladders. And a straightforward solution to the problem of saving the salmon is not now available, which points out that things are much more complex than we are usually able to foresee. Therefore, as Maser discusses, good implementation of a shared vision always incorporates monitoring and ways of responding to uncertain results, which in turn requires leadership.

The best leaders, I believe, not only lead unintentionally, even instinctively, but also inspire others. Merely good leaders can be effective, but they must understand that being successful takes concentrated effort and training. Leaders can be taught, and Maser provides us some valuable lessons in leadership within the context of developing and implementing a shared vision for a community's sustainable future.

The thoughtful reader of this book will likely conclude that the lifestyle to which we are accustomed needs to change and yet be uncertain how one's personal actions as an individual can alter our course for the future. Although we may not agree with all of Maser's *Prime Directive*, we cannot help but agree with much of it. Having said that, I believe readers will find that understanding both Maser's approach to visioning and the elements of leadership he identifies are essential to sustainable community development as we approach the 21st century.

Lee Schroeder
Vice President for Finance and Administration
Oregon State University, Corvallis, Oregon

PREFACE

The clearsighted do not rule the world,
but they sustain and console it.

Agnes Repplier
American essayist

Swiss psychiatrist Carl Jung was once asked if there was any hope for society. "Yes," he said, "if enough people do their inner work." What did he mean by "inner work"?

He meant consciously accepting the personal responsibility of healing the emotional wounds we receive from our parents, peers, teachers, and society at large as we travel the road to psychological adulthood, which translates into consciously, purposefully growing into a *psychologically mature* adult. This most arduous lifelong task requires the utmost courage, because once a person assumes the responsibilities of psychological maturity, the world seems to become a continuous test of one's mettle and willingness to grow. "But what," you might ask, "does this have to do with vision and leadership?"

As the peoples of Planet Earth are being drawn ever-closer together, they become more and more dependent on one another. Settlements worldwide (from hamlets, to villages, to towns, to cities, to megalopoli) are home to increasingly diverse populations.

The growing interdependence and the intensifying personal interactions among these diverse peoples pose fundamental challenges to old ways of thinking and acting, both within and between cultures. How we, as individuals and communities, respond to these challenges will, to a large degree, determine whether our communities become nurturing, cohesive, progressive, and sustainable or inhospitable, divided, and nonsustainable.*

I have, on the one hand, worked with vision statements, goals, and objectives for many years. My approach to helping people formulate collective visions has been through the medium of resolving environmental conflicts, where a statement of vision and its attendant goals are committed to paper as the culmination of the process of conflict resolution. In this sense, the frequent chaos of resolving a conflict is actually a prelude to creativity in which people are willing to craft a shared vision toward which to build as an alternative to the excruciating pain of conflict. In addition, they are willing to implement the vision as a means of avoiding further pain—but only as a last resort.**

On the other hand, I have taken part in so-called community visioning processes, in which it was patently clear that the people conducting the process knew nothing about a vision or how to create one. Under such circumstances, while collective "visions," in the loose sense of the term, have been forthcoming, animated by the people's desire for self-determination, they have not been implemented. The question is why the visions have not been implemented. Was it because there was no pain to avoid and hence no strong impetus to change? Was it because people really didn't care about their future (or that of their children and their grandchildren) as long as they knew how to muddle through in the present?

If there was no compelling reason to craft a shared vision in the first place, why did communities go to the trouble and expense to do so, only to abandon the process in the implementation stage? Was it a lack of true leadership, or was it the new set of uncomfortable social constraints for which the citizenry would hold city employees accountable if the vision were to be achieved? Of political discomfort, writer Glenda Holste says, "Today's radicalism is tomorrow's cursed gradualism."

In the years I have dealt with government, from that of a local community to the state and federal levels, my experience has been largely one of concerted resistance to change, even in the face of a progressive and undeniable decline in our quality of human life, which raises a curious condition of human idealism, aptly expressed by John

---

* The foregoing two paragraphs reflect a statement made by the Bahá'í International Community to the United Nations Conference on Human Settlements (Habitat II) June 3 to 14, 1996, Istanbul, Turkey.
** Chris Maser. 1996. *Resolving Environmental Conflict: Towards Sustainable Community Development.* St. Lucie Press, Boca Raton, Florida.

Galsworthy: "Idealism increases in direct proportion to one's distance from the problem."

A community, state, or nation is only as good as the home life of its people. In essence, our government is too big for the small, local, community-based problems of life and too small in bipartisan spirit for the big problems. Local communities must therefore begin accepting responsibility for their own care and their own future, which means they must always make full use of a good mistake, which brings us to the notion of leadership.

It has been my experience that the vast majority of people cannot lead because they do not know what the inner qualities of leadership are, let alone how to create and implement a viable shared vision for the sustainable future of a community, which demands the utmost skill in leadership. For this reason, the present book, *Vision and Leadership in Sustainable Development,* is not intended as a "how-to" book because there already exists a plethora of intellectual/mechanical models, especially for creating a shared vision and goals. Instead, this book is intended to probe the seldom-articulated philosophical underpinnings— the heart, if you will—of these models and examine the qualities of leadership it takes to implement them.

Finally, *Vision and Leadership in Sustainable Development* (which is divided into two parts, a shared vision and leadership) is built on and is an outgrowth of three other books in the Sustainable Community Development Series.* As such, there is of necessity some overlap for which I find no good alternative because the nature of sustainability in general and sustainable community development in particular is at once so dynamic and diffuse that abrupt edges of demarcation are nonexistent. I have, however, done my best to keep the overlap to a minimum while developing the interdependent role of vision and leadership in sustainable community development as the central theme of this book. If you have read one of the other books in the series in which vision was discussed, I thank you for your understanding and patience as I develop the subject in this book to what I think is its logical conclusion.

---

* Chris Maser. 1996. *Resolving Environmental Conflict: Towards Sustainable Community Development.* St. Lucie Press, Boca Raton, Florida; Chris Maser. 1997. *Sustainable Community Development: Principles and Concepts.* St. Lucie Press, Boca Raton, Florida; Chris Maser, Russ Beaton, and Kevin Smith. 1998. *Setting the Stage for Sustainability: A Citizen's Handbook.* Lewis Publishers, Boca Raton, Florida.

ACKNOWLEDGMENTS

As with every book I write, the reviewers who give graciously of their time and talents make the book better than I can as author. This book is no exception. Joyce Pytkowicz (a member of the Center for the Study of the First Americans at Oregon State University in Corvallis) and Lee Schroeder (Vice President for Finance and Administration at Oregon State University in Corvallis) both read and materially improved the entire manuscript. In addition, Lee Schroeder kindly agreed to write the foreword. My editor and friend, Sandy Pearlman, has once again nudged my work toward the excellence that I alone cannot achieve. I am deeply grateful for their courtesy and help.

And once again, I am profoundly indebted to my wife, Zane, for her patience while I worked on this book and for her ever-wonderful job of proofreading the final pages.

AUTHOR

C hris Maser spent over 25 years as a research scientist in natural
history and ecology in forest, shrub steppe, subarctic, desert,
and coastal settings. Trained primarily as a vertebrate zoologist,
he was a research mammalogist in Nubia, Egypt (1963–64) with the
Yale University Peabody Museum Prehistoric Expedition and a research mammalogist in Nepal (1966–67) for the U.S. Naval Medical
Research Unit #3 based in Cairo, Egypt, where he participated in a
study of tick-borne diseases. He conducted a three-year (1970–73)
ecological survey of the Oregon coast for the University of Puget
Sound, Tacoma, Washington. He was a research ecologist with the U.S.
Department of the Interior, Bureau of Land Management, for 12 years
(1975–87), the last 8 studying old-growth forests in western Oregon,
and was a landscape ecologist with the Environmental Protection Agency
for a year (1990–91).

Today he is an independent author as well as an international
lecturer and facilitator in resolving environmental disputes, vision statements, and sustainable community development. He is also a international consultant in forest ecology and sustainable forestry practices. He
has written over 260 publications.

Although he has worked in Canada, Egypt, France, Germany, Japan,
Nepal, Slovakia, and Switzerland, he calls Corvallis, Oregon, home.

PART I

A SHARED VISION: THE GATEWAY TO A COMMUNITY'S FUTURE

The trouble with our age is all signposts and no destination.

Louis Kronenberger, American author

S omeday, after we have mastered the winds, the waves, the tide and gravity, we shall harness for God the energies of love. Then, for the second time in the history of the world, man will have discovered fire." So wrote Teilhard de Chardin, the noted French Jesuit priest, paleontologist, and philosopher.

As we learn to master ourselves and thus our own creative processes, we have the potential not only to harness the energies of love but also to enlist them in helping us to become the dominant creative force in our own lives and in the lives of others. As individual adults and leaders, let us accept our responsibility to reconnect ourselves to the passion of our highest ideals and potential, to our deepest self-knowledge, and to our inner truth and knowing because each generation must be the conscious keeper of the generation to come—not its judge.

It is therefore incumbent upon us, the adults, to prepare the way for those who must follow. This will entail, among other things, wise

1

and prudent planning, beginning with a local shared vision to safe-guard the very best human values by carefully, purposefully interweaving them into the interpersonal fabric of our respective communities.

Alfred North Whitehead, English philosopher and mathematician, put it well: "The art of progress is to preserve order amid change and to preserve change amid order"; hence the importance of a shared vision builds on mutual respect and trust. Interpersonal relationships, after all, are the social glue that holds communities—and the world of interdependent human societies—together as they struggle with the notion of sustainable development.

A shared vision, like interpersonal relationships, must be heavily invested in from the very beginning, front-end loaded, as it were. To people who want action and instant gratification, creating a shared vision is like watching a multistory building under construction. It seems to take forever (months) for the foundation to reach the level of the street, but when it finally does, the stories appear to rise one per week.

At this juncture, when patience is called for as the foundation of a shared vision is about to be laid, it might be helpful to revisit part of a speech given on the first of June 1929 by I.L. Patterson, then governor of the state of Oregon, at the formal dedication of the Memorial Union on the campus of Oregon State Agricultural College (now Oregon State University). Speaking of the soldiers who died in the Spanish–American War and World War I, Governor Patterson said:

> ...let us look back on the campus of the Oregon State Agricultural College in the spring of 1918. Many volunteers among students and alumni had joined the allied forces before the United States definitely entered the war, and the first call for volunteers threatened to start a stampede to enlist. Then came a proclamation from the Secretary of War urging college men, especially those receiving military training in land grant colleges, to continue their studies until called upon by the War Department.
>
> Obedient to that counsel, the men of the Oregon State Agricultural College *took up the harder part* [emphasis added]. Although many were burning with eagerness to enlist at once, although their zeal to serve made *apparent inaction almost intolerable* [emphasis added], nevertheless they remained steadily at their work, and with such patience as their youth and patriotic fervor would permit, they waited quietly for the call of the government....

This was during an hour of crisis when men's emotions sometimes overrode their sense of justice, when words were warm
rather than carefully weighed. To realize how hard must have
been the task of holding to their daily routine in the midst of a
vast upheaval, we must remember that this irksome duty was
carried out in the face of unjust insinuations, of slurs which cut
to the quick the proud and impatient spirit of youth. No small
part of the honor which surrounds the war record of the State
Agricultural College belongs to those young men who, despite
the powerful temptation to cast aside restraint, could yet realize
that there are times when, *"They also serve who only stand and
wait"* [emphasis added].[1]

Thus, it is both wise and necessary to invest so heavily up front in
crafting a shared vision because that vision and its attendant goals are
the blueprint for a sustainable future. The objectives are analogous to
the individual projects (such as installation of the electrical wiring or
plumbing in the construction of a house) that in the collective form the
outcome of the goals and hence the achievement of the vision.

In short, people have within them the capacity to heal the world,
just as they do to destroy it. A leader's task is to help them find,
recognize, and hold onto the capacity to heal by helping them expand
the notion of self-interest from the individual to the community.

Ultimately, however, leadership must extend beyond the local shared
vision, even beyond its successful implementation, if local shared visions are to be anything more than interim stopgap measures while we
await the final demise of society as we know it. I say this because we
must understand that while a local shared vision of social/environmen-
tal sustainability is clearly a local act, the effects of such visions, when
taken in the collective, become a global consequence, the benefit of
which can be realized only when world leaders and their respective
nations do their part to clean up our common air, water, and soil.
Leadership of such high moral consciousness is sadly missing in the
world today, which brings me to *The Prime Directive.*

THE PRIME DIRECTIVE

1

- "Researchers warn Earth must get back in balance."[2]
- "Peru's highest snowcap has been slowly melting during the past 100 years....Benjamin Morales Arnao of the Andean Institute of Glaciology said the Broggi Glacier in north-central Peru has receded 2,527 feet since the turn of the century...."
- "'Unprecedented temperature increases are thawing huge swaths of the Arctic, including Alaska'....The Arctic is a harbinger—a canary in the mine shaft—of global warming, said Jonathan Overpeck, coordinator of a U.S.–Canadian government-sponsored study of climate in the far North. 'It's scary.'"
- "In an urgent plea for help, island states at a summit of the Earth's future told an alarming tale...of the here and now: The seas already may be encroaching on their fragile lands."

The threat of global warming has brought more than 140 governments together in negotiations to *try* [emphasis added] to limit the emissions of carbon dioxide and other "greenhouse gases" that trap heat in the atmosphere. [Trying *never* gets the job done.] But history, geography, economics and politics are driving them apart.

Island states fear the rising oceans that warming may cause. Oil producers fear what lessening the world's dependence on fossil fuels would mean to them. Big industrial nations [led by the United States] worry that emissions limits might slow their economies. Poorer nations say they should not have to bear the same burdens as the rich.

Much of the U.S. industry opposes controls. And [President] Clinton faces resistance in the U.S. Senate, which warns it will reject any new treaty commitments that do not also cover China and other developing nations, which have been exempted thus far from the cutback plans.

- The United States, land of big automobiles, air conditioners and coal, is by far the leading emitter of greenhouse gases. The amount of carbon dioxide poured into the atmosphere per American—about 19 tons a year—is twice the per-capita rate in such advanced nations as Germany and Japan.
- When it comes to the struggle against global warming, Japan sees the rest of the world as latecomers to a noble cause. That may help explain why it is reluctant now to commit to major new energy cutbacks.
- Once known for a daily blanket of sooty smog, Britain has cast itself as a leader in the drive to cut the carbon gas emissions blamed for global warming.
- No country highlights the developing world's struggle with global warming more vividly than China....The Chinese have become the world's No. 2 producers of carbon dioxide, shoveling abundant coal supplies into inefficient power plants to drive rapid economic growth.
- A relatively small contributor to greenhouse gases, Australia nevertheless may be the world's most strident opponent to binding targets for emission reductions. The reason: coal....Coal is both Australia's richest export and the biggest source of heat-trapping carbon dioxide among the fossil fuels.

The Australian government says demand for coal in the developing Asia–Pacific region will double by 2010. If the energy projects go ahead, it would mean 90,000 new jobs for Australians. But if new treaty commitments sink those coal-power plants, it could shave 1 percent from Australia's gross domestic product [bullets added].[3]

The Europeans objected to "loopholes" in the U.S. position [as the treaty to control global warming neared agreement], especially the American idea of international trading of emissions quotas—allowing U.S. plants, for example, to obtain the right to continue emitting [pollutants that contain greenhouse gases] by buying "rights" from countries that underutilize their quotas.[4]

The above quotes say that self-centered critics have once again, in their long parade of history, seized on the uncertainties of a situation, in this case the projections of global warming, to resist early action. This reticence to deal honestly with the creation and implementation of a shared vision for clean, healthy air in the world for all the reasons it is *necessary* for survival makes it worth quoting a salient paragraph from a speech Winston Churchill gave to the British Parliament in 1935, as he saw with clear foreboding the onrushing threat of Nazi Germany to international peace:

> When the situation was manageable it was neglected, and now that it is thoroughly out of hand we apply too late the remedies which then might have effected a cure. There is nothing new in the story....It falls into that long, dismal catalogue of the fruit-lessness of experience and the confirmed unteachability of mankind. Want of foresight, unwillingness to act when action would be simple and effective, lack of clear thinking, confusion of counsel until the emergency comes, until self-preservation strikes its jarring gong—these are the features which constitute the endless repetition of history.[5]

Where is there an unequivocal voice among national and international leaders that speaks for the children who must inherit the consequences of our other-centered wisdom or our self-centered blunders? Where is there an unequivocal voice among national and international leaders that speaks for protecting the productive capacity of the global ecosystem—our bequest to all the children of the future? Without such a singular voice of courage and unconditional commitment to the future in each nation, we, the adults of the world, are condemning the children—our children and grandchildren—to pay a progressively awful price for our petty psychological immaturities as we bicker amongst ourselves about who will do what rather than accept the sometimes bitter pill of our adult responsibilities.

Social insanity can be defined as doing the same thing over and over—despite the lessons of world history—while each time expecting new and dramatically different results. This is a simple summation of the way in which Western industrial society has navigated the 20th century, a century that has seen the deadly grapple between society's immediate wants and demands and what the environment can sustainably produce.

And what about the 21st century? Will it too be a century of deadly grapple between the polarized positions of "industrialists" and "preservationists," positions that are but symptoms of a spiritually bankrupt and morally sick society? Is this to be our legacy to the future?

I remember a time some years ago when I was employed as a research scientist, and I thought I had some answers. I now realize that I am not even sure of the questions. But there are a few things of which I am relatively certain, one of which is the obvious equivocating and timorous nature of most government leaders at all levels of society. I am certain that ecological–biological health must prevail in the world before social–economic health can. It is for this reason, and with a great deal of humility, that I commit the following notions to paper as *The Prime Directive* for human survival on Earth, for I see no other viable alternative.

THE PRIME DIRECTIVE

Our current mode of participating with Nature can be traced throughout human history as each successive society has experienced its own growth and evolution of consciousness. The singular lesson that I find in the history of human experience is that we, collectively, can heal our home planet only as we individually heal our own lives and therefore our respective societies. But such healing can take place only if we transcend science's objectification of Nature, manifested through rational knowledge, to honor the sacredness of Nature, manifested through intuitive knowing, which science can help elucidate but can neither explain nor replace.

I say this because we cannot answer our deepest fundamental social/environmental questions through science because they are not scientific questions. They are instead moral questions and questions of value that defy our current fragmented, mechanical–economic world view.

Preamble

The Prime Directive for human participation in the sacred evolution of Planet Earth is based on the moral evolution of society. A society is a group of human beings broadly distinguished from other groups by mutual interests, participation in characteristic relationships, a common culture, and shared institutions and agencies. Culture, in turn, is the totality of socially transmitted behavioral patterns, arts, beliefs, institutions, and all other products of human work and thought characteristic of a community or population. A society's culture is the product of its dominant mode of thinking.

There are two basic patterns of thinking: (1) a linear pattern of human thought that equates to the production and accumulation of material *products* as the primary purpose of life and (2) a cyclic pattern of human thought that equates to being an integral part of the *processes* that constitute the spiritual center of life's cycle. In turn, these patterns of thought determine the core of a society's culture.

The linear pattern of human thought produces a culture, such as our Western industrialized culture, in which economics is the force that drives the society, which determines its mode of institutions and relegates spirituality to the bottom rung of the social ladder. The cyclic pattern of human thought, on the other hand, produces a culture, such as that of the First Americans, the Maoris of New Zealand, or the Aborigines of Australia, in which spirituality is the force that drives the society and determines the mode of its economics and its institutions.

Given the same piece of land, each culture would produce a different design across its broad sweep, a design based on the culture's pattern of thinking, which is the template of the individual's sense of values expressed in the collective social mirror—the environment. Put a little differently, all people unite with the environment in one way or another and form their culture, because the environment and the people are inseparably one.

As the social values determine the culture and as the culture is an expression of those values, so is the care taken of the environment by the people the mirrored image of the hidden forces in their social psyche. These hidden forces, these secret thoughts guarded in the minds and hearts, ultimately express themselves and determine whether or not a particular society survives or becomes a closed chapter in the history books.

The path of development that we choose may be more or less cooperative and ecologically benign or more or less competitive and ecologically malignant, but whichever path we choose, that choice is ours, and we cannot escape it. To that end, a prime directive is necessary to guide whatever policies may be forthcoming to fulfill our participation as planetary citizens with Nature and with the sacred evolution of our home planet. We are all planetary citizens because our local behavior in the collective affects the world as a whole—witness depletion of the ozone layer and pollution in the oceans of the world.

The Prime Directive

The Prime Directive is intended as the guiding principle for both individual and social behavior of planetary citizens, present and future. "Planetary citizen" is to be understood as any individual human who inhabits Planet Earth. In addition, it is to be understood that all moral obligations of planetary citizenship—and *The Prime Directive*—apply to any human visiting another celestial body, because that human is a representative of his or her home planet.

The Prime Directive is meant as a standard of conduct for planetary citizens and is to be interpreted, reinterpreted, and amended when any part thereof can be improved for the mutual evolutionary benefit of the planet, its human society, and the cosmos at large. *The Prime Directive* is:

> Planetary citizens are to live in humility and harmony on Earth while simultaneously minimizing interference with any of Nature's evolutionary processes.

Articles of *The Prime Directive*

The following articles are written as examples of the behavior necessary for humans as planetary citizens, both as individuals and societies, to implement and faithfully follow in order to fulfill *The Prime Directive*.

Article I: Air

As air is the main transporting and integrating factor of human-caused pollution, its circulation around the planet affects the planet's soils and waters and all forms of life thereon and therein.

To clean the air, planetary citizens first and foremost must begin carefully managing what they introduce into the air so as to prevent any further contamination, which in turn will allow the air to begin ridding itself of human-caused pollutants. Concomitantly, planetary citizens must, with due diligence, clean and detoxify all existing industrial plants, modes of transportation, wood- and coal-burning stoves, and so on, regardless of the political and monetary costs. Such is their responsibility to all forms of planetary life for all generations, present and future.

Article II: Soil

As soil is the main terrestrial vessel, it receives, collects, and passes to the water all airborne, human-caused pollutants. In addition, such pollutants as chemical fertilizers, fungicides, herbicides, insecticides, rodenticides, and so on are added directly to the soil and through the soil to the water. At times, such pollutants make their way into the air and hence are redistributed more widely over the planet's surface through strong winds, which carry aloft the planet's topsoil following deforestation, desertification, and ecologically unsound farming practices.

As the air is cleaned so will the soil be cleaned, but that is not enough. Planetary citizens must begin carefully managing what they introduce into the soil so as to prevent any further contamination, which in turn will allow the soil to begin healing itself. Concomitantly, planetary citizens must, with due diligence, clean all toxic-waste sites, regardless of the political and monetary costs. Such is their responsibility to all forms of planetary life for all generations, present and future.

Article III: Water

As water is the great collector of human-caused pollutants, it washes and scrubs them from the air by rain and snow; it leaches them from the soil; and it carries them in trickle, stream, and river to be concentrated in the ultimate vessel, the combined oceans of the world.

As the air and soil are cleaned so will the waters be cleaned, but that is not enough. To clean the waters, planetary citizens must begin carefully managing what they introduce into the waters so as to prevent any further contamination, which in turn will allow the waters to begin diluting and dissolving human-caused pollutants. Concomitantly, planetary citizens must, with due diligence, clean and detoxify all polluted waters possible, regardless of the political and monetary costs. Such is their responsibility to all forms of planetary life for all generations, present and future.

Article IV: Life Forms—Nonhuman

1. Recognize that every form of life is equal in its service to the environment, even if we do not understand the way in which it serves. Each individual life, each individual species, each indi-

vidual function is equally important to the evolutionary success of the planet. Each species is not only different but also has its own excellence and is comparable to no other. Therefore, all differences among all forms of life are just that—differences— and the hierarchies or human valuation and judgment are social constructs that have nothing to do with reality. So it is that, because of and in spite of these differences, every life is a practice in biological conservation, and every form of life is equal before God.

2. Respect the integrity of the naturalness of all forms of life, which may mean letting an individual, individuals, or even a species die to fulfill a particular process in the evolution of Nature. This also means looking beyond the immediacy of the momentary emotion of seeing an animal in apparent distress and respecting a form of life for what it is and where it is in the naturalness of Nature's processes.

3. Cause no conscious or purposeful extinction of any form of life or life-form process for economic or political gain, regardless of the perceived short-term monetary costs in revenue foregone. Such is the responsibility of planetary citizens to all forms of life on their home planet for all generations, present and future.

4. Pet shops and other such establishments, except as strictly controlled and dealing only with recognized domestic pets, must be outlawed as an immoral affront to human decency and *The Prime Directive* in that they not only steal freedom from forms of life created to be free, and in so doing violate the life form's integrity, naturalness, and participation in the evolutionary processes of Nature, but also are a prime economic force in the growing extinction of wild indigenous forms of life.

   The reason domestic animals may be allowed in pet shops is that, while they cannot enter into a human culture, historically they have been cared for by that culture.

5. If human society is to survive as we know it, we must understand and accept that how we as individuals treat what we still consider to be the Earth's lesser creatures so we collectively treat the whole of Planet Earth. With time, animals will help to raise the level of our consciousness so that we will see the true image of the human spirit as reflected in a benevolent, loving attitude toward all forms of life.

Article V: Life Forms—Human

1. Inasmuch as humanity's habitation in and alterations of the environment on its home planet are a natural part of the creative–destructive–creative cycle and inasmuch as we are active participants in the redrafting of Nature's design simply because we exist, we therefore not only belong here and have a right to be here in the context of our "nativeness" but also have a duty to participate fully and accountably in the creation of our environment in the context of our "naturalness."

   It is in this context that we design and redesign the planet's surface and its attending environmental patterns. Be advised, however, that as planetary citizens we are accountable not to our ancestors or to our peers but to our children for the outcome of our endeavors.

2. It is neither the moral obligation nor the sacred duty of planetary citizens to rule the planet. It is, however, their moral obligation and their sacred duty to fulfill the role of planetary trusteeship for the benefit of all forms of life, present and future. To this end, all forms of life are to be treated with dignity and respect.

3. Planetary citizens are to control their population so as to remain within the cultural capacity established for any given area. Cultural capacity is the balance among how we want to live, the quality of our lifestyles and of our society, and how many people an area can support in that lifestyle on a sustainable basis. Cultural capacity is something we can predetermine and to which we can adjust the growth of our population accordingly. If, however, we continue to choose not to balance our cultural capacity with the land's capabilities, the *depletion of the land,* not of our desires, will continue to select the qualitative level of our cultural/social experience on our home planet.

4. To control the world's human population, even on a bioregional basis, will require unequivocal gender equality in male attitudes and behavior toward women. The world's human population will begin to decrease and stabilize at a sustainable level when and only when women can find self-esteem and social value through equal opportunities to be useful in their respective societies beyond the stereotype of male-envisioned motherhood. To this end, women must have guaranteed social rights and in-

dividual choice equal to that of men in all aspects of their daily lives.

Article VI: Habitats

It shall be the duty of planetary citizens to save an ecologically sound representation of all habitats for all known forms of life, regardless of the perceived short-term political and monetary costs. Such is the responsibility of planetary citizens to all forms of life on their home planet for all generations, present and future.

Article VII: Environment

1. It shall be the duty of every planetary citizen to pass on to the next generation the kind of environment in which he or she would choose to live in the best of all worlds.
2. To accomplish number one above, we, as individuals and as a global society, must ask how much of any given resource we *may* use for our immediate benefit and how much is *necessary* to leave intact in Nature as a biological reinvestment in the health and continued productivity of the ecosystem for the benefit of ourselves and all other forms of planetary life in the generations immediately succeeding ours and into the distant future.

Article VIII: Environmental Culturalization

Because we exist as citizens of Planet Earth and because we have no choice but to use this planet as our home, our culturalization of Nature's environment must be conducted in a way that not only ensures a balance between Nature's blueprint of naturalness and humanity's social desires but also ensures Nature's ability to continue evolving in a sustainable, productive, and desirable direction.

This means the environment must be designed and treated so that the degree of culturalness maintains and complements the connectivity of habitats across the broad sweep of the land while simultaneously allowing Nature's processes of disturbance, such as storms, fires, and floods, to guide the overall evolution of the environment.

To facilitate this possibility, planetary citizens must pay particular attention to and be totally committed to keeping their populations within the established limits of cultural capacity in whatever area they reside.

Article IX: Our Gift to the Future

Inasmuch as we, through our sexual acts, are responsible for the children's presence in the world;

And inasmuch as our present decisions and actions will determine the circumstances for all future generations;

And inasmuch as the great and only gift we have to give our children, their children, and their children's children, unto the seventh generation and beyond, is options, choices to be made, and some things of value from which to choose;

And inasmuch as a gift is free of all liens and encumbrances, which means to protect, maintain, and proffer the gift, not to judge how it may or may not be used;

We the people as planetary citizens must both understand and accept that, with increasing measure, we are the trustees of the future's options and the determiners of planetary evolution. We must therefore resolve—with firmness of mind and clarity of heart—to find and test our moral courage and political will and to act in an other-centered, future-oriented manner, regardless of the perceived short-term economic hardships and political uncertainties. Such is our responsibility to all forms of planetary life for all generations, present and future.

It requires neither scientific research nor technological marvels to heal Planet Earth. These are not necessary in order to follow *The Prime Directive*. Finding what we have lost, rediscovering our misplaced spirituality is, however, imperative. We must act now in adopting *The Prime Directive* if Planet Earth is to be a fit home for those who follow. The choice is ours. To all who are young and to those whose faces are yet unseen, we bequeath the consequences of our decisions and our actions.

The absolute necessity of fulfilling *The Prime Directive* if all generations are to have the options needed for a quality life is, to me, inescapable and thus constitutes the philosophical underpinnings of this book. While I have not explicitly interwoven *The Prime Directive* into the text, it is, nonetheless, both the thread of sustainability and the common bond of humanity within and among generations that stitches vision and leadership to one another and to the survival of society as we know it through the vast reach of time and space. Therefore, please keep *The Prime Directive* in mind as you continue to read this book.

WHY IS A SHARED VISION IMPORTANT?

2

The story of the Universe and the Earth has been told by many peoples in many ways since the beginning of humanity.[6] The story has been celebrated in elaborate rituals that have provided guidance and sustaining energy in shaping the course of human affairs. It has been the fundamental referent in establishing social authority regarding the modes of personal and community conduct.

We are, in the modern period, without a comprehensive story of the Earth and the Universe. Historians, even when articulating world history, deal not with the whole of the world but just with the human aspect, as though the human aspect is something apart from or an addendum to the story of the Earth and the Universe.

Scientists who have arrived at detailed accounts of the cosmos focus exclusively on the physical dimension and ignore the human dimension of the story. With all our learning, knowledge, and scientific insight or vision, we in the industrialized nations are psychologically and spiritually adrift when it comes to a meaningful relationship with our environment and the Universe, such as the indigenous creation stories of old, and thus we have at the present time a distorted approach to living on our home planet.[6]

Eyesight is nothing without vision, and "vision," according to Jonathan Swift, "is the art of seeing the invisible." To this, Dag Hammarskjöld adds: "Only he who keeps his eye fixed on the far horizon [the vision] will find his right road." Yet the meaning and purpose of a collective vision as a shared experience are something few people seem to understand, and because they fail to understand, many people simply take potluck with their future. When asked about their future, however, people often say, "I have a vision of what I want." But when pressed to explain their vision, it becomes clear that they don't have the foggiest notion that a vision is a strong organizing context built around interpersonal relationship in the present for the future.

As a strong organizing context, a shared vision has some distinctive traits: (1) it tends to focus a wide range of human concerns; (2) it is strongly centered in the community; (3) it can use alternative scenarios to explore a possible future by depicting in words and images that which a community is striving to become; (4) its creation relies on the trust, respect, and inclusivity of interpersonal relationships; (5) it is ideally suited to and depends on public involvement; and (6) it is ideally suited to the use of creative graphic imagery. Although a shared vision does not replace other kinds of land-use planning, it is the organizational context within which all other planning fits, a context that was recognized long ago but too often is forgotten.

More than 3,000 years ago, sages who belong not just to India but to the whole world gave humanity one of the earliest spiritual treasures known to history, the *Rig Veda*. In it is a prayer addressed to all of us, a prayer that is the heart and soul of a shared vision:

> Meet together, talk together.
> May your minds comprehend alike.
> Common be your action and achievement,
> Common be your thoughts and intentions,
> Common be the wishes of your heart,
> So there may be thorough union among you.

A vision consists of the self-determination that people ideally want to move toward, not what they fear and want to move away from, for, as William James noted, it is the ability to direct attention that "is the very root of judgment, character and will." As such, a vision, like the social/environmental sustainability of a community, is a perpetual work in progress. Sometimes the price of a vision for self-determination is the shedding of human blood. Always the price of a vision is courage because, at its center, it is *not* about preservation but rather is about doing the best we can to honorably push the limits of human possibility, a notion that is severely tested in times of turmoil. Pushing the limits of human possibility is a necessary condition of social evolution because, as Albert Einstein noted, "No problem can be solved from the same consciousness that created it."

Be that as it may, why does a vision work? A carving from a church in Sussex, England, suggests an answer: "A vision without a task is but a dream. A task without a vision is drudgery. A vision and a task are the hope of the world." And hope can be protected only in a true democracy, which is the spiritual and legal trust of human freedom and hence the only viable repository of a collective vision for popular self-determination.

A shared vision of a sustainable future toward which a community can build creates confidence, consensus, and energy in equal parts.[7] It also fits a Japanese proverb: "The old forget. The young don't know." At a deeper level, it engages our imagination and helps to ferret out which questions need to be asked, how to word them, and when to ask them.

By engaging their imagination and sense of possibility of the ideal through countless small-scale initiatives, such as shared community visions, people who are concerned with the health of their environment and social justice can create an opportunity to confirm a more positive sustainable future. Imagination, as Albert Einstein said, is more important than knowledge and is the most powerful tool for social change, but imagination without tenacity of purpose and persistence of action is all but useless, as noted by President Calvin Coolidge.

Coolidge asserted that "Nothing in the world can take the place of persistence. Talent will not; nothing is more common than unsuccessful [people] with talent. Genius will not; unrewarded genius is almost a proverb. Education will not; the world is full of educated derelicts. Persistence and determination alone are omnipotent."

Some people will point out that persistence and determination may have worked in the past because social change was slower in coming and easier to assimilate into cultural norms. But, they contend, we barely have time today to catch our cultural breath before another whirlwind of change descends upon us. So they excuse their respective communities for choosing to operate in a perpetual crisis mode, seldom getting beyond the next budget cycle, let alone creating a shared vision for a sustainable future through which change can be wisely accommodated.

As Winston Churchill said, "There is nothing new in this story." Consider the following modern-day example.[8] An aquatic weed called Eurasian water milfoil (known scientifically as *Myriophyllum spicatum*) was introduced into south Lake Tahoe, California, probably in the 1960s. Today it covers 200 acres, 170 of which are at the Tahoe Keys, which was constructed during the 1960s and may be the place the weed was introduced.

Because the green, viny weed, which grows to six to eight feet long in a month, winds itself around the propeller of a boat and gets sucked into the intake of the cooling system, which causes overheating, it requires constant control during the summer. The Tahoe Keys Property Owner's Association has activated its own eradication measure at a cost of more than $150,000 per year.

Experts on aquatic weeds, such as Dr. Lars Anderson (research leader of the Aquatic Weed Control Laboratory at the USDA Agricultural Research Service's center in Davis, California), predict that mass spreading of Eurasian water milfoil is imminent and will not only cause a drastic change in the biological makeup of Lake Tahoe but also exact huge financial losses. Despite these warnings, the local agency in charge of water quality (the Lahontan Division of the California Water Quality Control Board) has placed a "nonpriority" label on the issue.

Ossian Butterfield, director of the Lahontan Division's board, said that while the agency has known of the potential effect of the fast-spreading weed for about two years and has analyzed it carefully, eradicating it from the lake "doesn't seem to be a real priority at the moment. Maybe in the future it will be, but not right now." In the meantime, the weed has more than quadrupled in area in some places.

So the story continues, and still there is nothing new! Today, however, the story is not just being reenacted in a lake in a small corner of California. It is being enacted in our economy.

As local economies are being regionalized, then nationalized, then globalized through the centralization of corporate economic power, industries that were once the bedrock of communities are falling by the wayside as new industries and technologies offer a key to the future, but the question is what kind of future. In addition, many communities are being affected by shifting demographic trends (such as changes in the work force and increasing cultural diversity) and shifting social necessities of their citizens (such as the earliest of the "baby boomers" [those people born within a 15- to 18-year period following the end of World War II] approaching senior status), which will require a reexamination of social services and the supporting infrastructure.

Thus, while people talk about being "proactive" or "getting ahead of change," they rarely see change for what it is—an ongoing process of everything becoming something else; a process to be embraced for the opportunities hiding among the uncertainties; a process that can be guided to some extent for the sustainable benefit of human communities, present and future.

Seeing change only as a condition to be avoided at almost any cost, people continually reinforce Churchill's observation that they avoid uncomfortable situations until it is too late to effectively confront them. If, however, we humans want to live in a future of social quality, we must change our materialistic values and habits—and be determined and persistent in that change. We must also make sure that what we do is socially inclusive, which means that humanity must be physically *and* psychologically prepared for the opportunities and responsibilities that emerge as a result of people's growing interdependence.

People need to develop the attitudes, values, knowledge, and skills necessary to participate confidently and constructively in shaping their own communities on all levels so that each community might reflect into the global society the principles of love, justice, equality, unity, and social/environmental sustainability. Here, education is indispensable and must encourage thinking in terms of historical processes, seeing in history the inexorable movement toward a world civilization of ever-increasing consciousness, a movement whose successes are the legacy of all peoples and whose challenges we must now address as an increasingly single people.

A shared vision of a sustainable future must therefore be both ecologically and economically sound if it is going to enable people to think differently about their lives and in so doing commence to change them. But that change must be for and about the people themselves. If it does not have a human face out of which shine core human values, it will fail.

Indeed, history is replete with failed plans because omission of the human equation left them with a hollow ring. Yet, as American author Van Wyck Brooks observed: "Nothing is so soothing to our self-esteem as to find our bad traits in our forebears. It seems to absolve us."

The process of implementing or revisiting a community's vision statement is equivalent to negotiating a series of obstacles or *constraints* levied (consciously or unconsciously) by the community itself on itself through the vision. Some constraints, such as those imposed by Nature, are ecological and largely *nonnegotiable*. Although they can be—and often have been—circumvented, such circumvention has exacted an enormous cost in both human and environmental terms.

In contrast, other constraints (social, political, and economic) are essentially negotiable. The feasibility of a community's vision of a sustainable future can thus be determined in a process that considers the constraints imposed by nature and accepted by society through consciously mediated human behavior.

An important facet of social constraints that needs to be addressed is the *loss of community* and whether such loss represents a nonnegotiable constraint: Where there is no sense of community, there is no community, and no vision is possible. "If," as author Adrienne Rich says, "you are trying to transform a brutalized society, you begin with the empowering of the most powerless," which, in the United States today, means local communities.

Today's towns and cities frequently consist of fragmented communities (either virtual or geographic) that rarely act holistically. For those who seek to formulate a vision of sustainability for a town or city, first steps may necessarily include activities that build toward a truly integrated community. These activities not only build a bridge of trust but also increase the flow of information such that the pieces can better perceive the whole.

As such, a resident community, through its vision, accepts responsibility for its own survival, and outsiders must initially fit themselves into that vision if the community is to be sustainable. You, the reader, will understand why I say this when you read the chapter on community (Chapter 3). A vision can thus be likened to a human body in that the strong organizing context of the body's division of labor keeps the various cells functioning within acceptable bounds.

If, for example, cancer cells are removed from a cancerous animal, where they are defying the weakened organizational context of the body, and are placed in a healthy animal, they return to a normal functional pattern because they come under the influence of a strong organizing context. If, however, cells stay too long without the guidance of a strong organizing context, they reach a point where they can no longer be guided at all, and they become "rogue" cells or "cancer" cells.

If the context is disorganized, confused, or murky, then it is not surprising that the cells, whether of the human body, the body of a human community, or the body of humanity as a whole, tend to get out of control. The longer disorganization exists, the more difficult its effects are to reverse. Hence a community's need for the strong organizing context of a vision.

A vision can also be likened to an old story about an elephant and the blind people who describe the elephant as they are feeling it. One describes a thick pillar; another a rope; and a third a hard, curved horn. Although this story may be familiar, the Sufi version has an interesting twist. The people are not blind but rather are in a dark room. Thus, when they all light their candles, they can see the full shape, dimension, and movement of the elephant. The point of this story, says editor Sarah van Gelder, is that no one person can grasp the breadth and depth of the changes that are permeating our culture today—it requires the light of many candles burning simultaneously to perceive the whole.

Therefore, a strong organizing context perceived from many points of view not only establishes the need to monitor the results of implementing the community's vision but also determines what needs to be monitored, which simply means that for a community to become sustainable, it must be able to understand how it influences the health of its life-support systems. Monitoring itself is the formal process of observing and interpreting changes in ecosystems associated with human-caused disturbances, such as urban development, logging, farming, and so on.

Like a telescope or a microscope, monitoring acts as a lens through which we detect events and trends not normally within the range of human perception. For example, only long-term global-scale monitoring can determine the consequences of the "greenhouse effect" (first proposed as a theory in 1894 by a Swedish scientist studying the effects of burning fossil fuels) on the Earth's atmosphere, which in turn affects the quality of human life and perhaps even human survival.

With sufficient coordination, scientific programs may fulfill the objectives of monitoring. But the specific goal of monitoring is to *detect ecologically significant change in ecosystems* using scientific methods. Unlike science, however, monitoring emphasizes the process of risk analysis and decision making.

Unfortunately, monitoring inevitably reveals uncertainties that often cloud decisions. Decision making will thus eventually turn around the question of risk: How much risk are we capable of and willing to assume by our collective actions or inactions? What are the consequences of that risk? Can they even be measured?

There are two basic approaches to dealing with such uncertainty. First, as we have traditionally done, we can seek to increase our knowledge in order to decrease the uncertainty associated with manipulating ecosystems. Second, and still largely untried, we can act more conservatively. The latter approach assumes that, in our ignorance, the risks of making mistakes outweigh the potential payoff of being correct. A farmer decides *not* to grow a certain cash crop because she cannot assume the risk of increased soil erosion and subsequent declines in her ecological and economic productivity.

As this example depicts, monitoring and decision making on a small farm can be rather straightforward. In such a place, disasters are very personal events.

On the other hand, decision making is rather more impersonal and the circle of sustainability that monitoring seeks to close is more vast and tenuous in agribusiness, on national forests, or within the reciprocal relationship of a community to its landscape. There, decisions are made in a collective and are laden with corporate and social values, especially within the immediate vicinity of a community working its way toward social/environmental sustainability. In this sense, monitoring closes the circle of sustainability at the interface between Nature and society.

This circle of social/environmental sustainability will be only as vibrant and successful as the psychological maturity of those involved in the process will allow. My experience has been that those people in a community who tend toward psychological maturity speak for the children (present and future), whereas those who tend toward psychological immaturity speak only for themselves. With the former, sustainability is possible. With the latter, it is not—because the children have no voice.

Knowing intuitively that children need a voice, it was an ancient custom of the indigenous Americans to call a council fire when decisions that would affect the whole tribe or nation needed to be made. To sit in council as a representative of the people was an honor that had to be earned through many years of truthfulness, bravery, compassion, sharing, listening, justice, being a discreet counselor, and so on. These qualities were necessary because a council fire by its very nature was a time to examine every point of view and explore every possibility of a situation that would in some way affect the whole of the people's destiny. In today's terminology, this might be called a "visioning process."

When someone called a council fire, that person had to have the courage to accept the council's decision with grace, because when the good of the whole is placed before the good of the few, all are assured a measure of abundance. The timeless teaching of the council fire is that until *all* of the people are doing well, *none* of the people are doing well.

Borrowing from the days of old, the modern visioning process is designed around the same timeless teaching of the ancient council fire, namely that until *all* of the people are doing well, *none* of the people are doing well. Thus, for the sake of sustainability, present and future, the good of the whole must be placed before the good of the few.

The council fire worked well for the First Americans because they knew who they were culturally, and they had a sense of place within their environment. Today, however, societies around the globe are in transition, which robs many people of their original sense of place and substitutes some vague idea of location. With so many people feeling adrift in their lives, the whole concept of a vision, much less one that includes future generations, seems inconsequential at best if not an exercise in abject futility.

This transition is largely the result of massive shifts in human populations over the last three centuries. These shifts have altered the composition of peoples and their cultural structures throughout the world. All of this activity results in growing interconnectedness, interdependence, and cultural uncertainty as some political lines change physically and others blur culturally.

Cultural uncertainty is particularly true for those people caught between two cultures, such as the warring religious factions around the world, where millions of refugees not only have their sense of culture disrupted but also their sense of place transformed into an alien location in which their lives hang in limbo. A large number of these people are immigrating to the United States, where many are trying to reconstruct the foundations of their own cultures while fitting compatibly into a new culture and thus a new sense of community.

These shifts in population are forcing even some of the most parochial communities to see themselves from new and different points of view. Others are being forced to look at themselves anew because today's social/environmental conditions, currently driven by economy and technology, are changing so fast that many of our known and comfortable self-views are obsolete. Hence, there are some preliminary subjects, beginning with our own perception of our community and world, that need examination prior to dealing with the notion of a vision itself.

THE CONCEPT
OF COMMUNITY

3

Community, as English historian Arnold Toynbee said of civilization, "is a movement and not a condition, a voyage and not a harbor." The word community comes from the Latin *munus,* which means gift, and *cum,* which means together, among one another. Thus community literally means to give among one another. Community can therefore be thought of as a group of people who welcome, honor, and exchange one another's gifts, which are unique to each person.

This central core of community is then expanded to a group of people with shared interests living under and exerting some influence over the same government in a shared locality. To understand the limitations of this notion of community, consider an extended family. The strongest bond is between a husband and wife, then between the parents and their children. But as the family grows, the bonds between the children and the various aunts and uncles and first, second, and third cousins tend to become progressively weaker as relationships become more distant with the increasing size of the family and the continual addition of more and more distantly related newcomers.

Thus, in each higher level of complexity and organization there is an increase in the size of the system and a corresponding decrease in the energies, or closeness of personal relationships, holding it together. Thus, as a family or town grows, the forces that hold together the bonds of personal relationships—of community, if you will—weaken as the size of the system increases. This is why the concrete notion of community cannot extend beyond the local without becoming an untenable abstraction.

I think President Lincoln had a grasp of this concept when discussing the role of government with respect to community: "The legitimate objective of government is to do for a community of people whatever they need to have done, but cannot do at all—or cannot so well do—for themselves in their separate and individual capacities."

Lincoln's "objective of government" means addressing local problems first and with local resources, if at all possible. It means keeping local earnings circulating within a community for as long as possible. And it means developing and practicing new forms of full-cost accounting that will result in least-cost planning so that local government, to the maximum extent possible, is the highest level of government needed to solve a community's problems.

People in a local community also share social interactions with one another and organizations beyond government and through such participation are able to satisfy the full range of their daily requirements within the local area. However, human nature, which I believe is fundamentally spiritual, must be taken into account. Communities are unlikely to be prosperous or sustainable until the spiritual dimension of human reality is accounted for in the culture, where the moral, ethical, emotional, and intellectual development of the individual are of primary concern. This notion brings to mind a statement by German-born missionary and Nobel laureate Albert Schweitzer: "Man must cease attributing his problems to his environment, and learn again to exercise his…personal responsibility in the realm of faith and morals."

A community also interacts with the larger society, both in creating change and in reacting to it. Finally, the community as a whole interacts with the local environment, molding the landscape within which it rests and in turn molded by it. In this sense, community is about the oneness of the whole and the wholeness of the one.

Although humankind has been concerned about the health or wholeness of communities since earliest times, it is only in recent years that emphasis has shifted to a broader model of community health and long-term sustainability. The broader view reflects a modern understanding of the determinants of both environmental and social health, including the spiritual, behavioral, political, economic, biological, and medical aspects of society.

We are finally recognizing that health is more than the absence of disease. A comprehensive framework of health includes prevention and treatment, equity, lifestyles conducive to both mental and physical health, and a comprehensive, integrated healthy environment.

For perhaps the first time in human history, professional experts from different disciplines are agreeing with one another. The best and the brightest people from the physical and mental health professions, science, agriculture, the conservation movement, and both Eastern and Western religions are urging people to recognize that we are part of— partners with and within—a living system.

Every thought, every word, every action creates a reaction that affects the health (ease) or dis-ease of the whole system. It is from the dictates of our own conscience and consciousness that we have the greatest potential to effect change. It is from an integrated "whole systems" perspective that together we can realize the possibility of sustainable community development.

TRUE COMMUNITY IS FOUNDED ON A SENSE OF PLACE, HISTORY, AND TRUST

Community is rooted in a sense of place through which people are in a reciprocal relationship with their landscape. As such, a community is not simply a static place within a static landscape but rather is a lively, ever-changing, interactive, and interdependent system of relationships. Because a community is a self-organizing system, it does not simply incorporate information, but through its activities changes its environment as well.

In a sense, therefore, the distribution of communities across a landscape is analogous to nations across a continent, which is the stuff of geography. Discussing geography, author–editor Robert D. Kaplan feels that the study of geography as a serious discipline has declined in recent decades and today is often thought of as "a grade-school social-studies course or perhaps a 'triptik' published by the American Automobile Association." To Kaplan, "geography is nothing less than the social, environmental, and political implications of humanity's interaction with the landscape."[9]

"I wonder," muses Kaplan, speaking of the United States, "if this map might one day look like the map of Europe after Rome fell." A hundred years before Rome fell, he continues, it was a world power, defended by its great military, but growing ethnic diversity, an imperial strength for so long, eventually helped to undermine the mighty Roman Empire. "As it entered its final century, the empire was a place of old decaying cities, a threatened middle class, terrorists, and lawyers who paralyzed government through unending legal challenges." Are we any different today?

The United States, writes Kaplan, was founded in a state of Nature. Our form of self-government, we are reminded by such historians as Fredrick Jackson Turner and Daniel J. Boorstin, "evolved not from ideology, as in Europe, but from encounters with the landscape by the early settlers." Thus, as a community in its living alters the landscape, so the landscape in its reaction alters the community.

Reciprocity is the self-reinforcing feedback loop that either extends sustainability to or withholds it from a community and its landscape. We therefore create trouble for ourselves in a community when we confuse order with control. Although freedom and order are partners in generating a viable, well-ordered, autonomous community, a community is nevertheless an open system that uses continual change to avoid deterioration. But "if we cannot cultivate people who are able to bear responsibilities, to recognize their impact on the world, then freedom," asserts Geoff Mulgan, "becomes a pathology."

A person who is mindful and feels a deep sense of place can bring about change that is beneficial to the continual health of his or her community. But if, after some time, a person is told by the company he or she works for that a transfer is likely within two years, then that person tends to go from a resident at heart with a sense of place to a transient who is reluctant to invest any more money or time in his or her home, which must be sold, or in community, which must be left. As more and more people are put in such a position, the kinds of changes that take place in a community tend to increasingly stray from the community's sense of its own history.

History is a reflection of how we see ourselves and thus goes to the very root of how we give value to things. Our vision of the past is shaped by, and in turn shapes, our understanding of the present—those complex and comprehensive images we carry in our heads by which we decide what is true or false.[10]

Alas, "the lack of a sense of history is the damnation of the modern world," writes author Robert Penn Warren, which is a thought akin to that of German philosopher Georg Wilhelm Friedrich Hegel, namely that "...experience and history teach...that people and governments have never learned anything from history." Our apparent disregard for history is indeed tragic, because, as military historian Robert Epstein points out: "Ancient history has everything. There is nothing that can ever happen that won't have an echo from the classical past." To this, author–editor Robert D. Kaplan adds: "The underlying message is that knowledge of the past helps foresight, and those with foresight accrue power" (read equals empowerment).

A community's history must therefore be passed from one generation to the next if the community is to know itself throughout the passage of time. In this sense, it is no small irony, writes James Howard Kunstler, that during the greatest era of prosperity in the United States, the decades following World War II, only the cheapest possible buildings were constructed, including civic buildings.[11] Compare, he says, any richly designed post office or city hall built at the turn of this century with its modern, dreary, concrete-box counterpart.

Kunstler's point is a good one. When the United States was a far less wealthy nation (by monetary standards), things were built to endure because it would have seemed immoral, if not insane, in our great-grandparents' day to throw away hard-earned money and honest labor on something guaranteed to disintegrate within 30 years.

The buildings erected in those earlier days paid homage to history in their design, including elegant solutions to the age-old problems posed by the cycles of weather and light. They paid respect to the future because they were consciously built to endure beyond the lifetimes of the people who constructed them. Kunstler accounts for this continuum of past, present, and future in what he calls "chronological connectivity."

Chronological connectivity, says Kunstler, is a fundamental pattern of the Universe: "an understanding that time is a defining dimension of existence—particularly the existence of living things, such as human beings, who miraculously pass into life and then inevitably pass out of it." It puts us in touch with the ages and connects us with a sense of eternity, indicating that we are somehow part of an organism that is significantly larger than ourselves.

The notion of chronological connectivity suggests that the large organism we help to compose even cares about us and that we in turn must respect ourselves and all life that will follow us in time, just as those who preceded us respected those who followed them. This notion is important, asserts Kunstler, who practices no formal religion, because it puts us in touch with the holy, that which is at once humbling and exhilarating. Connectivity with the countries of the past and the horizons of the future leads us in the direction of enchantment, grace, and sanity.

But if the connective continuity of a community is disrupted, the community suffers an extinction of identity and begins to view its landscape not as an inseparable extension of itself but rather as a separate commodity to be exploited for immediate financial gain. When this happens, community is destroyed from within because trust is withdrawn in the face of growing competition from increasingly transient members.

We have rejected both the past and the future since 1945, says Kunstler, a repudiation that is plainly manifest in our graceless constructions built to disintegrate within a few decades. This consciously built-in decline is euphemistically termed "design life," which may last 50 years. Since today's buildings are expected to serve only our era, we seem unwilling to expend money or effort for either their beauty or their service to the generations of the future.

Nor do we care about those elegant solutions to the problems created by the cycles of weather and light; after all, we have such technology as electricity and central heating. Thus, many new office buildings have windows that cannot be opened or virtually no windows at all. This process of disconnecting from the time continuum of the past, through the present, into the future and from the cycles of weather and light diminishes us spiritually, impoverishes us socially, and destroys the time-honored cultural patterns we call community. As an Army major at Fort Leavenworth, Kansas, put it in reference to the electronic media, they are about *"now, now, now,* with all the depth of a credit card." Unfortunately, the same can be said of most modern planners and developers.

No community today is untouched by the interplay between its traditional self and the greater, more expedient industrial–commercial society. It is not surprising, therefore, that conflicts over the value of place are arising with increasing frequency between those members of a community who hold traditional values and those who hold more modern transient values. In this sense, many communities are in transition between sets of values, which must be carefully assessed in terms of both human attitudes and the ways in which land is used.

As authors James and Roberta Swan point out: "There is a need to find a common language and conceptual framework to promote mutual understanding about the power of place. It is easy to feed the fires of conflict in such situations. The more difficult task is to build bridges of respect and cooperation."[12]

Community can also be lost another way: when citizens become reticent to think in terms of maintenance. We Americans seem eager to build but then begrudge providing the tax dollars necessary to maintain our highways and schools, let alone our downtowns, which we effectively abandon.

One of the reasons a number of townspeople may be reluctant to spend money on maintenance is their lack of long-term commitment to the town. Where they live while earning a living does not hold sufficient value for them to retire there. Thus, while they are committed to working in and living as a part of the town, they plan to move somewhere else to spend the rest of their lives upon retirement. With such thinking, why would they be committed to spending their hard-earned money on maintaining a place they are eagerly planning to leave?

Be that as it may, what we neglect we lose, be it a house, a street, or a downtown. Communities are not made to be disposable; they are not designed in terms of planned obsolescence. This could be partially remedied if each member of a community would tithe 10% of his or her time to do something that would improve the quality of that community.

Tithing a portion of one's time is the beginning of recognizing the difference between real wealth and money. Conventional money knows no loyalty to a sense of place, a local community, or even a nation, and so it flows toward a global economy in which traditional social bonds give way to a rootless quest for the highest monetary return. The real price we pay for money, the real cost, is the hold it has on our sense of what is possible—the prison it builds around our imagination.

According to Bernard Lietaer, of the Center for Sustainable Resources at the University of California at Berkeley, "Money is like an iron ring we've put through our noses. We've forgotten that we designed it, and it's now leading us around. I think it's time to figure out where *we* want to go—in my opinion toward sustainability—and then design a money system to get us there."[13]

Lietaer goes on to say that while textbooks on economics claim that people and corporations are competing for resources and markets, they are in reality competing for money, and in so doing are using resources and markets. "A more fascinating aspect of money," remarks author Caroline Myss, "is the fact that it can weave itself into the human psyche as a substitute for the life-force." Through the way in which we spend money, says Myss, we make our private beliefs into public declarations.

"Modern money," explains David Korten, author of *When Corporations Rule the World,* "is only a number on a piece of paper or an electronic trace in a computer that by social convention gives its holder *a claim* on real wealth," which Korten goes on to say has concrete value in meeting the necessities of and fulfilling our desire for a quality life.[14] But in our confusion over where real wealth lies, we chase the "Almighty Dollar" and neglect those things that actually sustain a life of quality, both spiritual and material. Money has no intrinsic value, only the potential of being converted into something else that may have real value.

It is striking, notes Korten, that our language makes it so difficult to express the critical difference between money and real wealth. But, he suggests, picture yourself alone on a desert island with nothing to sustain you but a large trunk filled with hundred-dollar bills, and the difference between money and real wealth becomes clear.

Think of the modern money economy, he suggests, as a system comprised of two subsystems: one creates wealth and the other creates and distributes money as a convenient means of allocating that wealth. Wealth means healthy ecosystems, social/environmental sustainability, human equality and dignity, meaningful work, having a home and food, and so on. In a healthy economy, money serves the people in helping to create and protect the real wealth. Money, in a healthy economy, is neither the dominant value nor the sole or dominant medium of exchange.

One of the most important indicators of economic health is social/ environmental sustainability, which means not only quality interpersonal relationships but also quality relationships between people and their environment. A healthy economy is based on love and reciprocity, where people do kind and useful things for one another with no expectation of financial gain. Such mutual caring is the soft social capital that both creates and maintains the fabric of trust, which in turn is the glue of functional families, communities, and societies.

Pathology enters the economic system, writes Korten, when money, once a convenient means of exchange, becomes the factor that defines the purpose of life for individuals and their communities. Then the human, social, and biological capital on which the well-being of any community depends is sacrificed on the altar of making money, at which time those who already have money prosper at the expense of those who do not.

The growing dominance of money as master is also revealed in the increasing "monetization" of human relationships. Not long ago, even in such rich, industrialized countries as the United States, half of the adult population worked without salary to create and maintain home and community, which are among the most fundamental functional values of a healthy, sustainable economy.

Today, financially supporting a household usually requires that two adults hold two, and sometimes three or four, paying jobs between them, but at the expense of quality human relationships because, of necessity, they rarely see each other and the care of children and the home is either neglected or hired out. In addition, the once shared mutual caring becomes "community service," which is the work of hired public employees, to the extent the public is willing to pay for it.

As the soft social capital of mutual caring dwindles and the resulting quality of family life withers, a community becomes fragmented and its members increasingly apathetic or competitive. As human relationships become more and more dysfunctional, a community's infrastructure crumbles into ever-greater disarray—exacting a cumulative social cost.

Nestled into a wooded hillside in the Pocono Mountains of eastern Pennsylvania is the tiny hamlet of Roseto.[15] Although the bricks and mortar that hold the ethnic Italian–American enclave together may not be distinguishable from its neighboring towns, Roseto is nonetheless distinct. Researchers in the 1960s found the citizens of Roseto, who numbered just over 1,600, to be among the healthiest people in the United States.

Rosetan death from heart disease was half the national average, in addition to which Rosetans tended to live many years longer than their peers. They also exhibited greater resistance to mental illness and peptic ulcers than did other Americans. Their good health and longevity defied medical logic because they smoked and drank as much as other Americans, experienced as much stress, exercised as infrequently, and ate a high-fat diet in traditional Italian style. How could one account for such good health in a group with such traditionally unhealthy habits? In a word: community.

Dr. Stewart Wolf, M.D., who discovered Roseto more than 30 years ago, found that the tight-knit community that had evolved in Roseto fostered an atmosphere of friendship and mutual caring and support that buoyed and protected its residents from the stresses of everyday life and thereby protected them against heart disease. He named the health-giving benefit of living in a close community the "Roseto Effect."

After punching out on the time clocks at the local slate quarries and blouse factories, the people of Roseto returned home to close, extended families, where grandparents, parents, and children lived under one roof, each nurturing and supporting the other. They also invested themselves in the larger community by walking around the neighborhood after supper to chat and joke with one another, and they joined and socialized formally at the many civic and community organizations and functions, from the Marconi Social Club to the Parent–Teacher Association. In addition, religion played an important role is this predominantly Catholic town.

In the 1970s, however, the close-knit community of Roseto began to unravel as the younger generation increasingly began to look for work elsewhere, attendance slipped in church, and the number of three-generational households diminished. The social conformity that had maintained narrow differences between the haves and have-nots disappeared as well, tearing the fabric and spirit of the community.

As the class differences between the haves and have-nots progressively widened, the social glue that had once held Roseto together dissolved, and so did the now legendary health benefit of living there. The very first fatal heart attack in anyone under 45 was recorded in 1971. Today, the health benefit of living in Roseto is history. The rate of heart disease mirrors the national average, and Rosetans live no longer than anyone else.

From the above scenario, it is clear that the fabric of communities needs to be rewoven. "In a society in which relationships are defined by love, generosity, and community," Korten feels, "the importance of money in mediating personal exchange and allocating resources is likely to decline markedly."

Reweaving the social fabric will require reducing one's dependence on money and restoring nonmonetary exchanges. To do this, people must selectively delink themselves, their families, and their communities from dependence on the predatory institutions of a global economy. They must also downscale consumption to reduce their dependence on paid work while increasing their reliance on local products to meet basic necessities and strengthening the engagement of all persons in the productive life of family and community.

It seems clear, therefore, that the sense of true community literally cannot extend itself beyond local place, mutual caring, and its history. Community, says Wendell Berry, "is an idea that can extend itself beyond the local, but it only does so metaphorically. The idea of a national or global community is meaningless apart from the realization of local communities."[16]

For a community to be founded in the first place and to be healthy and sustainable, it must rest on the bedrock of trust.

> ...a community does not come together by covenant, by a conscientious granting of trust. It exists by proximity, by neighbor-

hood; it knows face to face, and it trusts as it knows. It learns, in the course of time and experience, what and who can be trusted. It knows that some of its members are untrustworthy, and it can be tolerant, because to know in this matter is to be safe. A community member can be trusted to be untrustworthy and so can be included. But if a community withholds trust, it withholds membership. If it cannot trust, it cannot exist.[16]

Trust, according to the *American Heritage Dictionary*, is firm reliance on the integrity, ability, or character of a person or thing; confident belief; faith. But trust cannot really be defined because it is based on faith that someone is "trustworthy" or faithful to his or her word. Trust can only be lived in one's motives, thoughts, attitude, and behavior; thus the admonishment of American poet and journalist Ella Wheeler Wilcox: "Distrust the man [person] who tells you to distrust."

Trust must be based on truth. To make this point, Marc Luyckx, a member of the Forward Studies Unit of The European Commission, a think-tank within the administration of the European Union in Brussels, Belgium, related the following story, which was told to him by the president of the World Business Academy.[17] The story takes place in northern Australia, where some reporters tape-recorded two policemen insulting an Aboriginal person. The reporters then printed the transcript on the front page of the newspaper.

The chief of police, an intelligent and open-minded man who had for some time been trying to reshape his police force, was to be interviewed about the incident on television. Hearing this, the minister of justice told the chief to fire the two policemen and warned him to be careful of what he said publicly or he would be fired also.

But instead, on camera, the chief said: "I must tell the truth, and the truth is those two policemen are not an exception. The rest of the police could have done the same. But I will tell you more. The rest of the population of my region of Australia could have done the same as well. We are becoming racists."

There was an explosion in the press and on television, and the chief of police was fired the next day. The firing had not been approved by the Parliament, however, and the opposition party in the Parliament applauded him for one full minute for telling the truth in public. This action forced the government party to applaud as well, which resulted in the minister being fired and the chief being reinstated.

The upshot is that the police in that area of Australia became the best in the country because the truth had been spoken. After truth has been spoken, there is not only room for but also permission for spiritual growth and personal authenticity, which leads to trust—the stuff communities are made of.

It is important here to understand that communal trust (the very foundation of a shared vision for a sustainable future) is built *gradually,* through levels of communication, which means people must be given the time to get to know one another.[18] The first level of communication is "small talk." Small talk includes comments about the weather, one's immediate surroundings, and current events. Although such small talk may seem superficial and meaningless, it has a purpose. Exchanging small talk for a moment or two gives each person a chance to "size up" the other person and find out what, if anything, each has in common with the other and whether further conversation would be fruitful. This level of communication is "safe" because one is not expected to reveal anything about oneself.

The second level of communication is the disclosure of facts. Should the initial "small talk" go well, either or both of the participants might feel the desire to get to know the other better. If both people feel this way, the conversation goes to the next level, as both people begin disclosing rather impersonal facts about themselves, such as the work they do or the hobbies they have. In this way, common interests (or the lack thereof) are discovered.

The third level of communication is the sharing of opinions and points of view. In this phase of communication, one shares more personal points of view or opinions on such things as politics, religion, or concerns over the direction in and the speed with which one's community is growing.

As trust builds, one reaches the fourth level of communication—sharing personal feelings. At this point, both people disclose feelings of a more personal nature than those of level three. One might, for example, speak of problems at work, or of one's personal sense of loss as the trees are cut down on a neighboring hillside to make way for a new housing subdivision, or of concern for the future of one's children in the face of unplanned urban growth.

Unfortunately, a growing number of people have trouble learning to trust, and some never learn. Trust versus mistrust is the psychosocial crisis in the first of psychologist Erik Erikson's eight stages of human development.[19] Trust versus mistrust is the dominant struggle from birth to age 1. Erikson assigned hope as the virtue of this stage in which the mother–baby relation lays the foundation for trust in others and in oneself. But as everything has within itself the seed of its opposite, this stage also presents the challenge of mistrust in others and a lack of confidence in oneself.

Hope, as the virtue of trust, is the enduring belief that one can achieve one's necessities and wants. Trust in human relationships is thus the bedrock of community and its sustainable development.

If trust is not developed, none of Erikson's other stages of development can take place: *autonomy* versus shame and doubt, *initiative* versus guilt, *industry* versus inferiority, *identity* versus identity confusion, *intimacy* (relationship) versus isolation, *generativity* versus stagnation, and *integrity* versus despair—all of which are part and parcel of a sustainable community. Community is therefore the melding of how people in different developmental stages relate both to themselves as individuals within a community and with others as a community.

In sum, community is relationship, and meaningful relationship is the foundation of a healthy, sustainable community. In this connection, Ralph Waldo Emerson penned the following: "It is one of the most beautiful compensations of this life that no man can sincerely try to help another without helping himself." William James said it thusly: "Wherever your are, it is your own friends who make your world."

As such, a resident community serves five purposes: (1) social participation—where and how people interact with one another to create the relationships necessary for a feeling of self-worth, safety, and shared values; (2) mutual aid—services and support offered in times of individual or familial need; (3) economic production, distribution, and consumption—jobs, import and export of products, as well as the availability of such commodities as food and clothing in the local area; (4) socialization—educating people about cultural values and acceptable norms; and (5) social control—the means to maintain those cultural values and acceptable norms.[20]

Community also reminds one that the scale of effective organization and action has always been small local groups. As anthropologist Margaret Mead said: "Never doubt that a small group of thoughtful, committed citizens can change the world; indeed it is the only thing that ever has."

It is therefore logical that community not only is a way of valuing the independent voluntary or nonprofit organization but also relies for its expression on such institutions as neighborhood schools, family centers, and volunteer organizations. Further, creating sustainable communities strengthens one's fidelity to a sense of place and is the best possible immigration policy because it raises the value of staying home. These things top-down government cannot fulfill.

With the current disintegration of family and local community in American life, it is unlikely that most people in this country really have an intimate sense of trust and belonging. We have largely lost our sense of connection to and with community that once impressed French political figure and traveler Alexis de Tocqueville to the point that he wrote in the 1830s:

> Americans of all ages, all conditions, and all dispositions constantly form associations...religious, moral, serious, futile, general or restricted, enormous or diminutive. The Americans make associations to give entertainments, to found seminaries, to build inns, to construct churches, to diffuse books, to send missionaries to the Antipodes; in this manner they found hospitals, prisons and schools.[21]

He went on to argue that it was no accident that "the most democratic country on the face of the earth is that in which men have, in our time, carried to the highest perfection the art of pursuing in common the object of their common desire." Why then the progressive disintegration of trust?

Consider that only 30% of the people surveyed in 1966 said they did not trust the government in Washington, D.C., some of the time or all of the time, and 75% of the people surveyed in 1992 responded in the negative.[21] What has happened to the most democratic country on Earth? Why have we lost our sense of community? There at least three possibilities.

One reason for this loss of community may be our lopsided expansionist economic world view in which material possessions and the incessant push for continual economic growth take the place of spirituality, as once manifested in quality relationships and mutual caring. The economic world view translates into both adults in many households having to work outside the home just to make ends meet, which raises the question of who is left at home to forge community ties and act as parents.

This is an important question, as author James Baldwin asserts when he says: "For these are all our children....We will all profit by, or pay for, whatever they become." If, therefore, human society and its environment are ever to become sustainable, it is necessary to rediscover or recreate our sense of local community in order to balance the material with the spiritual, the piece within the whole.

The second reason is summed up by Abraham Maslow: "We [as human beings] fear our highest possibilities (as well as our lowest ones). We are generally afraid to become that which we can glimpse in our most perfect moments, under the most perfect conditions, under conditions of greatest courage. We enjoy and even thrill to the god-like possibilities we see in ourselves in such peak moments. And yet we simultaneously shiver with weakness, awe, and fear before these same possibilities."[22] Is it, as Maslow says, our fear of our own greatness and success that is the inner enemy made manifest in the moral decay that is consuming communities in this country? But there is yet a third possibility.

Have you ever wanted to abdicate your adult responsibilities in the face of an uncomfortable situation and return to an earlier stage in your life, such as childhood or adolescence, when someone else took care of your basic needs? We all face this kind of psychological immaturity at one time or another.

A logger once said that he knew the current logging practices were detrimental to the ecological health of the forest, but couldn't the remedy wait until he had retired? What he really wanted was to pass his errors to the next generation so he would not have to be responsible for the discomfort of owning them and being adversely affected financially by that ownership.

This feeling—this longing to "cop out"; to go backward in time; to regress to an earlier, safer, more self-centered stage in one's psychological development (or for some people to never grow out of it)—is termed the "mother complex," according to Jungian analyst Robert Johnson.[23] Although the mother complex is not owned exclusively by men, Johnson, speaking of men, says that the darkest qualities in a man's life appear in connection with his regressive nature or mother complex, which he stresses is a phenomenon of a man's inner life and is not associated with his human mother.

Nothing, says Johnson, is as dangerous to a man's (or woman's) psychological well-being and maturity as an unresolved mother complex. "Skid row or a drug-and-alcohol rehabilitation center lies not far ahead of a man with a heavy [unresolved] mother complex." Unfortunately, this regressive desire to abnegate our adult responsibilities toward ourselves, one another, or our common environment is a pervasive attitude in American society.

Of its many manifestations, there is one that emerges as increasingly influential in modern America—the ever-more transient nature of the American people. A person who is transient is continually beginning a new job and/or moving to a new location and has no time to form a sense of place, with its demand of commitment and fidelity. A person who is perpetually beginning is so distracted, so dissipated in focus and energy that he or she seldom reaches a point of resolving his or her deep emotional issues, those which pertain to psychological maturity and wholeness.

Such transience is a problem not only in secular life but also in monastic life, which brings me to the notion of *stabilitas*.[24] Simply put, the monastic concept of *stabilitas* or steadfastness implies not only abiding in a particular place but also identifying oneself with the community in all its works, its ups and downs, its tensions, joys, and sorrows. *Stabilitas* means perseverance in and with a community over the long term for its common good.

In monasticism, the vow of *stabilitas* is based on the fact that a monk, under the appearance of greater potential, which one might call a "greener pasture," may follow a path from one monastic community to another and in so doing lose the good already at hand. The purpose of the vow is to make a monk realize that steadfastness in and of itself is an immense good and that in a vast majority of cases constitutes a much greater good than might be gleaned by changing monasteries.

If a monk will retain *stabilitas,* he or she will be able to effect the greatest and most important change—that of oneself, the inner transformation to a more conscious human being open to the balance between spirituality and materiality. This may be likened to a thought by Minnie Richard Smith: "Diamonds are only chunks of coal that stuck to their jobs." So it is that if we in secular life continually seek outer distractions by moving from place to place and job to job, we too may lack the focus to achieve the inner transformation that not only could be ours here and now but also is necessary for wise land-use planning, which is based on quality relationships among people and between people and their environment.

Robert Johnson, in his book *Lying with the Heavenly Woman,*[23] refers to the gentle way the Chinese have of talking about friendship (relationship): Their proverb is that the best cup of tea between friends is the fifth cup. Tea in old China was made by simply pouring hot water over loose tea leaves in a cup. The essence of the proverb lies in steeping the tea leaves.

When friends meet, busy and tense from their daily lives in the outside world, they pour hot water over new tea leaves, which, turning quickly into tea, is drunk in haste and without much grace. Since the same tea leaves are used for each cup of tea, the second pouring of water requires a longer time to steep the leaves. This is better. The third cup requires still more time, as does the fourth. The fifth cup stands for an appreciable length of time before the nearly spent tea leaves render up a brew of the required strength. Hence, the fifth cup of tea is the symbol of friendship at its best because even an introverted person needs the quiet passage of time, measured in cups of tea, to realize the deepest friendship.

There seems scant place in our Western, industrialized psyche for this kind of leisure because the American proverb is time is money. Our materialistic societal appetite seems to have reached a compulsive, addictive state in which to want is to have to have! We have made synonyms of "desire," "want," "need," and "demand," and in so doing we have lost sight not only of the land's ecological capability but also of our inner sense of leisure.

The Chinese character for leisure is composed of two elements, which by themselves mean open space and sunshine. Hence, an attitude of leisure creates an opening that lets the sunshine in. Conversely, the Chinese character for busy is also composed of two elements, which by themselves mean heart and killing. This character points out that for the beat of one's heart to be healthy, it must be leisurely.[25]

We tend to think of leisure, according to Brother David Steindl-Rast (a Benedictine monk), as the privilege of the well-to-do. "But leisure," says Brother Steindl-Rast, "is a virtue, not a luxury. Leisure is the virtue of those who take their time in order to give to each task as much time as it deserves....Giving and taking, play and work, meaning and purpose are perfectly balanced in leisure. We learn to live fully in the measure in which we learn to live leisurely."

You might wonder what leisure has to do with sustainable community. To create a viable community and a shared vision for its sustainable future, people must take the time to drink the fifth cup of tea together. They must give both their community and their vision for its future as much time as they each deserve by creating each with the appropriate leisure, as in olden times, which means slowing down to recapture the *quality* of human relationships—the social glue of community.[26]

Author Jeremy Rifkin has observed that as our pace of life becomes faster, we become more impatient. As we become more organized, we become less spontaneous and hence less joyful. We are better prepared to react to some aspects of the future but less able to enjoy all aspects of the present or reflect on the past. And wisdom requires reflection.

"As the tempo of modern life has continued to accelerate," says Rifkin, "we have come to feel increasingly out of touch with the biological [and spiritual] rhythms of the planet, unable to experience a close connection with the natural environment." Our human perception of time is no longer joined to the ebb and flow of the tides, the rising and setting of the sun, or the eternal parade of the seasons. We have instead created an environment governed by artificial time punctuated by electronic impulses from the heart of technology. But technology, contrary to the thinking of many people, is not the culprit in our ever-faster pace of life; the culprit is economics.

Danny Hillis, pioneer of the conceptual design behind high-speed supercomputers, joins our discussion by warning that our obsession with speed causes us to lose sight of the future and remain trapped in the present. To this, prominent German environmental thinker Wolfgang Sachs adds that speed is also an unrecognized factor that fuels environmental problems.

It is possible, contends Sachs, to talk about the ecological crisis as a collision between scales of time—the fast scale of human modernity crashing into the slow scale of Nature and the Earth. In our fast-paced world, he says, we put more energy into arrivals and departures than we do into the experience itself. In this sense, our obsession with constant motion virtually guarantees that we miss the very experience to which we are rushing.

The speeding internal clock of our constantly go-faster society is not only difficult to escape but also precludes most of us from thinking in terms of consciously varying the pace of our lives to find therein the hidden beauty, because our culture at large deems speed to be "productive." It is, nevertheless, imperative to break the sense of time as taskmaster because raising children, making close friends, and creating works of art all require various scales of time since all are practices in the aesthetics of relationship.

The aesthetics of relationship in scales of time is illustrated in a story Danny Hillis tells about the recent replacement of the gigantic oak beams in the ceiling of one of the dining halls at Oxford University. University officials were concerned that they would not be able to find lumber large enough and strong enough to replace the worn-out beams. But the replacement beams were of the same quality as when the hall had been built 500 years earlier. How could this be?

"Simple," explained the university's forester. "When the dining hall was originally constructed 500 years ago, our predecessors were thoughtful enough, considerate enough, and farsighted enough to plant a grove of oak trees so that the university could, when necessary, replace the beams with others of the same quality." By planting the oaks all those centuries ago, one could say that the people who planted them not only understood and appreciated time in its various scales but also may well have seen time as a mystery to be contemplated, rather than a foe to be vanquished.

Here it is important to understand that slowness is not in opposition to speed, but rather is the middle path between *fast* and *inert*. Therefore, if one will give up always looking beyond the task at hand, such as crafting a shared vision of a sustainable future, one inevitably finds that one not only has the required time for the task at hand but also that the task is done well the first time and thus actually saves time and money somewhere in the future.

Because true community and its shared vision are founded on the rare beauty of quality relationships, such a community and its vision are possible only when we individually take the time to do our inner work and transcend the regressive nature of our unresolved mother complexes. Resolving our mother complexes in conjunction with a vow of *stabilitas* in our respective communities (and the leisure to adequately fulfill that vow) is critical *if* a true shared vision for a sustainable future is to be forthcoming. Such a vision and its implementation are the cardinal responsibility of psychologically mature adults to the generations of the future. It we fail in this responsibility, local communities will come under ever-increasing stress.

LOCAL COMMUNITY UNDER STRESS

Although the last two centuries may have nurtured such institutions as political freedom and the rights of private property, they have done little for the quality of relationship—the trust—that holds traditional American communities together. The last two centuries have done even less to nurture the concept, let alone the reality, of multiracial communities. But this softer value of trust is the social capital that enables people to work together and commit to common causes. And there is yet another value that we have all but lost—the spiritual health of our reciprocal relationship with our environment.

Although there are major environmental catastrophes looming on our horizon, as James E. Haklik affirms, perhaps the greatest catastrophe has already occurred "and we are now fumbling about trying to cope with its effects, pretty much unaware that it even happened." What catastrophe is Haklik talking about? He is referring to the modern loss of our spiritual relationship with our environment, a spiritual relationship that in olden times committed humanity to do its conscious best to protect the health of the very environment on which it depended for livelihood.

The catastrophe is not only the loss of this spiritual connection but also the fact that we, as a whole, have too little concern for or understanding of its effects, which are manifested in part through our loss of relationship to place and community as well as our environment. Having said this, it is clear to me that relationships of high quality and integrity are absolutely critical to the success of a community in translating its cultural identity into a shared vision of the future toward which to build.

To this, Mikhail Gorbachev might add: "Economic prosperity must go hand in hand with social cohesion [community] and ecological sustainability. What good is a lot of money when the social fabric is destroyed and the environment polluted?"

For a community to fulfill its vision, it must be grounded in personal ethics, which are translated into social ethics. This puts the responsibility for one's own conscience and behavior where it rightfully belongs—squarely on one's own shoulders. With a strong sense of personal and social ethics, communities will be spared wasting time and money policing socially unacceptable behavior, which ultimately leads to the destruction of both a community and its landscape. With a strong sense of personal and social ethics, neither the environment nor future generations will be the dumping ground for personal and social irresponsibility.

While for some community may simply be a useful new concept to wrap around old ideas and institutions, for others it will be a new set of ideas, a new frame of reference about how and why people relate to one another and to the wider world. Its value lies in building a bridge between people's core values and principles for action and governance, which will help shift perceptions about what politics and government are really for, such as balancing growth in the population of a community with the biologically sustainable capacity of its landscape.

There is in each community an upper limit to population beyond which the overall quality of life becomes unalterably diminished and the immediate landscape irretrievably damaged with respect to human values. If an upper limit to population size is selected, a certain percent of the population would reply that the community is already too large. Another segment of the community would respond that it is big enough right now. Still another portion would assert that if things were done better, such as all phases of careful strategic planning, a much larger population could be accommodated. But at some point, no matter how well growth is "managed," people realize that the upper limits of a population do count.[27] To this Ogden Nash might add: "Progress is a good thing, but it has been going on too long."

Once a certain size, a critical mass, is reached, there is no reclaiming the more comfortable scale of a community with its ambiance. Beyond some point, the indescribable sum total of population, traffic, human activities, commotion, noise, the clarity of stars at night, the quality of air and water, demand on public services, quality of personal relationships, and the ability to put it all in the context of a place of *quality* called "home" is irretrievably lost.

Why should 10 to 15% of the people (those who will never accept limits to a community's size because of vested interests in continual growth) be able to determine the long-range future of a community's population? Urban growth boundaries are designed to limit the size of a community within the context of its landscape as long as development meets certain criteria. But those with vested interests in continual growth would push for increasing the size of the urban growth boundary once filled to capacity, which negates the whole concept of containing population growth.

So the question becomes one of how a community can be given the legal right to limit the growth of its population if it so chooses. The decision, once made, needs to be written into the city charter and used to provide a context for all documents and any further planning.

Amending the city charter is important because there is an increasingly common yearning for a more defined and authentically lived set of ethical values (trust) with which to rekindle meaning and purpose in life and politics. The language of community is one way of reconnecting people to a set of shared values and principles with which to embrace daily uncertainties. Shared ethics must therefore be nurtured as one of the most valuable assets in making human communities work. In many places, however, such as West Africa, the notion of shared personal and national ethics is rapidly becoming a foreign emotional–intellectual territory that is giving way to anarchy—the cancer that spreads when the strong organizing context of a shared vision of sustainable community is in disarray or absent.[28]

"West Africa," according to Robert D. Kaplan, "is becoming *the* symbol of worldwide demographic, environmental, and societal stress, in which criminal anarchy emerges as the real 'strategic' danger."

Overpopulation, scarcity of resources, disease, crime, migrations of refugees, and the increasing erosion of nation-states and international borders, along with the empowerment of private armies, security firms, and international drug cartels, are now most convincingly evident through a West African prism. In Kaplan's mind, these sorts of issues, which are often extremely unpleasant to discuss, will soon confront our own Western industrial society.

He then goes on to discuss four compelling reasons why he thinks this will happen: environmental scarcity, cultural and racial clashes, remapping the world politically, and the transformation of war as we know it. To further our discussion of the critical importance of a shared vision for a sustainable future, we will focus only on environmental scarcity.

"For a while," writes Kaplan, "the media will continue to ascribe riots and other violent upheavals abroad mainly to ethnic and religious conflict. But as these conflicts multiply, it will become apparent that something else is afoot, making more and more places like Nigeria, India, and Brazil ungovernable." However, should "the environment" or "diminishing natural resources" be mentioned in foreign-policy circles, one would meet the proverbial brick wall of skepticism or boredom, especially from conservatives to whom "the terms seem flaky."

"It is time," asserts Kaplan, "to understand 'the environment' for what it is: *the* national-security issue of the early twenty-first century," which he then proceeds to detail in one long sentence: "The political and strategic impact of surging populations, spreading diseases, deforestation [desertification], and soil erosion, water depletion, air pollution, and possibly, rising sea levels in critical, overcrowded regions like the Nile Delta and Bangladesh—developments that will prompt mass migrations and, in turn, incite group conflicts—will be the core foreign-policy challenge from which most others will ultimately emanate, arousing the public and uniting assorted interests left over from the Cold War."

Beyond this, he specifically targets the coming scarcity of water in such diverse places as Saudi Arabia, Central and Southeast Asia, and the southwestern United States as a cause of future conflicts. In North Africa, for example, a war could erupt between Egypt and Ethiopia over the waters of the Nile, whereas tensions have already arisen in Europe between Hungary and Slovakia over the damming of the Danube.

And then there is the proposed damming of the Mekong River in Sambor, Cambodia, which would create an impoundment 309 square miles in extent and displace 60,000 people. These 60,000 would be added to the 30 to 60 million people worldwide who have already been displaced by large dams during the past 50 years, mainly in China and India.[29]

As often happens under such circumstances, an environmental dispute fuses with an ethnic and historical one, in which case the cause of the conflict is often clouded and thus misunderstood. Today's environmental crises are not unlike modern warfare, of which Kaplan writes: "As [Colonel Thomas] Suitt [of Fort Leavenworth, Kansas] ran me through the…[computer screen] battle, displaying all…[300 to 400] vehicles and the terrain as combat progressed and asking me what I would do at each stage, I felt as if I were playing multidimensional chess with thirty seconds allowed between moves. More and more information has to be processed with less and less time to reflect."[9] It is in these murky waters of human struggle that the clarity of a shared vision for a sustainable future must be created, implemented, and adhered to—one community at a time—if the 21st century is to be lived with any semblance of human dignity.

Community, a deliberately different word than society, may refer to neighborhoods or workplaces, but to be meaningful it must imply membership in a human-scale collective, where people encounter one another face to face. Community must therefore nurture human-scale structural systems within which people can feel safe and at home in a particular place to which they feel a measure of fidelity. And it is precisely this sense of safety in and fidelity to a particular place that is being called into question as the face of community is being redefined in a more worldly context.

SHADES OF COMMUNITY: A LESSON FROM BIRDS

Here it is instructive to consider communities of birds in a given area as ornithologists think of them. First, there is the resident community, which is that group of birds inhabiting the area to which they have a strong sense of fidelity all year. In order to stay throughout the year, year after year, they must be able to meet all of their ongoing requirements for food, shelter, water, and space. These requirements become most acutely focused during the time of nesting, when young are reared, and during harsh winter weather.

Then there are the summer visitors, which overwinter in the southern latitudes and fly north to rear their young. They arrive in time to build their nests, and in so doing must fit in with the year-long residents without competing severely for food, shelter, water, or space, especially space for nesting. If competition is too severe, the resident community will decline and perhaps perish through overexploitation of the habitat by summer visitors, which have no lasting commitment to a particular habitat.

There are also winter visitors, which spend the summer in northern latitudes, where they rear their young, and fly south in the autumn to overwinter in the same area as the year-long residents, but after the summer visitors have left. They too must fit in with the year-long residents without severely competing with them for food, water, shelter, and space during times of harsh weather and periodic scarcities of food. Here, too, the resident community will decline and perhaps perish if overexploitation of the habitat through competition is too severe. And like the summer visitors, the winter visitors are not committed to a particular habitat, but use the best of two different habitats (summer and winter).

On top of all this are the migrants, which come through in spring and autumn on their way to and from their summer nesting grounds and winter feeding grounds. They pause just long enough to rest and replenish their dwindling reserves of body fat by using local resources of food, water, shelter, and space, to which they have only a passing fidelity necessary to sustain them on their long journey.

The crux of the issue is the carrying capacity of the habitat for the year-long resident community. If the resources of food, water, shelter, and space are sufficient to accommodate the year-long resident community as well as the seasonal visitors and migrants, then all is well. If not, then each bird in addition to the year-long residents in effect causes the area of land and its resources to shrink per resident bird. This, in turn, stimulates competition, which under circumstances of plenty would not exist. If, however, such competition causes the habitat to be overused and decline in quality, the ones who suffer the most are the year-long residents for whom the habitat is their sole means of livelihood.

"What," you might ask, "does this have to do with a resident human community?" It relates to the statement previously made by Wendell Berry: a true community can extend itself beyond the local, but *only* if it does so *metaphorically*. This means that if the resident community is rendered nonsustainable, then the trust embodied in the continuity of its history is shattered, as is the self-reinforcing feedback loop of mutual well-being between the land and the people.

Having lost the cohesive glue of trust embedded in its fundamental values, the community loses its identity and is set adrift on the ever-increasing sea of visionless competition both within and without, where "growth or die" becomes the economic motto that drives the cultural system. Such visionless competition inevitably rings the death knell of community.

THE EXISTENCE OF COMMUNITY DEPENDS ON HOW WE TREAT ONE ANOTHER

To protect a resident community's sustainability within that of its landscape, the community's requirements must be met before other considerations are taken into account; if this does not happen, no other endeavor will be sustainable. As an example, let's consider the First Americans.

First Americans

Prior to the invasion of foreigners from Europe, the First Americans had unlimited natural resources per capita on a long-term basis, although such resources as food may have been limited seasonally. (Today, however, local communities face increasingly permanent limitations on natural resources, both renewable and nonrenewable, in addition to which seasonal limitations must also be taken into account.)

When the Europeans arrived and began competing for those same resources, the inevitable outcome was not readily apparent. But as the numbers of Europeans continually increased, through both local births and rapid immigration, the First Americans were increasingly pushed out of the way by superior numbers of Europeans, each of whom demanded his or her "fair share" of the available resources.

Moreover, the First Americans shared the land, whereas the Europeans took forcible ownership thereof to the exclusion of a whole indigenous culture. The Europeans superimposed their mythology on that of the First Americans and consciously set about destroying not only the culture of the First Americans but also the mythology upon which it was based. With the demise of their resources and culture, the First Americans lost their sense of place, hence their sense of mythology, hence their sense of identity, hence their sense of community, and finally their cultural soul.

"Company" Towns

Many of today's local communities are in a similar type of jeopardy as were the First Americans because they are little more than the economic colonies of large national and international corporations. Most corporations, whose fidelity is to the profit margin as opposed to a sense of people, community, or place, increasingly siphon off as much of the local capital as possible and give as little in return as possible. (This is how the Europeans treated the First Americans.)

When the corporations withdraw their presence, because the resources on which they count become depleted or markets fail, communities that were built around the corporations are left to fend for themselves. This often means that they must use all available natural resources in their local landscapes if they are to diversify enough to survive.

Outside Pressures

Today, local communities are facing increasing outside pressures from people who move seasonally into their local landscapes to harvest renewable natural resources, such as the mushrooms that the local people in the Pacific Northwest often need to survive as a community. When the harvest is over, the seasonal visitors leave. The issue, therefore, is no longer job stability but rather community sustainability. And because the people coming into an area are often from other countries and nationalities, there is a clash of mythologies and a corresponding lack of communication, as often happens when people are forced together through perceived necessity.

In some cases, people who move into an area for the seasonal harvest of its resources, like the birds, may be able to fit in without overharvesting. There is a caveat to this statement, however: There must be a firm limit to the number of seasonal gleaners and the quantity they harvest, which unequivocally takes into account the requirements of the local residents and the sustainable productive capacity of the landscape.

In other cases, where the necessities of the local year-long residents and the sustainable productive capacity of the land are not put first, the seasonal gleaners operate de facto in a fashion similar to that of the corporations, which use local communities and their landscapes solely as economic colonies in a competitive bid for their resources.

Competition

In contrast to the preceding, there are communities where wealthy people move in, drive up land prices, and effectively take over the town by forcing out the community's original inhabitants. The displaced members are forced to live elsewhere but are allowed to commute from their new homes to their original community, where they may work to serve the wealthy. Whether this happens by default or by design, the effect is the same: trust is irrevocably broken, as is the historical continuity of the community.

Many people would say that all this is simply the way of competition and that makes it okay. But a vision directed solely by competition cannot long endure; it must deplete itself. Continual depletion of natural resources, and with them local communities, is a danger we daily face because we are so overdependent on and mesmerized by competition that it is our predominant model for learning and change.

Although conventional wisdom says there is nothing intrinsically wrong with competition, that it can even be fun and promote invention and daring, we have lost the balance among competition, cooperation, and coordination at precisely the time we most need to work with one another. Economic competition, which today is being globalized, increasingly pits workers in each enterprise against workers in all enterprises, workers in each ethnic group against workers in all ethnic groups, and workers in each country against workers in all countries.

Economic competition as practiced in the strict, narrow sense can only destroy social/environmental sustainability, never forge its links. We thus find ourselves oftentimes competing with the very people with whom we need to collaborate, which frequently leads to destructive conflicts over the way in which resources are used and who gets what, how much, and for how long.

Our challenge, therefore, is to redesign and develop our communities around such universal principles as love, honesty, moderation, humility, hospitality, justice, and inclusive unity, all of which promote social cohesion. Without these ingredients, no community, no matter how economically prosperous, intellectually endowed, or technologically advanced, can long endure.

Communities will thrive and be sustainable in the new millennium only to the extent that they acknowledge, respect, and nurture the spiritual dimension of human nature by making the moral, emotional, spiritual, and intellectual development of the individual a central prior-

ity. Further, their centers of learning must cultivate the limitless potentialities of the human consciousness and must pursue the equal participation of all people in generating and applying their unique gifts of
knowledge.

Remembering at all times that the interests of the individual and the
community are inseparable, not only from one another but also from
the landscape within which they reside, these communities must promote respect for both the rights and responsibilities that foster equality
and partnership between men and women to protect and nurture
families. They must also nurture both natural and cultural beauty and
use such beauty to stitch the community into its surrounding landscape.

QUESTIONS WE NEED TO ASK

4

When Margaret Shannon, a professor of natural resource policy and sociology at the State University of New York, said that "the world does not define itself for us; rather we choose to see some parts of the world and not others," she opened the door to a whole new way to think about culture: through our individual and collective perceptions. Her statement puts us on notice that we do not *see* clearly our own culture, but rather we have some perception of it, which in itself creates our culture, because my perception is more or less different from yours, sometimes vastly different.

The amount of chaos and conflict in a community is therefore a direct measure of not only how different people's perceptions really are but also how committed they are to defending their individual points of view, regardless of their narrowness in scope. The purpose of a vision is to render the present chaos into the greatest possible harmony for the collective benefit of the community as a whole through time, recognizing that each person's perception is part of the community's living culture.

Living culture is thus embodied in the people themselves, and it is there one must search for an understanding of a people as a whole. In this sense, each person is both the creator and the keeper of a unique piece of the cultural tapestry, an understanding of which one can glean only by seeing it simultaneously from many points of view, much as an insect sees.

Our perceptions can be thought of as similar to an insect's compound eyes because it is through perception that we "see" one another and everything else. An insect's compound eyes are formed from a group of separate visual elements, each of which corresponds to a single facet of the eye's outer surface, which may vary from a few hundred to a few thousand facets, depending on the kind of insect. Each facet has in turn what amounts to a single nerve fiber that sends optical messages to the brain. Seeing with an insect's compound eyes would be like seeing with many different eyes, with many different perceptions simultaneously.

Each perception of a component of one's community is like a facet in the compound eye of an insect, with its independent nerve fiber connecting it to the local community and hence expanding outward to the regional, national, and global society (the various levels of our increasingly collective and abstract brain). Thus, each perception, composed of many elements, including an individual's personal and cultural foundation, has its unique construct. This of course establishes the limits of an individual's understanding.

A person who tends to be positive or optimistic, for example, sees a glass of water as half full, while a person who tends to be negative or pessimistic sees the same glass of water as half empty. Regardless of the way it is perceived, the level of water is the same, which illustrates that we see what we choose to see, which has everything to do with perception but may have little to do with reality.

The important implication is that the freer we are as individuals to change our perceptions without social resistance in the form of ridicule or shame, the freer is a community (the collective of individual perceptions) to adapt to change in a healthy developmental or evolutionary way. On the other hand, the more people are ridiculed or shamed into accepting the politically correct ideas of others, the more prone a community is to the cracking of its moral foundation and to the crumbling of its social infrastructure, because social change cannot long be held in abeyance, which poses questions to which we must respond. As Sam Goldwyn once said, "For your information, let me ask you a few questions."

Before the people of a community are ready to craft a shared vision of their future, they must ask and answer two questions: (1) Who are we today as a culture? (2) What legacy do we want to leave our children?

WHO ARE WE AS A CULTURE?

Who are we culturally—now, today? This is a difficult but necessary question for people to deal with because a vision is the palpable nexus between a fading memory of the past and the anticipation of an uncertain future. The people of a community must therefore decide, based on how they define their present cultural identity, what kind of vision to create. A people's self-held concept (individual, cultural, and universal values) is critical to their cultural future because their personal and cultural self-image will determine what their community will become socially, which in turn will determine what their children will become socially.

The question of who we are culturally may be a more important question today than it would have been in the recent past because there are times in history, such as today, when two eras run parallel to each other, when one is dying while the other is struggling with its infancy.[30] This can be a deeply disturbing, confusing, and divisive time as different world views, cultural patterns and assumptions, and predominant means of livelihood compete with one another in an effort to give meaning and direction to life.

Such a time of raw chaos and naked transition can be terribly frightening and thus lead people to retreat into the simplistic solutions often associated with fundamentalism. Fundamentalism (which can ensnare both the political right and left or the spiritual and secular) is characterized by a rigid, impervious belief system that relentlessly widens the polarity between the safe "us" and the dangerous "them." Because it is founded in fear (which is always divisive) and becomes the embodiment of fear that feeds on itself, fundamentalism is not only incapable of tolerating diverse views and backgrounds but also far less capable of creatively asking new questions and discovering new answers within a context of dynamic complexity.

Fundamentalism, which is so prevalent in today's political discourse, is simply not up to the challenge of our times. Instead, the next stage of cultural evolution must focus inward, into each person's consciousness, because this is the only realm out of which can grow creative, self-organizing innovations that offer sustainable ways of living, which are, after all, based on the quality of both interpersonal relationships and those between humanity and its environment.

Cultural evolution, like all evolution, thrives in a context rich in diversity and complexity, wherein myriad opportunities for interaction exist. Self-organizing innovations can emerge out of such a setting as people search for ways to live consciously and sustainably in every sense of the word. These innovations become "attractors," which draw us out of the chaotic soup into further experimentation with social/environmental sustainability.

The most powerful attractors are those that respond to people's basic requirements for survival and to their deepest yearnings for such things as connection, meaning, and transcendence, all of which add up to personal wholeness. When these attractors resonate among large numbers of people (a critical mass), society shifts, but people must first be aware of these "attractors" amid the flotsam and jetsam of change in which the decay of the dying era seems, at least momentarily, to overwhelm the formative one.

Of course, there initially is a multitude who, preferring the devil they know to the devil they don't, steadfastly swear allegiance to the passing era by clinging tenaciously to old views and old ways of doing things. But there is also an expanding group of younger people who find the present and future ripe with possibilities. And it is here, in the present, that small choices and actions can have major, albeit unpredictable, effects in determining what comes next and how it manifests.

And somewhere among the millions of choices and thousands of experiments with conscious living is the possibility that they will coalesce into a new society that is founded on and protects true community while endowing life with real meaning. For such a civilization to be viable, however, it would have to be anchored on the bedrock value of social/environmental sustainability in all its various aspects.

Thomas Jefferson gave good counsel on values: "In matters of principle, stand like a rock. In matters of taste, swim with the current." To identify those principles and/or values on which we stand firm, we can ask ourselves: What are the fundamental principles that I believe in to the point of no compromise? What values are central to my being?

Categories of Value

The Ch'an masters who carried Zen to Japan brought Confucian ethics with them. In discussing these fundamental values as a guide to personal behavior, Confucius said, "If a man will carefully cultivate these in his conduct, he may still err a little, but he won't be far from the standard of truth."[31, 32] When we as individuals clearly understand and can explicitly articulate our personal values, then we can live in keeping with them.

Let's consider three categories of values: universal, cultural, and individual.[33] Universal (or archetypal) values reveal to us the human condition and inform us of our place therein. Through universal values, we connect our individual experiences with the rest of humanity (the collective unconscious) and the cosmos. Here, the barriers of time and place, of language and culture disappear in the ever-changing dance of life. Universal values must be experienced; they cannot be comprehended. Can you, for example, know a sunset? Fathom a drop of water? Translate a smile? Define love?

Universal values are the timeless constants brought to different cultures at various times throughout history. "Even as the hands of a clock are powered from the center, which remains ever still, so the universal values remain ever at the center of human life, no matter where the hands of time are pointing—past, present, or future."[33] These are the truths of the human condition toward which people aspire (such as joy, unity, love, and peace); of these, the sages have spoken in many tongues.

Cultural (or ethnic) values are those of the day and are socially agreed upon. They are established to create and maintain social order in a particular time and place and can be highly volatile. Cultural values concern ethics and human notions of right and wrong, good or evil, in terms of customs and manners.

In culture we see reflected the ideas and behaviors that a society rewards or punishes according to their perceived alignment to its values. Hence, cultural values are for an individual a mixed bag, especially in a highly complex society that has lost its sense of family, community, and mythology, like that of the United States, where there is much that may resonate with an individual and much that may not.

Every culture is a person in a sense, and, like people, there is the potential for creative interaction and/or conflict when cultures meet. Although we are all too familiar with cultural conflicts and the destruction they have wrought, it is well to remember that a meeting of cultures also triggers tremendous explosions of creativity in such things as language, ethics, education, law, philosophy, and government.

Individual (or personal) values are constituted by the private meanings we bestow on those concepts and experiences (such as marriage vows or spiritual teachings) that are important to us personally. These meanings are in large part a result of how we are raised by our families of origin and what of our parents' values we take with us in the form of personal temperament. These meanings may change, however, depending on our experiences in life and how much we are willing to grow psychologically and spiritually as a result of our experiences. As such, individual values are reflected in such things as personal goals, humor, relationships, and commitments.

Thus, how well a people's core values are encompassed in a vision depends first on how well the people understand themselves individually and as a culture, which means how well they understand their core values, and second on how well that understanding is reflected on paper, where there can be no question about what has been stated and how. Let's consider the First Canadians.

The First Canadians have departed from their old culture because they have, against their will, been forced to adopt European–Canadian ways, which means they have given up or lost ancestral ways. Yet they have not, by choice, totally adopted white culture and want to retain some degree of their ancestral culture. Thus, the three questions they must ask and answer are: Which of our ancestral ways still have sufficient cultural value for us to keep them? Which of the white ways do we want to or are we willing to adopt? How do we put the chosen elements of both cultures together in such a way that we can today define who we are culturally?

For example, in 1993, I was asked to review an ecological brief for a First Nation in western British Columbia, Canada, whose reservation is located between the sea and land immediately downslope from that which a timber company wanted to cut. The problem lay in the fact that the timber company could only reach the timber it wanted to cut by obtaining an easement through the reservation, which gave the First Nation some control over the timber company. The First Nation wanted this control to have an active voice in how the timber company would log the upper-slope forest, because the outcome would for many years affect the reservation.

By virtue of the company's required easement through the First Nation's land, the First Nation was the strong organizing context that would control the behavior of the timber company as it logged the upper-slope forest. If, however, the timber company had not been required to pass through the First Nation's land, it could, through self-serving logging practices, easily have become the uncontrollable cancer that would have destroyed the cultural values of the First Nation's land for many generations.

Before meeting with the timber company, the First Nation's chief asked for some counsel. My reply was as follows:

> Before I discuss the ecological brief I've been asked to review, there are three points that must be taken into account if what I say is to have any value to the First Nation. What I'm

about to say may be difficult to hear, but I say it with the utmost respect.

Point 1: Who are you, the First Nation, in a cultural sense? You are not your old culture because you have—against your will—been forced to adopt some white ways, which means you have given up or lost ancestral ways. You are not—by choice—white, so you may wish to retain some of your ancestral ways. The questions you must ask and answer are: What of our ancestral ways still have sufficient value that we want to keep them? What of the white ways do we want to or are we willing to adopt? How do we put the chosen elements of both cultures together in such a way that we can today define who we are as a culture?

Point 2: What do you want your children to have as a legacy from your decisions and your negotiations with the timber company? Whatever you decide is what you are committing your children, their children, and their children's children to pay as the effects of your decisions unto the seventh generation and beyond. This, of course, is solely your choice, and that is as it should be. I make no judgments. But whatever you choose will partly answer Point 3.

Point 3: What do you want your reservation to look like and act like during and after logging by the timber company? How you define yourselves culturally, what choices you make for your children, and the conscious decisions you make about the condition of your land will determine what you end up with. In all of these things, the choice is yours. The consequences belong to both you and your children.

What about you, the reader? Who are you today? We each change personally as we grow in years and experience. So do our respective communities. Each community that wishes to create a vision for a sustainable future must therefore ask of itself: Who are we today in a cultural sense? Then, based on how a community sees itself, each community must ask: Who do we want to be or to become in the future? These are important questions and must be clearly answered on paper for all to see, because how they are answered will determine the nonnegotiable constraints that set the overall direction of a community's vision and thus the legacy inherited by its children. To answer who we are as a community today and what we want as a community in the future, it is advantageous to begin by honestly evaluating your own set of values.

Identifying Those Values That You Personally Want to Safeguard for Yourself and Your Children

Although it may not seem important at any particular moment in a given day, it is critical in the long run to know what values to safeguard in one's community. After all, values shape the contours of our lives. For example, a simple act by the very people who went to Phoenix, Arizona, to find relief from their allergies has placed Arizona among the top 10% of states in pollen count during the six-week allergy season.[34]

Before urban sprawl began consuming the desert, the area around Phoenix was a haven for people who suffered from allergies. Doctors in the 1940s and 1950s sent patients there because the dry air was virtually pollen-free. But many of those people also brought with them their nondesert plants, which subsequently matured and now fill the air with pollen during the spring of each year.

In addition, the dry climate causes pollen grains from nonindigenous plants to stay aloft and ride the air currents, wafting in every zephyr. They are not washed from dry desert air, as they are in nondesert areas that experience spring rains. So the allergy sufferers themselves made their own haven into their worst nightmare by not identifying and protecting the very value that brought them to Phoenix, Arizona, in the first place—air virtually free of pollen.

Mikhail Gorbachev, in an interview with Fred Matser, is concerned that "we are witnessing a breakdown of the proper relationship between human kind and the rest of nature. I believe...this situation has arisen," says Gorbachev, "because we have retreated from the perennial values. I don't think that we need any new values. The most important thing is to...revive the universally known values from which we have retreated."[35]

With the above in mind, you would be wise to pause for a moment and describe to yourself how you feel about your community before you begin to craft your vision and goals. What types of images come to mind? Who do you think about in your community and why? What places do you think about (open space, shopping malls, schools)? Do activities present themselves? If so, which ones? In short, characterize your community, and be sure to do so either by recording your questions and answers on tape or by putting them in writing.

If you find that you are unsure how you feel about something, take the time to consciously observe your community; see how it functions and how you feel about the way it functions. How friendly is it? How safe do you feel living and moving about in it during the day and at night?

If you are still not sure you have covered all the bases, put yourself in the position of a consultant who has been hired to characterize your community. What questions would you, as a consultant, ask the residents? Why did you select these particular questions? What are you hoping they will tell you? Why do you think these particular questions are important? Now continue your observations and answer the questions for yourself.

Based on what you see and feel, what values do you hold that are met in your community and why? Which values are not met and why?

By asking these question of oneself, it becomes clear that framing good questions is the key to crafting a good vision statement and goals. Now, using this technique, characterize and design the community of your dreams. What would it be like? Can you see where, how, and why your interests and talents would fit into your vision? Describe in writing its primary elements, remembering that the most important part of community, by the very nature of the concept, revolves around the quality of human relationships and the reciprocal partnership between the community and its landscape.

If even a small group of community members is willing to participate in such a personalized exercise, it would quickly become apparent that the makings of a sound vision and goals are contained in the collective of the personal observations, feelings, and values. But taken alone, personal values are not enough. The pulse of the community as a whole must also be taken.

Ferreting Out Community Values

To ask a relevant question about where you are going, you must know not only where you want to go but also where you are, which means taking stock of who you are. Whereas a shared vision is a statement of where you want your community to go, assessing your community, including the reciprocity of its relationship to the immediate landscape, as it is today allows you to determine your starting point for the journey.

One way of assessing a community is by entering into its routines.[36] This means selecting people to attend school events, such as football games and meetings of the Parent–Teacher Association; visiting people in their kitchens and living rooms; and going into cafes, gas stations, laundromats, and other places where people gather, such as taverns and churches. The purpose of these visits is to interact with residents to determine such things as what they do for work and what their work routines are, their personal interests, recreational patterns, what support services are important to them, and how they feel about changes within the community and between the community and its landscape.

To really understand how a community sees itself, one must ask people not only what they like about their community and its landscape and why but also what they do not like and why. One must ask people what they most want to change about their community and its landscape. Questions also help one find out which informal networks people use both to communicate with one another and to solve problems, as well as those whom they trust and rely on as communicators and caretakers.

Alternatively, a consultant can be hired to design the questions and derive the answers by visiting personally and informally with community members in both their places of business and their homes. Here the watchword is *trust*. The people *must trust* the consultant(s), because people do not care how much a person knows until they know how much that person genuinely cares about them.

It is, after all, the quality and sustainability of one's own community that are being mapped into the future, and that is no small matter. It is thus important to understand that trust is heightened and the community's purpose is served to the extent that members of the community become actively engaged in the process.

The purpose of asking such questions is to make the informal system of community clearly visible in such a way that by understanding the range of issues people are concerned about and how they see themselves in relationship to those issues, one can help the community recognize and express its current cultural identity. This kind of information is called ethnography in anthropology, or "the story of the people."

The story of the people as a baseline description of how the people identify themselves culturally is a sound preparatory step toward crafting a shared vision. A sustained process of interaction within a community at the informal level has two important effects.

One, it fosters empowerment of the people themselves and as a community because personal and social reflection not only determines the intelligence and possible consequences of any given action but also leads citizens to see what the next step might be and to take it. It is thus important, as French philosopher Henri Bergson observed, to "think like a man [person] of action, and act like a man [person] of thought."

Two, it can prompt social institutions into becoming more responsive because people within agencies gain insight into the concerns of citizens and thus into a community's cultural identity by participating in the ongoing "story of the people." Such participation gives agency people good and relevant information that makes sense to the citizens and allows them to understand why citizens say what they do. This notion is reminiscent of a statement made by Mahatma Gandhi to an audience of India's bureaucrats and social elite: "Until we stand in the hot sun with the millions that toil every day in the fields, we will not speak for them."

In this statement, Gandhi showed that he understood the basis of real public opinion, which ranges from a vague general feeling to a specific set of beliefs for which people are willing to die.[37] Public opinion is characterized as much by emotions as by logic and is determined by self-interest, which, with your help, can be expanded from a strictly individualistic, self-centered self-interest into an "enlightened" (more conscious), broader (community) self-interest.

One important fact must be kept in mind, however; information alone will rarely change the ideas and opinions held by people, especially if the information is in a purely abstract form. Good public relations works more on the "hidden" levels of thought and feelings, those exemplified by the trust embodied in genuine mutual goodwill, as opposed to the level of logic that is purely intellectual.

Gandhi, by insisting on meeting the downtrodden masses of India on their own ground, established the credibility and genuineness of his understanding of their plight and of his love for them, and this made all the difference because they felt not only that they knew him but also that they could trust him. And trust is the key to one's belief in and willingness to follow the lead of another person.

One of the ways Gandhi garnered the people's trust was to deal fairly with all sides (including the British, regardless of their behavior), which is critical because in almost any subject there is controversy when viewed from more than one perspective. This means that one must guard carefully against arrogance in one's own point of view and one's behavior because arrogance will almost always cause the listeners to resent whatever is being said, no matter how well founded it may be.

Consider that in today's world, the intangible asset of "goodwill," which is analogous to trust, is rated surprisingly high in value as part of the total price of purchasing a business. Building the intangible asset of goodwill takes many years of diligent, consistent effort; once earned, few organizations are willing to relinquish it. Individuals, such as leaders, not only can but also must build this asset over time if they are to be effective.

For example, someone trying to lead a community toward social/ environmental sustainability must make it his or her business to supply accurate information and other useful services to those citizens involved in the visioning effort. It would be folly to try and mislead them with exaggerated statements and facts of dubious merit, although I have seen it. In return for such steadfast honesty, one's fellow citizens listen attentively to and consider carefully what one says, even though they may not agree.

Earning the trust and goodwill of one's fellow citizens is critical today because, having been lied to so often by experts, people are more skeptical than ever before and thus reluctant to place their trust in people they do not personally know. Even then, they may be cautious. Nothing persuades an audience to examine your point of view as much as personal trust. Be that as it may, the conclusions to which your presentation may bring an audience is only useful if there is a powerful drive to act in accord with those conclusions.

Whether we like it or not, what usually motivates people is their own self-interest. With this in mind, experience shows that a persuasive message is more likely to be accepted and acted upon if it meets the following criteria:

- It provides for a personal necessity or desire ("If you do this, it will protect your quality of life.").
- It is in harmony with group beliefs ("We all know that social/ environmental sustainability is…").
- The audience is led to the final conclusion and then left to discover it for themselves ("Based on past experience and current knowledge, it seems self-evident that…").

Whatever method is used to gather the information, it must be based on personal trust and goodwill, in addition to which the people must ultimately craft the vision and goals themselves, with the help of a neutral third-party facilitator. The group could then craft a "straw" document that contains a statement of vision and goals to which the community at large can respond. Unless the whole community partakes of the process, a straw document must be produced for the community to comment on.

This straw document is not a "buy-in" vote, however, which is no more than a wolf in sheep's clothing. The purpose of a buy-in, which is often used by self-centered governments, agencies, and special-interest groups, is to win agreement with a self-serving point of view by convincing members of the community that they cannot reason for themselves and should therefore "trust" those of superior knowledge to know what is good for the community as a whole. *This approach will not work.*

Instead, the comment period must be long enough to give people the time they require to really consider so important a document. And then, the people must really be listened to, and their comments must be collected, collated, and incorporated into the vision. A vision, to be effective, must be finalized by consensus. And finally, a vision and goals must periodically be reenvisioned to keep them dynamic and relevant in the present to the present and to the future, something that is seldom done.

Such small-scale change, done with and by people rather than for or to them, when multiplied over a whole community, becomes a clear signpost toward a community's vision of social/environmental sustainability and hence the legacy people leave their children.

WHAT LEGACY DO WE WANT TO LEAVE OUR CHILDREN?

Once a group of people, whether a community such as an indigenous peoples or your own hometown, has defined itself culturally (present and future), it can decide what legacy it wants to leave its children. This must be done consciously, however, because the consequences of whatever decisions the group makes under its new cultural identity are what the group is committing its children, their children, and their children's children to pay.

The rest of my reply to the First Nation in Canada applies here:

> Now to my comments: This is a difficult task at best. As with any definition, it is a human invention and has no meaning to Nature. Therefore, you must tell the timber company, clearly

and concisely, what the terms in this ecological brief mean to you and how you interpret them with respect to the company's actions that will affect your reservation.

1. Every ecosystem functions fully within the limits (constraints) imposed on it by Nature and/or humans. Therefore, it is the type, scale, and duration of the alterations to the system—the imposed limits—that you need to be concerned with.

If your reservation looks the way you want it to and functions the way you want it to, then the question becomes: How must we and the timber company behave to keep it looking and functioning the way it is? If, on the other hand, your reservation does not look the way you want it to and does not function the way you want it to, then the question becomes: How must we and the timber company behave to make it look and function the way we want it to?

But regardless of your decisions or the company's actions, your reservation will always function to its greatest capacity under the circumstances (constraints) Nature, you, and the company impose on it. The point is that your decisions and the company's actions, excluding what Nature may do, will determine how your reservation both looks and functions. This reflects the importance of the preceding Point 3, which is: what you want your reservation to look like and how you want it to function *after* the timber company has left. It also reflects the importance of what you decide.

2. If you want the landscape of your reservation to look and function in a certain way, then how must the timber company's landscape look and function to help make your reservation be what you want it to be? Keep in mind that the landscape of your reservation and the company's timber holdings are both made up of the collective performance of individual stands of trees or "habitat patches" (a stand is a human-delineated group of standing trees). Therefore, how the stands look and function will determine how the collective landscape looks and functions.

3. Remember that any undesirable ecological effects are also undesirable economic effects over time. Your interest in your reservation will be there for many, many years, generations perhaps, but the company's interest in the forest may well disappear just as soon as the trees are cut. So, the company's short-term economic decision may be good for them immediately but may at the same time be a bad long-term ecological and thus a bad long-term economic decision for you.

4. To maintain ecological functions means that you must maintain the characteristics of the ecosystem in such a way that its processes are sustainable. The characteristics you must be concerned about are: (1) composition, (2) structure, (3) function, and (4) Nature's disturbance regimes, which periodically alter the ecosystem's composition, structure, and function.

The composition or kinds of plants and their age classes within a plant community create a certain structure that is characteristic of the plant community at any given age. It is the structure of the plant community that in turn creates and maintains certain functions. In addition, it is the composition, structure, and function of a plant community that determine what kinds of animals can live there, how many, and for how long. If you change the composition, you change the structure, hence the function, and you affect the animals. People and Nature are continually changing a community's structure by altering its composition, which in turn affects how it functions.

For example, the timber company wants to change the forest's structure by cutting the trees, which in turn will change the plant community's composition, which in turn will change how the community functions, which in turn will change the kinds and numbers of animals that can live there. These are the key elements with which you must be concerned, because an effect on one area can—and usually does—affect the entire landscape.

Composition, structure, and function go together to create and maintain ecological processes both in time and across space, and it is the health of the processes that in the end creates the forest. Your forest is a living organism, not just a collection of trees—as the timber industry usually thinks of it.

5. Scale is an often-forgotten component of healthy forests and landscapes. The treatment of every stand of timber is critically important to the health of the whole landscape, which is a collection of the interrelated stands.

Thus, when you deal only with a stand, you are ignoring the relationship of that particular stand to other stands, to the rest of the drainage, and to the landscape. It's like a jigsaw puzzle where each piece is a stand. The relationship of certain pieces (stands) makes a picture (drainage). The relationship of the pictures (drainages) makes a whole puzzle (landscape). Thus, the relationships of all the stands within a particular area make a drainage, and the relationships of all the drainages within a particular area make the landscape.

If one piece is left out of the puzzle, it is not complete. If one critical piece is missing, it may be very difficult to figure out what the picture is. So each piece (stand) is critically important in its relationship to the completion of the whole puzzle (landscape). Therefore, the way each stand is defined and treated by the timber company is critically important to how the landscape, encompassing both the company's land and your reservation, looks and functions over time.

6. Degrading an ecosystem is a human concept based on human values and has nothing to do with Nature. Nature places no extrinsic value on anything. Everything just is, and in its being it is perfect (intrinsic value). Therefore, when considering intrinsic value, if something in Nature changes, it simply changes—no value is either added or subtracted. But superimposing the extrinsic value of human desires on Nature's intrinsic value creates a different proposition. Thus, whether or not your reservation becomes degraded depends on what you want it to be like, what value or values you have placed on its being in a certain condition, to produce certain things for you. If your desired condition is negatively affected by the company's actions, then your reservation becomes degraded. If your desired condition is positively affected by the company's actions, then your reservation is improved. Remember, your own actions can also degrade or improve your reservation.

7. It is important that you know—as clearly as possible—what the definitions in this brief really mean to you and your choices for your children and your reservation. Only when you fully understand what these definitions mean to you can you negotiate successfully with the timber company.

If you, the reader, substitute the name of your own community wherever "reservation" occurs in the above brief, and if you substitute "land-use zoning" or "land-use planning" wherever "timber company" occurs in the above brief, you have an outline to follow for your own community, perhaps with a few modifications to fit specific local conditions.

In addition to the above, we must exercise the good sense and humility to sincerely *ask* our children (beginning with second- and third-graders) what they think and how they feel about their future as we build our shared visions of a sustainable future in which each person's core values (including our children's) are acknowledged.

WHAT LEGACY DO OUR CHILDREN WANT US TO LEAVE THEM?

Consider for a moment that the children must inherit the world and its environment as we adults leave it for them. Our choices, our generosity or greed, our morality or licentiousness, will determine the circumstances that must become their reality.

Why, then, do we adults assume that we know what is best for our children, their children, and their children's children when adults as a whole are destroying their world through greed and competitiveness? Why are children never asked what they expect of us as the caretakers—the trustees—of the world they must inherit? Why are they never asked what they want us to leave them in terms of environmental quality? Why are they never asked what kinds of choices they would like to be able to make when they grow up? (For that matter, why do we not ask our elders where we have come from based on their legacy to us, how we are repeating history's mistakes, and what we have lost, such as fundamental human values, along the way?)

Where do we, the adults of the world, get the audacity to assume that we know what is good for our children when all over the world they are being abused at home by parents who are not in control of themselves, are being slaughtered in the streets in the egotistical squabbles of adults over everything imaginable, and are being starved to death by adults using the allocation of food for political gain? We do not even know what is good for us. How can we possibly speak for them?

This lack of responsible care was keenly felt at the June 1992 worldwide Conference on the Environment, held in Rio de Janeiro. A 12-year-old girl delivered to the entire delegation a most poignant speech about a child's perspective of the adult's environmental trusteeship. I saw a video of the speech in which a child was pleading for a more gentle hand on the environment so that there would be some things of value left for the children of the future. The adult audience was moved to tears—but not to action!

If our human society is to have a sustainable future, it is increasingly important to listen to what the children say because they represent that which is to come. Children have a beginner's mind. To them, all things are possible until adults with narrow minds, who have forgotten how to dream, put fences around their imagination.

We adults, on the other hand, too often think we know what the answers should be and can no longer see what they might be. To us, whose imaginations were stifled by parents, schools, and frightened social peers, things have rigid limits of impossibility. We would do well, therefore, to consider carefully not only what the children say is possible but also what they want.

In asking children what kind of world they want us to leave them, one must know how best to talk the matter over with them on their level. The following are some tips.[38]

According to people who commonly work with children, the same basic principles that apply to speaking with adults apply to speaking with children. The difference is changing the emphasis and intensity to fit the children's age and circumstances.

In speaking to adults, for example, one makes eye contact, uses visuals, encourages participation by the audience, and varies one's vocal delivery and gestures. People who tell stories to children or in other ways educate them use the same techniques, only in an exaggerated manner, and the younger the children, the greater the exaggeration.

In general, this means one needs enthusiasm combined with lots of hand motions and facial expressions to captivate children. One must also make sure that the children are interested in what is being said and that the topic, such as what they want their future to be like, is presented in such a way that it is important to them and they understand how and why that is so.

The younger the children, the more they enjoy the here and now, and the less they relate to the notion of past tense; after all, to them, yesterday is a long time ago. The older children are, the more readily they can relate to past, present, and future tense, but it can be made much easier for them if the ideas can be connected to something they already know.

Here are some specific points to consider:

1. Arrange the room for optimum attention. Arrange the room for optimum attention by asking yourself: Will everyone be able to see? Will they be comfortable? Will each child feel like she or he is a part of the group?

The best seating arrangement for a young audience is a circle or semicircle because the children can interact more easily with the speaker, and making them part of the circle is the first step in helping them feel like they are really involved in the discussion. Children tend to lose interest if they do not feel really involved with the group.

It is best if the speaker can sit down close to the children because it is less threatening for them to be at eye level than to peer upward at a looming giant of an authority figure. Some people have the best results when everyone, including the speaker, sits on the floor.

2. Involve the children. Although young children can be asked to act out their feelings, middle-school and high-school kids are too self-conscious to participate in such a manner because they do not want to appear foolish in front of their peers. With older children, ask a question and have them think about it or raise their hands in response. Ask questions in the beginning that everyone can answer positively, and then incorporate the information into the discussion.

3. Know the audience. Before speaking to a group of children, do a little fact-finding. What have they been studying in school that relates to what they want their future to be like? Then use this material to draw and hold their attention.

Ask the children about themselves. What do you like best or are you most interested in? Do you know what you want to be when you grow up? How do you feel about the world around you? What do you want the world to be like when you are grown up? What do you want the world to be like for your children? Although finding out about the kids helps you connect with them, it is even more important for the kids to know that you genuinely care about them and their future. It is thus important to relate your points to what they are thinking about.

You must also adjust your presentation to the age group you are visiting with. For example, exaggerated gestures are okay with young children but must be toned down for older ones. And while young children can deal with open-ended questions (What do you think?), older kids are often too embarrassed to say what they think in front of their peers. In this case, open-ended questions inhibit participation.

4. Variety. Everyone responds to variety, especially children. Variety can be created with a story (including how one projects one's voice, which is important in holding kids' attention), listening and learning (lecture), speaking and sharing (questions and answers, including a list of questions of your own gleaned from things the children say to you or one another), and open participation (discussion), all of which work best if appropriately laced with drama and humor. In addition, visual aids (such as a flip chart, showing a film or slides) help to emphasize or clarify your point, and props (such as giving a demonstration, putting on a skit, reciting a poem, even giving a short assignment) promote involvement. Of course, any combination of these can be used.

Pictures are also a good way to get to know children, especially young children, and to incorporate variety into one's discussion of what they want us, as adults, to leave for them as a legacy. My next-door neighbor, Justin Lewis, teaches a combined class of second- and third-graders. Each year I speak to his class about some aspect of Nature, usually forests. Together, we have developed a way of helping young children express what they want the forests to be like when they grow up—in other words, what legacy they want us to leave for them.

Justin begins the process before I come into his class by asking the children to draw individual pictures of what they think a forest is, and he has them write an explanation to accompany the picture. He gives me the pictures before I visit with the children, so I can evaluate their perceptions of a forest.

I then visit with them in their classroom and show them slides of a forest with its plants and animals. We talk about plant and animal relationships within the forest (including people). Next, we take a field trip into a real forest so that I can help the children transfer any abstract ideas into concrete experiences in order to further their understanding.

Once again, Justin has them draw individual pictures of a forest so they can incorporate their new understanding. Justin and I then discuss the difference between their first and second pictures. Finally, so the children can begin to understand that it is everyone's responsibility to save, protect, and care for the forests for the future, which is not always easy, Justin has them work collectively to draw a mural of the forest they want us, the adults of the world, to leave for them. The mural is important so they begin learning to work together toward a common goal, the precursor to a full-fledged vision.

5. Keep it short. Time is a critical factor when visiting with children because a child's attention span is much shorter than that of an adult. For the younger elementary-school children, 10 to 15 minutes generally works well, while older children will generally pay attention for 30 to 50 minutes.

6. Make sure the children understand you. The language and concepts must be kept simple for small children, which by no means precludes teaching them some new things, such as words or ideas. Be sure to check with the kids when using words that might be unfamiliar. Ask, "Can anyone tell me what this is (or means)?" Make sure everyone understands before moving on.

If you are in doubt about how to make sure children of different age groups will understand you, take the time to visit teachers and librarians. They have a wealth of tips on different ages, developmental stages, and interests to help you ask the children what they want us, as their guardians, to protect for them as our legacy to their livable future.

The future, after all, is theirs, which brings us to the necessary topic of vision, goals, and objectives. For your community to negotiate effectively for the future, for yourself, for your children, and for their children, your community must have a clear vision, goals, and objectives.

UNDERSTANDING A VISION, GOALS, AND OBJECTIVES

5

Having defined who they are culturally, having determined what legacy to leave their children, and having taken into account the legacy their children want them to leave, the people of a community are now ready to craft a vision of what they want as a sustainable future. Although the word vision is variously construed, it is used here as a strong organizing context in the form of a shared view of the future, which is based on its three separate but overlapping aspects: world view, perception, and imagination.[33]

WORLD VIEW

Our world view is our way of seeing how the world works; it is our overall perspective from which we interpret the world and our place in it. However, it can also be seen as a metaphysical window to the world, which cannot be accounted for on the basis of empirical evidence any more than it can be proved or disproved by argument of fact. "Metaphysical" simply means "beyond" (*meta*) the "physical" (*physic*), of which Albert Einstein said, "The more I study physics, the more I am drawn to metaphysics."

There are in the most general terms two world views: the sacred and the commodity. One need not be religious in the conventional sense to hold a sacred view of life, because a sacred view focuses on the intrinsic value of all life. As such, it gives birth to feelings of duty, protection, and love while emphasizing the values of joy, beauty, and caring, which in turn erects *internal* constraints to destructive human behavior against Nature. "Sacred" comes from the Latin *sacer,* which has the same root as *sanus,* sane. A sacred view of life is therefore a sane view, which corresponds to the Sanskrit *sat, cit, ananda,* or being, consciousness, and bliss.

A commodity view of life is interested in domination, control, and profit and seeks to "gain the world" by subjugating it to the will of the industrial mentality. At the core of the commodity world view are several economic seeds, such as self-interest, the economy versus ecology dilemma, the growth/no-growth tug-of-war, Rational Economic Man, and others.[39] It is necessary with respect to a commodity world view to protect the health of the environment in the present for the present and the future through *external* constraints placed on destructive human behavior.

Eighteenth-century British philosopher and statesman Edmund Burke, considered the founding father of modern conservatism, understood well the need for external constraints on the destructive appetites of humanity when he penned:

> Men [people] are qualified for civil liberty in exact proportion to their disposition to put moral chains upon their own appetites....Society cannot exist unless a controlling power upon will and appetite be placed somewhere, and the less of it there is within, the more there must be without. It is ordained in the eternal constitution of things that men [people] of intemperate minds cannot be free. Their passions forge their fetters.

If, therefore, we are going to change life, to improve it in any appreciable way, we must begin with attitudes, not facts. An outer change always begins with an inner shift in attitude, which Albert Einstein called "a new level of thinking."

"The world we have made," Einstein said, "as a result of...[the] level of thinking we have done thus far creates problems we cannot solve at the same level at which we created them." Ray Anderson, CEO of Interface, a company that makes carpet tiles, is a case in point.[40]

About two years ago, Ray Anderson was happily running his company when he received what he calls a "spear through the heart." Anderson's company consists of 26 factories in 6 countries, customers in 110 countries, 5,800 employees, and nearly a billion dollars in annual sales. Everything was rosy.

Then he was asked by the director of research to address a staff meeting and present an environmental vision for the future of the company.

"I sweated for three weeks," he said, "over what I would say to that group." During those three weeks, someone sent him a book that was to change his level of thinking, a book in which he would find his spear and his vision. The book was *The Ecology of Commerce* by Paul Hawken.

Anderson, an engineer from Georgia Tech, understood the message. His carpet tiles, made from nylon and polyvinyl chloride, come from oil through processes that contribute to pollution. They also last forever in landfills.

Herein lay his "spear through the heart." His company not only was a liability to the planet but also was not sustainable. So he rose to the challenge Hawken presented in his book: "Industry, the largest, wealthiest, and most pervasive institution on Earth," wrote Hawken, "must take the lead in saving the Earth from...[human]-made collapse."

First came Anderson's speech to his staff in which he said his vision was "to make Interface the first name in industrial ecology worldwide, through substance, not words. To convert Interface into a restorative enterprise—putting back more than we take from the Earth. To achieve sustainability and then to help others achieve sustainability, even our competitors."

Anderson says his speech "surprised me, stunned them, and galvanized us into action." Two years later, Interface is proceeding with its commitment to clean up its act.

Some of his business friends think Anderson is crazy and give him books to counter the one by Hawken and other environmental writers. In considering what he has read, Anderson calls one side "alarmists" and the other "foot draggers."

"The alarmist perceives the Earth to be in crisis, sees our actions as totally inadequate, and predicts the outcome to be collapse. The foot dragger perceives things as not so bad, even getting better; sees our actions as good enough, maybe too good—meaning expensive and misguided; and sees the outcome as an abundant future for all. Here's the paradox: The surest way to realize the alarmists' outcome, collapse, is to accept the foot draggers' view. The surest way to realize the foot draggers' outcome, abundance, is to believe the alarmists' view that we are in trouble and have to change."

So Ray Anderson and his company are changing. He is having a blast, while both he and his colleagues are thrilled by the vision and excited by the challenge. "We are all part of the continuum of humanity and life," he said in a recent speech to other corporate CEOs. "We will have lived our brief span and either helped or hurt that continuum and the Earth that sustains all life. It's that simple. Which will it be?"

That is indeed the question. Which will it be: to hurt the continuum of life out of self-centeredness or to help the continuum of life out of concern for others? If we shift our view of life from one that is self-centered to one that is other-centered, we create a new set of facts and conditions as well as a new perception of the old facts and conditions because new perception represents a new level of thinking and thus of perceiving.

PERCEPTION

Our perception is the vision with which we see the world and interpret what we see in that we create our own world by both our attitudes toward it and our perceptions of it, a point clearly made by Army Major Susan P. Kellett-Forsyth, one of the first female graduates of West Point: "It matters less what you read than where you live and where you come from, because that determines how you interpret what you read." Perception comes from perceive, which is from the Latin *percipere,* to seize wholly. "It is one of the great marvels of consciousness," writes author Laurence Boldt, "that whatever situation we clearly perceive, we improve."

To see wholly is to see a better way; therefore, to perceive a problem clearly is to begin formulating its solution. To solve a problem or resolve a conflict, we need the wisdom to keep searching and the confidence of love to hold what we find up to the light of understanding. It is when we doubt our capacity to love and to create, which we then replace with fear and isolation, that we begin to distort our perceptions of the world. When our view of the world is based on the love and confidence of clear perception, the world becomes a better place. It cannot be otherwise.

Nevertheless, we are usually moved from avoidance and confusion to attention and clarity only when we perceive the necessity to do so. "Necessity," wrote Plato, "is the mother of invention." Necessity, in this sense, is simply the perception that a current situation has become intolerable and that something must be done about it, which means the perceiver is the one who must act.

Once necessity is acknowledged and *accepted*, we begin searching for a solution to our problem by examining our old perceptions, which forces us out of our current prejudices and conceptual limitations in such a way that we can sift through those old ideas and concepts that we have in the past overlooked and/or discarded. Fortunately, necessity has an intense urgency about it, without which we too easily and too often give up searching for a better way of being or doing.

"Of course," Laurence Boldt says, "necessity, like beauty, is in the eye of the beholder." No matter how deplorable a situation seems to an observer, the individual in the situation finds no reason to improve it until such improvement becomes for him or her a personal necessity. Until our discontent is moved to necessity and we demand a better way, we will accept that which is of lesser quality. Because we fear and thus hate the things that seem to trap us, we find no way out until we supplant our fear with love and its counterpart, confidence.

We are stuck with our perceived problems until we have the determination, strength, and confidence to view them with love; this applies to problems on the scale of the Earth and our respective communities, as well as to our own personal troubles. The gift of the discoverer and innovator is the ability and tenacity to keep focused on what most of us avoid, the often lonely search for a better way, about which historian Daniel J. Boorstin writes: "The obstacles to discovery—the illusions of knowledge—are also part of our story. Only against the forgotten backdrop of the received common sense and myths of their time can we begin to sense the courage, the rashness, the heroic and imaginative thrusts of the great discoverers. They had to battle against the current facts and dogmas of the learned."[41]

By the very questions he or she asks, the discoverer and innovator elevates finding a new way to a necessity to which she or he is committed in a personal quest. Yet time and again we accept limitations because, not knowing what questions to ask or how to ask them, we cannot see the alternatives in front of our noses.

"Remember," says Laurence Boldt, "people were once told that bleeding was the best cure for disease and that slavery was an economic necessity." And in our present generation, we are told not only that we must prostitute our principles to get along but also that many, if not most, of the problems in the world today are all but insurmountable.

Even though our current problems are by and large fixable, "Man is much more afraid of the Light than he is of the Dark," asserts astrologer Alan Oken, "and will always shield his eyes against a truth which is brought to him prematurely. He will throw stones at it or even crucify it in order to remain in the comfortable shadow of his ignorance. But that is human nature and Man must not be condemned for his unconsciousness."

These notions call forward our individual and collective choices, namely, to yield to the comfortable blindness of ignorance or to summon our courage and make resolute our determination to search until we find a better way. It has been wisely said that anything will reveal its secrets if you love it enough.

IMAGINATION

Imagination, or seeing that which can be, is the third aspect of vision. Even as we open our physical eyes and see the world as we think it is, with all its problems and opportunities, so we can open the eye of our mind and see the possibilities of as yet unseen realities. To open our physical eyes fully, we must learn to trust so we can accept "what is, as it is" through the eyes of love. To open the eye of our mind, we must learn to trust that what we see in our imagination we can bring forth in the physical world.

Whereas perception involves seeing that which already exists in the outer world, imagination involves seeing in one's inner world that possibilities can be made manifest in one's outer world. Albert Einstein penned it nicely: "Your imagination is your preview of life's coming attractions," to which William Butler Yeats added, "In dreams begin responsibility." Consider, therefore, that everything humanity has ever created (or ever will create), both tangible and intangible, began as a single idea in the privacy of someone's mind, be it this book, a religious order, or going to the moon. Our imagination is the source of our power to create and the driving force behind our choices—the prerequisites of a shared vision toward which to build.

DEFINING VISION, GOALS, AND OBJECTIVES

> *Most worthwhile achievements [such as crafting a vision]*
> *are the results of many little things done in a single direction.*
>
> Quebin

Defining a vision and committing it to paper goes against our training because it must be stated as a positive in the positive, something we are not used to doing. Stating a positive in the positive means stating what we mean directly. For example, a local community has an urban growth boundary that it wants to keep within certain limits, which can be stated in one of two ways: (1) we want our urban growth boundary to remain within a half a mile from where it is now situated (a positive stated as a positive), or (2) we don't want our urban growth boundary to look like that of our neighbor (a negative that one is attempting to state as a positive).

Further, to save our planet and human society as we know it, we must be willing to risk changing our thinking in order to have a wider perception of the world and its possibilities, to validate one another's points of view or frames of reference. The world can be perceived with greater clarity when it is observed simultaneously from many points of view. Such conception requires open-mindedness in a collaborative process of intellectual and emotional exploration of that which is and that which might be, the result of which is a shared vision of a possible future.

Two sayings are pertinent here: If you don't know where you're going, any path will take you there, and if you stand for everything, you soon find that you stand for nothing. Would you for a moment consider flying in a commercial airplane if the pilot did not know where he or she was going, how much fuel was aboard, and roughly when you would arrive? Even nomadic hunter-gatherers and nomadic herders knew where they were going; their livelihood—and their survival—depended on it.

Without a vision, we take "potluck" in terms of where we will end up, which was Alice's dilemma when she met the Cheshire-Cat in Lewis Carroll's *Alice's Adventures in Wonderland*.[42] Alice asked the Cheshire-Cat:

> "Would you tell me, please, which way I ought to go from here?"
>
> "That depends a good deal on where you want to get to," said the Cat.
>
> "I don't much care where—" said Alice.
>
> "Then it doesn't matter which way you go," said the Cat.
>
> "—so long as I get somewhere," Alice added as an explanation.
>
> "Oh, you're sure to do that," said the Cat, "if you only walk long enough."

The movie *Spartacus,* which depicts the true story of a Roman slave who as a boy of 13 had been sold into slavery, is an excellent illustration of the power of a collective vision. Bought as a young man, Spartacus was taken to a highly organized school, where he was forced to learn fighting and become a gladiator. There was, however, a revolt early in his career and he, along with his fellow gladiators, escaped.

For a time, they ran roughshod over the countryside, disorganized and out of control. They robbed, raped, and murdered the Roman gentry and encouraged their slaves to join the growing mob. But Spartacus was uncomfortable with the out-of-control mob because he recognized that it had simply become what it was against; it had become like the Romans. He therefore organized the slaves into an army that would fight its way across Italy to the sea and escape.

Thus, in 71 B.C., Spartacus led his army in an uprising. Now a highly organized fighting machine that opposed Roman rule, Spartacus' army had become a dangerous, out-of-control cancer (by Roman standards) that threatened the Roman sense of superiority, because it was, after all, just an army of slaves. Although the slaves twice defeated the Roman legions, they were finally conquered by General Marcus Licinius Crassus after a long siege and battle in which they were surrounded by and had to simultaneously fight three Roman legions.

The battle over, Crassus faces the thousand survivors seated on the ground as an officer shouts: "I bring a message from your master, Marcus Licinius Crassus, Commander of Italy. By command of his most merciful excellency, your lives are to be spared. Slaves you were, and slaves you remain. But the terrible penalty of crucifixion has been set aside on the single condition that you identify the body or the living person of the slave called Spartacus."

After a long pause, Spartacus stands up to identify himself. Before he can speak, however, Antoninus leaps to his feet and yells, "I am Spartacus!" Immediately, another man stands and yells, "No, I'm Spartacus!" Then another leaps to his feet and yells, "No, I'm Spartacus!" Within minutes, the whole slave army is on its feet, each man yelling "I'm Spartacus!"

Each man, by standing, was committing himself to death by crucifixion. Yet their loyalty to Spartacus, their leader, was superseded only by their loyalty to the vision of themselves as free men, the vision that Spartacus had inspired—and Crassus could not take away, even on pain of death. The vision was so compelling that, having tasted freedom, they willingly chose death over once again submitting to slavery. And they were, to a man, crucified along the road to Rome. But by withholding their obedience from Crassus, they remained free because slavery requires that the oppressed submit their obedience to the oppressor.

In more recent times, a vision of freedom and equality inspired 13 colonies to formally declare their independence from England on July 4, 1776. The vision of human freedom and equality was so strong that a whole nation, the United States of America, was founded on it. In 1836, the fall of the Alamo, the Franciscan mission in San Antonio, Texas, and the slaughter of the men defending it inspired Texans in their vision of freedom from Mexican rule. In both cases, the strength of the vision carried a people to victory against overwhelming odds.

In contrast to the above examples, however, is the movie *Braveheart,* a true story about Sir William Wallace (1272?–1305). In 1296, Edward I, king of England, claiming the Scottish throne for himself, drove out the king of Scotland, stationed English soldiers in the country, and stole the "Stone of Scone," also known as the "Stone of Destiny," which was the ancient symbol of Scottish sovereignty.

William Wallace, known for his courage and strength, led bands of Scottish patriots in a bitter war against the invaders. The English raised an army and advanced against Wallace, only to be defeated at the battle of Stirling Bridge. At that point, Edward hurried home from France and led a great army against the Scottish clansmen, whom he defeated at Falkirk in 1298. Wallace escaped, however, and carried on the fight in the mountains. He was captured seven years later (1305) and executed.[43]

The story is also about Robert The Bruce (1274–1329), who became king of Scotland in 1306 and reigned until 1329. He defeated the British at Bannockburn in 1314 and finally won recognition of Scottish independence from England in 1328.

During the life of William Wallace, however, Robert The Bruce had sworn allegiance to Edward I, king of England, although he occasionally changed sides and aided Wallace.[43] In the movie *Braveheart,* Robert The Bruce and the greedy noblemen of Scotland kept changing sides, which meant that Wallace was often betrayed by his own countrymen in the struggle for Scottish independence from England.

The betrayals came about because, in order to defeat Wallace, the king of England needed to weaken the resolve of the vision of Scottish freedom from England that Wallace represented. Edward I would therefore bribe Robert The Bruce and the Scottish noblemen with lands and titles in England, which they accepted—proving the maxim united we stand, *divided we fall.*

It was precisely this divided loyalty that undermined the vision of freedom held by Wallace and the other Scottish patriots. It was this divided loyalty that caused Robert The Bruce to take another 23 years, until 1328, to finally fulfill the vision of Scottish independence. Had Robert The Bruce and the Scottish noblemen united unconditionally with Wallace and the Scottish patriots behind the vision of freedom, might Wallace have lived to see a free and independent Scotland with Robert The Bruce as king seated on the Stone of Scone (a rough-hewn block of grey sandstone weighing 458 pounds) prior to the year 1300? Most likely!

They did not unite however, so it was not until November 14, 1996—700 years after its theft (although it was briefly reclaimed by Scottish Nationals in 1950–51)—that the Stone of Scone was returned from underneath the Coronation Chair at Westminster Abbey in London, England, to Edinburgh Castle, Scotland.[44] Then, finally, was Scotland's vision of freedom complete.

Although a vision may begin as an intellectual idea, at some point it becomes enshrined in one's heart as a palpable force that defies explanation. It then becomes impossible to turn back, to accept that which was before, because to do so would be to die inside. Few, if any, forces in human affairs are as powerful as a shared vision of the heart. Consider Mahatma Gandhi's inspired fight to free India from British rule.

In its simplest, intellectual form, a shared vision asks: What do we want to create? Why do we want to create it? Beyond that, it becomes the focus and energy to bring forth that which is desired, because, as John F. Kennedy said, "Those who anticipate the future are empowered to create it," which is similar to Gandhi's statement: "The future depends on what we do in the present." It is also similar to Franklin Delano Roosevelt's statement: "The only limit to our realization of tomorrow will be our doubts of today." Alas, few people know what a vision, goal, or objective is; how to create them; how to state them; or how to use them as guidelines for sustainable development.

A statement of *vision* is a general declaration that describes what a particular person, group of people, agency, or nation is striving for. A vision is like a "vanishing point," the spot on the horizon where the straight, flat road on which you are driving disappears from view over a gentle rise in the distance.

As long as you keep that vanishing point in focus as the place you want to go, you are free to take a few side trips down other roads and always know where you are in relation to where you want to go, your vision. It is therefore necessary to have at hand a dictionary and a thesaurus when crafting a vision statement. It must be as precise as possible, because through it you must say what you mean and mean what you say.

Gifford Pinchot, the first chief of the U.S. Forest Service, had a vision of protected forests that would produce commodities for people in perpetuity. In them he saw the "greatest good for the greatest number in the long run." Through his leadership, he inspired this vision as a core value around which everyone in the new agency could, and did, rally for almost a century.

In a more recent example, I spoke in 1989 to a Nation of First Canadians who owned a sawmill in central British Columbia. I had been asked to discuss how a coniferous forest functions, both above- and belowground, so that the First Canadians could better understand the notion of productive sustainability, something they were greatly concerned about. After I spoke, a contingent from the British Columbia provincial government told the First Canadians what they could and could not do in the eyes of the government. The government officials were insensitive at best. The First Canadians tried in vain to tell the officials how they felt about their land and how they were personally being treated. Both explanations fell on deaf ears.

After the meeting was over and the government people left, I explained to the First Canadians what a vision is, why it is important, and how to create one. In this case, they already knew in their hearts what they wanted; they had a shared vision, but they could not articulate it in a way that the government people, whose dealings with the First Canadians were strictly intellectual, could understand.

With my help, they committed their feelings to paper as a vision statement for their sawmill in relation to the sustainable capacity of their land and their traditional ways. They were thus able to state their vision in a way that the government officials could understand, and it became their central point in future negotiations.

In contrast to a vision, a *goal* is a general statement of intent that remains until it is achieved, the need for it disappears, or the direction changes. Although a goal is a statement of direction, which may be vague and is not necessarily expected to be accomplished, it does serve to further clarify the vision statement. A goal might be stated as "My goal is to see Timbuktu."

An *objective,* on the other hand, is a specific statement of intended accomplishment. It is attainable, has a reference to time, is observable and measurable, and has an associated cost. The following are additional attributes of an objective: (1) it starts with an action verb; (2) it specifies a single outcome or result to be accomplished; (3) it specifies a date by which the accomplishment is to be completed; (4) it is framed in positive terms; (5) it is as specific and quantitative as possible and thus lends itself to evaluation; (6) it specifies only "what," "where," and "when" and avoids mentioning "why" and "how"; and (7) it is product oriented.

Consider the previous goal: "My goal is to see Timbuktu." Let's now make it into an objective: "I will see Timbuktu on my 21st birthday." The stated objective is action oriented: I will see. It has a single outcome: seeing Timbuktu. It specifies a date: my 21st birthday, and it is framed in positive terms: I will see. It lends itself to evaluation of whether or not the stated intent has been achieved, and it clearly states "what," "where," and "when." Finally, it is product or outcome oriented: to see a specific place.

As one strives to achieve such an objective, one must accept and remember that one's objective is fixed, as though in concrete, but the plan to achieve the objective must remain flexible and changeable. A common human tendency, however, is to change the objective—devalue it—if it cannot be reached in the chosen way or by the chosen time. It is much easier, it seems, to devalue an objective than it is to change an elaborate plan that has shown it will not achieve the objective as originally conceived.

It is important to understand what is meant by vision, goal, and objective because collectively they tell us where we are going, the value of getting there, and the probability of success. Too often, however, we "sleeve shop." Sleeve shopping is going into a store to buy a jacket and deciding which jacket you like by the price tag on the sleeve.

The alternative to sleeve shopping is to first determine what you want by the perceived value and purpose of the outcome. Second, you must make the commitment to pay the price, whatever it is. Third, you must determine the price of achieving the outcome. Fourth, you must figure out how to fulfill your commitment—how to pay the price—and make a commitment to keep your commitment. Fifth, you must act on it.

Alexander the Great, the ancient Greek conqueror, provides an excellent example of knowing what one wants and how to achieve it. When he and his troops landed by ship on a foreign shore that he wanted to take, they found themselves badly outnumbered. As the story goes, he sent some men to burn the ships and then ordered his troops to watch the ships burn, after which he told them: "Now we win or die!"

Although it is we who define our vision, goals, and the objectives for achieving them, it is the land that limits our options, and we must keep these limitations firmly in mind. At the same time, we must recognize that they can be viewed either as obstacles in our preferred path or as solid ground on which to build new paths. How we choose depends on how we approach life.

MAKING ABSTRACTIONS INTO CONCRETE EXPERIENCES

In a sense, generalized personality traits are an amalgamation of the mechanisms with which one navigates life. They thus become the essence of one's interpretation of life's experiences and the springboard of one's personal capabilities. These traits, which we each possess to a greater or lesser degree, are not cut-and-dried, but rather are overlapping tendencies with varying shades of gray. Nevertheless, they can be substantial barriers to communication and thus to the creation of a shared vision.

For example, some people can take ideas seemingly at **random** from any part of a thought system and integrate them; these people have mental processes that instantly change direction, arriving at the desired destination in a nonlinear, intuitive fashion. Others can think only in a **linear sequence**, like the cars of a train; these people have mental processes that crawl along in a plodding fashion, exploring this avenue and that, without assurance of ever reaching a definite conclusion. If the random thinker is also at ease with **abstractions** but the linear-sequence thinker requires **concrete** examples, their attempts to communicate may well be like two ships passing in a dense fog.

There are also **piece thinkers**, the people who tend to focus on individual pieces of a system, or its perceived products, in isolation of the system itself. **Systems thinkers**, on the other hand, tend more toward a systems approach to thinking. A person oriented to seeing only the economically desirable pieces of a system seldom accepts that removing a perceived desirable or undesirable piece can or will negatively affect the productive capacity of the system as a whole. This person's response typically is, "Show me; I'll believe it when I see it."

In contrast, a systems thinker sees the whole in each piece and is therefore concerned about tinkering willy-nilly with the pieces because he or she knows isolated tinkering might inadvertently upset the desirable function of the system as a whole. A systems thinker is also likely to see himself or herself as an inseparable part of the system, whereas a piece thinker normally sets himself or herself apart from and above the system. A systems thinker is willing to focus on transcending the issue in whatever way is necessary to frame a vision for the good of the future.

The more a person is a piece thinker, the more reticent he or she is to change. This type of individual sees change as a condition to be avoided because he or she feels a greater sense of security in the known elements of the status quo, especially when money is involved. But, as Helen Keller once said: "Security is mostly a superstition. It does not exist in Nature. Life is either a daring adventure or nothing." Conversely, the more of a systems thinker a person is, the more likely he or she is to agree with Helen Keller and risk change on the strength of its unseen possibilities.

A piece thinker is likely to be very much concerned with land ownership and the rights of private property and wants as much free rein as possible to do as he or she pleases on his or her property, at times without regard for the consequences for future generations. The more of a piece thinker a person is, the greater the tendency to place primacy on people of one's own race, creed, or religion, as well as on one's own personal needs, however they are perceived. The more of a piece thinker a person is, the greater the tendency to disregard other races, creeds, or religions, as well as nonhumans and the sustainable capacity of the land. Also, the more of a piece thinker a person is, the more black and white one's thinking tends to be.

A systems thinker, on the other hand, is likely to be concerned about the welfare of others, including those of the future and their nonhuman counterparts. Systems thinkers also tend to be concerned with the health and welfare of Planet Earth in the present for the future. And they more readily accept shades of gray in their thinking than do piece thinkers.

These traits come in a variety of combinations, which indicates how different and complex people can be in response to their life experiences and hence in their concepts of a shared vision. These differences and complexities naturally carry over into people's patterns of communication. None of these patterns is better than any other as far as communication is concerned; each is only different and needs to be understood, which brings us to the use of abstractions.

Concrete words refer to objects a person can directly experience. Abstract words, on the other hand, represent ideas that cannot be experienced directly. They are shorthand symbols used to sum up vast areas of experience or concepts that reach into the trackless time of the future, such as "best management practices." Albeit they are convenient and useful, abstractions can lead to misunderstandings.

The danger of using abstractions is that they may evoke an amorphous generality in the receiver's mind and not the specific item of experience the sender intended. The receiver has no way of knowing what experiences the sender intends an abstraction to include, especially when dealing with one's own core values projected into the process of creating a shared vision. For example, it is common practice to use such abstract terms as "proper method" or "shorter than," but these terms alone fail to convey the sender's intent. What exactly is the "proper method"? "Shorter than" what?

When abstractions are used, they must be linked to specific experiences through examples, analogies, illustrations, and/or actual experience. It is thus better to use, as much as possible, simple, concrete words with specific meanings. In this way, the sender gains greater control of the images produced in the receiver's mind, and language becomes a more effective tool.

When dealing with communities in relationship to their landscapes, especially cross-cultural communities or cross-cultural community interactions, it is advisable to get people into the field, where they can physically wander through an area, such as one being considered for the open-space component of a shared vision, and discuss it. Abstractions can thus be transformed into concrete examples, which one can experience through sight, touch, smell, sound, taste, or any useful combination thereof and then discuss with a common frame of reference.

This kind of concrete experience is important because a major barrier to communication is the inability to transfer the outcomes of experience from one kind of situation to another; again, this is especially true when people of different nationalities or ethnic backgrounds come together in discussing contentious issues. The potential ability to transfer results of experiences from here to there is influenced by the breadth of one's personal experiences. Every nationality or ethnic group represents a vast array of experiences, some broad, others narrow, all different.

Experiential transfer, however, is critical to understanding how ecosystems and their interconnected, interdependent components function, including the bridge between a community and its surrounding environment. It is also a necessary ability in dealing with contentious issues between a community's sustainability and that of its landscape to be able to show how potential outcomes can be projected to a variety of possible future conditions.

When a person cannot make such transfers for lack of the necessary frame of reference, he or she will find the ideas to be abstractions, whereas others, with the required experience, will feel them to be concrete examples, based on their accumulated knowledge. This is where analogies are useful.

To make sure that an analogy will be understood, one must ask the person or people to whom one is speaking if he/she or they are familiar with the concrete example that one proposes to use in helping to extend the frame of reference to include the abstraction. If, for instance, one is talking about the value of understanding how the various components of an ecosystem interact as a basis for the system's apparent stability, one can use simple examples, as follows:

1. What happens when just one part is removed? Let's say a helicopter crashes and people are injured. The immediate question is what happened and why.

A helicopter has a great variety of pieces with a wide range of sizes. Suppose the particular problem here was with the engine, which is held together by many nuts and bolts. Each nut and bolt has a small sideways hole through it so that a tiny "safety wire" can be inserted; the ends are twisted together to prevent the tremendous vibration created by a running engine from loosening and working the nut off the bolt.

The helicopter crashed because a mechanic forgot to replace one tiny safety wire that kept the lateral control assembly together. A nut vibrated off its bolt, the helicopter lost its stability, and the pilot lost control. All this was caused by one missing piece that altered the entire functional dynamics of the aircraft. The engine had been "simplified" by one piece—a small length of wire.

Which piece was the most important part of the helicopter? The point is that each part (structural diversity) has a corresponding relationship (functional diversity) with every other part. They provide stability only by working together within the limits of their designed purpose.

2. What happens when a process is "simplified"? A newly elected mayor of a city whose budget is overspent guarantees to balance the budget; all that is necessary, in a simplistic sense, is to eliminate some

services whose total budgets add up to the overexpenditure. A "simplistic sense" is used here because it is not quite that simple. What would happen, for example, if all police and fire services were eliminated? Would it make a difference, if the price were the same and the budget could still be balanced, if garbage collection were eliminated instead?

The trouble with such a simplistic view is in looking only at the cost of and not the function performed by the service. The diversity of the city is being simplified by removing one or two pieces or services, without paying attention to the functions performed by those services. To remove a piece of the whole may be acceptable, provided we know which piece is being removed, what it does, and what effect the loss of its function will have on the stability of the system as a whole.

Once it is certain that an analogy is understood, one can help another person transfer the concept to the abstraction. As the principle of transfer becomes clear, the abstraction begins to take on the qualities of a concrete idea, which usually dissolves this barrier to communication and thus enhances the person's ability to grasp the shared vision.

When dealing with a shared vision of social/environmental sustainability, for example, we must remember always that Nature deals in trends over various scales of time. Habitat (food, cover, space, and water) is a common denominator among species (including humans). We can use this knowledge to our benefit by understanding that long-term social/environmental sustainability requires short-term economic goals and objectives to be stated in the *positive* within the primacy of environmental postulates and sound long-term ecological goals and objectives.

REFRAMING A NEGATIVE AS A POSITIVE

There is great power in learning to reframe negatives into positives. In so doing, the participants in creating a shared vision not only understand their community from several vantage points but also understand that much of the confusion in communication comes from trying to move away from negatives. Trying to move away from a negative precludes people from saying what they really mean because they are focused on what they do *not* want. As long as people express what they do not want, it is virtually impossible to figure out what they *do* want.

Although our educational systems in the United States, beginning with parents and ending with universities, stress the positive, they usually teach in terms of the negative. What does this statement mean?

Suppose your neighbor lives along a busy street and has a little boy named Jimmy. Your neighbor is concerned about Jimmy because of the increasing automobile traffic in the neighborhood.

One day Jimmy's mother says to him, "Jimmy, don't go into the street." The directive words (those telling Jimmy what to do) are *don't go* (a confusing contradiction), and the last word Jimmy hears is *street*; he thus follows the direction of the two congruous words he hears, "go" and "street," and gets hit by a car.

What Jimmy's mother really meant and needed to have said was, "Jimmy, stay in the yard." Then the directive word (the one telling Jimmy what to do) would have been *stay* (singularly clear and concise), and the last word Jimmy would have heard would have been *yard*. He would still have followed the two congruous words he heard, "stay" and "yard," but with very different results—he would be alive.

This example illustrates that, having been raised trying to make positive statements out of negative ones, we spend most of our lives trying to move away from the negative—and we cannot. We can only move toward a positive.

Let's look at an example from the Northwest Territories of Canada. Some time ago, I was asked to help a community of First Canadians create a vision for 800 square kilometers of forest for which they had to draft a management plan that was acceptable not only to them but also to the Canadian territorial and federal governments.

After going through the educational part of the workshop (how forests, streams, and rivers function and how humans can fit into the processes), the workshop participants went into the forest, where they were instructed to sit down and be silent for 20 minutes. They were told to listen to the forest and feel its heartbeat, something they acknowledged never having done.

Afterward, they discussed how they were feeling, what they were thinking, and what the experience had meant to them. Then, with a much heightened awareness of their forest and its cultural significance, we went back to the conference room, where I asked them what their vision of the future was, what they wanted their forest to look like.

"We don't want it to look like British Columbia," was the answer. (The northern part of British Columbia, just south of the border with the Northwest Territories, is laced with gigantic clear-cuts to which the First Canadians objected.)

"I appreciate what you're saying," I replied. "So, what do you want your forest to look like?" I queried again.

"We don't want it to look like it does south of the border," was the reply.

After two or three more such exchanges, I was sure that the participants did not know how to frame their vision, their desire for the future, in a positive statement. All they could do was try to move away from the perceived negative.

I thus helped them reframe the negative into a positive by asking a series of questions.

"What is your staple diet?"

"Moose" was the reply.

"What kind of habitat do moose need?"

"Willow and birch thickets."

"When do you hunt moose?"

"In the late summer and autumn."

"Do you have any medicinal plants that are important to you?"

"Yes, such and such."

"Where do they grow?"

"In this kind of place and that kind of place."

"I notice that birch bark is used to make various domestic objects. Are birch trees important to you?"

"Yes."

The exchange continued. Finally, I asked if anything had been omitted or forgotten. A few things came to mind.

While I was asking these questions and the participants were responding, someone was writing both questions and answers on a large flip chart. The filled sheets were then fastened to the walls of the room. After completing this initial phase of reframing, the participants forgot about the clear-cuts in British Columbia and began focusing on the cultural requirements that needed to be translated into their forest plan.

After taking the positive ideas from the sheets on the walls and crafting an outline, then sentences and paragraphs, the final prose was distilled into a vision statement and a series of goals. Through the simple process of questions and answers, the participants' negative fears were translated, by the participants themselves, into a shared vision and goals for the positive future of their forest and hence their culture.

There is great power in learning to reframe negatives into positives. In so doing, the participants not only understand their community from several vantage points but also understand that much of the confusion in communication comes from trying to move away from negatives. Trying to move away from a negative precludes people from saying what they really mean because they are focused on what they do not want. Let's consider another example, one broader than a community—the coho salmon of the Pacific Northwest. To understand the problem of the coho salmon, however, we need a little history.[45]

Aware of a precipitous decline of wild coho salmon in Oregon, the Oregon Department of Fish and Wildlife implemented "Oregon's Coho Plan" in 1982, which emphasized the "management" of coho as a single species with strong reliance on fish hatcheries to produce large numbers of hatchery-reared coho for release into the wild.

In March of 1991, the American Fisheries Society published its landmark study, *Pacific Salmon at the Crossroads: Stocks at Risk from California, Oregon, Washington, and Idaho.* The study identified 214 genetically different stocks of salmon, 101 of which were at a high risk of extinction, 58 at moderate risk, and 54 of special concern. The study also noted that at least 106 major stocks had recently become extinct.

Although Oregon Governor Barbara Roberts launched an effort to restore the salmon in 1992, the coho continued to decline in 1993, which resulted in severely restricted fishing seasons. Sport and commercial fishing for coho salmon was halted on the West Coast in 1994. That same year, the National Marine Fisheries Service (the fishery arm of the federal government), under tremendous pressure from conservation groups, individuals, and personnel from state agencies, announced that it would investigate salmon and steelhead stocks between Canada and California.

By 1995, the amount of data gathered on salmon, which is housed at the Marine Science Center in Newport, Oregon, already measured in many linear feet of storage space, but the coho numbers were still declining. The National Marine Fisheries Service announced its intent to list coastal coho as threatened in that year, but the 104th Congress placed a moratorium on listing species as threatened or endangered under the Endangered Species Act.

The National Marine Fisheries Service announced in 1996 that ten stocks of Northwest steelhead were at risk of extinction. The congressional moratorium on listing species under the Endangered Species Act was lifted in May of 1996, and the National Marine Fisheries Service announced that April 25, 1997 would be the deadline for listing the coastal stocks of coho salmon.

Against this background, Oregon Governor John Kitzhaber commenced "The Oregon Approach" to resolving the salmon crisis. In

August 1996, the first draft of the Oregon Coastal Salmon Restoration Initiative was released. The Oregon Forest Industry Council pledged $15 million to the governor's salmon recovery effort, but only on the condition that coastal coho *not* be listed under the federal Endangered Species Act, which would have little effect on the industry's forestry practices.

The second draft of the Oregon Coastal Salmon Restoration Initiative was released in early 1997, and Governor Kitzhaber traveled to Washington, D.C., to gain federal support for his plan to restore salmon in Oregon waters.

Despite all of this activity, however, the huge effort to guide the recovery of salmon in Oregon has a fatal flaw: the major goal of the recovery plan is to *prevent* the coastal coho salmon from being listed as threatened or endangered under the federal Endangered Species Act, which is trying to move *away* from a perceived negative, highlighted by the conditional support of the timber industry. For the recovery plan to work, however, it must move *toward* a positive—to *save* the salmon.

This is the third time Oregon has tried to solve the salmon problem in the last 15 years, but the coho continue to dive toward extinction because the focus (even in the present plan) is based more on maintaining the economy than on restoring the populations of wild salmon to ecological health. "We're about to lose the most complex and valuable species on this earth," says Paul Englemeyer of Yachats, Oregon, an advocate for the salmon and a member of the Oregon Watershed Council, "and we're more worried about protecting our personal agendas than the salmon."

Salmon are a barometer of the health of the land. When the populations of salmon are healthy, the land is healthy in like measure. The problem is not just that humanity abuses the salmon; the problem is that humanity abuses the land. Fifty years from now, our children will care about only one thing—the presence of salmon. After all, the salmon are part of the intergenerational commons and belong as much to the children of today and tomorrow as they do to us, the current adults.

Having said all this, it must be understood that there is only one way to save the salmon in Oregon. To understand this, however, one must contrast the Karluk River on Kodiak Island, Alaska, with the coastal rivers in Oregon.

The Karluk River, which flows 21 miles, has 2.5 million salmon returning annually, despite the fact that it is only about 50 feet wide (approximately the width of two side-by-side city streets). In contrast, the Columbia River system, with its roughly 2,500 major watersheds and 266,000 miles of streams, once had an estimated 10 to 16 million salmon, but today the returning number is about 2% and declining. In addition, the Karluk River has more returning wild salmon than all the combined coastal streams in Oregon. Why? What is the difference between the Karluk River and Oregon's coastal rivers?

During the salmon boom of the late 1800s, one of Alaska's biggest fish canneries was situated at the mouth of the Karluk River, where for decades tens of millions of salmon were taken from dams, weirs, traps, and nets stretched across the Karluk's slender girth. The Karluk River was not alone, however; similar stories were unfolding in Oregon. The unrestricted cannery era finally ended along the coast of the Pacific Northwest after laws were passed in the 1930s to protect the few remaining salmon.

But today, while the graveled Karluk River and other streams on Kodiak Island are once again choked with salmon, the number of salmon has steadily declined in the streams and rivers of Oregon. Why has a species so critical to the web of life along the west coast of North America restored itself to robust abundance in one small area and yet been forced to the brink of extinction along a broad front in another, both within the same 150 years?

Blame for the decline of salmon in Oregon covers the gambit from overfishing to dams across the rivers, from predation by seals and sea lions to sport fishing, the introduction of hatchery-reared fish into the wild, and the mysteries of the Pacific Ocean, as well as the unbridled activities of such extractive industries as logging, mining, and the grazing of livestock.

Overfishing? Despite the cannery, the waters of Kodiak Island support one of the world's most active fisheries.

Predation by seals and sea lions? The populations of seals and sea lions were greater in the 1800s, and the salmon of Kodiak Island still face a formidable array of predators.

The ocean? The ocean is a scapegoat, one that is easy to use in absolving us humans of ecological malfeasance. Clearly, the numbers of salmon have remained relatively steady during changes in the condition of the Pacific Ocean. And if they declined, they rebounded, as evidenced by their teeming abundance at the time of European settlement along the West Coast.

None of these factors explains why the salmon are in danger of extinction in the coastal rivers of Oregon. These factors do not explain why only 4,000 coho salmon remain in the Siuslaw River when there were nearly 500,000 in the late 1800s. Or why the annual run of coho salmon in the Alsea River is less than 1% of its estimated 125,000 wild coho. Or why the entire Tillamook drainage system has a mere 1,000 coho, where once more than 180,000 flourished.

There are no roads on Kodiak Island, no plowed fields, and no paved cities sprawling across the landscape. The estuaries are not channeled to aid the passage of ships, domestic livestock do not graze in and trample the riparian zones, streams are not poisoned with chemicals from industry and agriculture, mines do not gouge into the streams, and the forests have not been clear-cut from mountains. Kodiak Island is still a healthy, functioning ecosystem, whereas Oregon has seen 12,000 miles of streams become so degraded in the last 150 years that they are today in noncompliance with standards set by the Environmental Protection Agency.

"But why," you might ask, "is this difference so stark?" Kodiak Island does not have mountain after mountain denuded by decades of clear-cut logging; it does not have economic tree farms where healthy forests once stood; it does not have thousands of miles of roads throughout its landscape and along the margins of its streams; it does not have livestock trampling the soil of and stripping the vegetation from the banks of its streams; it does not have its soil and water polluted with industrial chemicals, including those from intensive agriculture; and it does not have unregulated urban sprawl, with its strip malls and super-highways spreading amoeba-like across its landscape. Oregon, on the other hand, has all of these simultaneously.

The problem with the declining coho salmon in Oregon is not the effect of some one thing in the environment, nor does it rest with some one thing that we humans have done or are doing. And it is not a result of the Endangered Species Act. The problem lies with us—in our thinking, attitudes, and behavior as the dominant species on this planet. The problem lies in the fact that we focus not on the health of the ecosystem that sustains us but only on maximizing the extraction of whichever commodity interests us at any given moment in time.

If the people of Oregon truly want to restore coho salmon to healthy populations, then their focus must be on what they *want*—to *save* the salmon. The focus cannot be on what they do *not* want—to have the salmon *listed* as threatened or endangered under the federal Endangered Species Act.

Efforts to restore the coho salmon to health will depend on the sincerity and diligence of the people of Oregon in their effort to restore the state's environment to ecological health rather than just treat a few isolated symptoms thought to be the cause of the salmon's decline in a vain attempt to prevent it from being listed as threatened or endangered. This means that the people must change their thinking, attitudes, and behavior to simultaneously accommodate the ecological requirements of the salmon—all of them. But as long as people focus on what they do not want, it is virtually impossible to figure out what they *do* want and to achieve it, which brings us to the notion of constraints.

THE OUTCOME OF A VISION IS EXPRESSED IN THE NEGOTIABILITY OF CONSTRAINTS

The vision of some future desired condition, by its very nature, elicits the singular social constraint (the fixed point around which everything else turns, like the hub of a wheel) that must be met if the terms of the vision are to be fulfilled. A constraint in this sense means being restricted to a given course of action or inaction, which in this case connotes something that restricts, limits, or regulates personal human behavior.

A vision does not in and of itself create a single constraint where there was none before. It cannot because everything in the world is already constrained by its relationship to everything else, which means that nothing is ever entirely free. What a vision does is determine the degree to which a particular socially chosen constraint is negotiable. In addition, a vision forces a blurring of all interdisciplinary lines in its fulfillment because the power of the vision rests with the people who created it and those who are inspired by it, not those whose sole job is to administer the bits and pieces of everyday life, as important as they might be.

What does "negotiable" mean here? It means to bargain for a different outcome, to cut the best possible deal. For example, most changes in climate are determined by Nature and are nonnegotiable. Consider that the Pacific Northwest is supposedly entering a 20-year wet cycle after a 20-year dry cycle. According to historical weather records, this would be correct. The Pacific Northwest recently finished the wettest year on record (1996). Other really wet years on record, beginning with 1896, include 1904, 1937, 1968, 1971, 1983, and 1995.[46]

Can we negotiate with Nature to give us sunnier, drier winters without flooding when we deem the winters too dark and wet? Can we negotiate for more rain during winters we deem too dry? Well, we could try, but it would be to no avail. Nature at times does not negotiate; therefore, some of the conditions Nature hands us are non-negotiable; we cannot cut a "better" deal, one that is more to our liking.

Our challenge, therefore, is to learn what is negotiable and what is not. Beyond this, we must learn to accept with grace that which is not negotiable and learn to account for and accept responsibility for the price of that which is negotiable, because negotiability is not free. When we negotiate, we trade one set of behavioral freedoms for another in that we impose a particular constraint on ourselves through a vision in order to alleviate or free up some other potential constraint in the future—the desired outcome of our vision. But if "freedom is not linked to morality," contends Mikhail Gorbachev, "it is not freedom. It is permissiveness. It is just self-seeking, rather than freedom."

"But what kinds of things," you might ask, "does Nature negotiate?" Nature has recently negotiated a new hybrid variety of wheat that gives good yields in arid land. It matures early, which is particularly important in dry years.[47]

Although the agricultural industry has been trying to introduce such a variety of wheat for years, it was unable to overcome a major obstacle, namely, wheat's self-pollination. Wheat is self-pollinating because it has both male and female organs that function in one plant. To produce a hybrid, therefore, the male component of one variety must be in contact with the female component of another as geneticists seek to coax the desired traits out of each variety. However, wheat's dual-sex attributes had complicated the process of cross-breeding, that is until recently when one company finally invented a method of getting rid of one sex in the wheat plant, which allowed scientists to create the hybrid.[47]

Is there anything that we humans can negotiate amongst ourselves wherein Nature does not have the final word? The answer is yes, but with the caveat that the outcome of our behavior must not breach one of Nature's guiding principles.

We can, for instance, negotiate our self-created rules and regulations, our self-created economic theories and self-imposed practices. And it is exactly because our self-created, self-imposed theories, rules, and regulations are negotiable that their degrees of negotiability are also open to those who would dicker for a better deal. Hence the question is: What does the creation of a shared vision do to the negotiability of our self-created, self-imposed theories, rules, and regulations?

A shared vision determines, by its defined outcome, the degree of negotiability that can be afforded to those of our self-created, self-imposed theories, rules, and regulations that are in question. In other words, a vision determines the negotiability of any particular social constraint, and the constraints with which we have to deal in everyday life are, in a human sense, social because they are behavioral, be it how one interprets the rights of private property, how one conducts oneself in church, or where one chooses to build one's house (for example, in the floodplain of a river or on high ground).

At this juncture, let's examine the way in which constraints work by looking at four examples: flooding in California, potential land-use decisions in Oregon, and two processes of visioning with indigenous First Nation peoples of Canada.

California

Sixteen crews worked to shore up some of the 1,100 miles of levees in the Sacramento–San Joaquin Delta.[48] In other areas, crews used sandbags and plastic sheets to shore up critical sections in the 6,000-mile network of levees in northern California.

A dozen major breaks in the levees occurred along the San Joaquin, Mokelumne, and Consumnes rivers, and many other places are threatened because of the pressure of the water day after day. "It's a race with Mother Nature, but right now we're ahead," said Captain Mark Bisbee of the state Forestry Department.

A levee failed on the San Joaquin River on January 10, 1997, sending work crews fleeing through dense fog as a 90-foot gap opened and water began rushing into neighboring fields, where it might have swamped up to 5,000 acres. A break in a levee near Lathrop allowed the flooding of more than 25 square miles and damaged as many as 400 homes.

Water from a ruptured levee on the Feather River, 100 miles northeast of San Francisco, flooded a farm. The farmer and his wife lost $300,000 worth of cattle. "The sheriff's department just wouldn't let us in," said the farmer, "so 200 head died a slow death. It was gruesome." Some of the farmer's cattle were ensnared in ditches or fences; one cow, snagged on a small gate, had to be burned free with torches. The stench of the rotting animals was everywhere. Thus, floods have given way to fields of death across northern California, where hundreds of drowned cows, horses, and other farm animals—their bloated carcasses tangled in barbed wire or mired in ditches—lie strewn across the soggy landscape.

Although major losses of farm machinery, barns, homes, and wells appear to be the immediate headache for farmers (as well as losses to livestock for some), others are concerned about the survival of their crops. Although an estimated 150,000 acres of red winter wheat could be damaged, it is too early to tell because wheat is a grass and can tolerate being under water for awhile. What wheat farmers are most worried about is the potential loss of topsoil to erosion from running water.

With at least three reservoirs nearing their capacities, California water officials said the danger from flooding was far from over as runoff from rain and melting snow continued to build. Some rivers, including the Central Valley's Stanislaus and San Joaquin rivers, would continue bulging with runoff within their eroding levees until February, well after the storm event had passed. "It's unfortunate," said Jeff Cohen, of the California Water Resources Department, "that there is damage downstream, but it's the requirement [draining water from the reservoirs]." He added that the U.S. Army Corps of Engineers requires water to be drained from reservoirs before they reach capacity.

You may be wondering what this story about flooding has to do with a vision and constraints. It has to do with the priority of people's choices. Consider, for example, the people who originally moved into California's Central Valley. In those bygone times, people lived on and farmed the land in concert *with* the rivers, including their periodic floods, because they knew where the floodplain was and respected it. However, it has long been American tradition to wrest every useable acre from Nature, lest an acre be thought of as "unproductive."

If the rivers could be controlled and the flooding stopped, then more "unproductive" acres could be made to produce that which Americans thought desirable. So dams and levees were constructed. If they failed to produce the desired control, more dams and levees were built. In the end, however, they are proving no match for Nature, as the above story illustrates. But there is something left unsaid by the story, namely that the choices people made brought all this about.

Let's look at just four possible choices people could have made prior to the floods of 1996/1997. The choices are: (1) do not live or farm in the floodplain; (2) live and farm in the floodplain *without* dams and levees and plan for, be prepared for, and accept the risk of periodic flooding; (3) live and farm in the floodplain *with* dams and levees in place, thinking the problem of flooding is solved, but move after a levee breaks once or twice; or (4) live and farm defiantly in the floodplain *with* dams and levees in place, regardless of the dire consequences of periodic flooding.

All of these choices represent different levels of self-imposed constraints on one's own behavior based on different perceived values for monetary gain and lifestyle. The choice that seems to have been generally accepted over time is the last one: live and farm defiantly in the floodplain regardless of consequences. This, then, becomes the primary social constraint or "fixed point" around which all human residential, rural, and commercial development is made to revolve, despite the fact that sooner or later the rivers will remember their floodplains and reclaim them—at least temporarily.

When their irresponsible risk taking fails, people want the government (hence society at large) to bail them out, when in fact the risk of building in the floodplain was not only theirs alone but also ill-advised with inevitable consequences. But why should the people at large, through personal taxes paid to the government, be expected to bail out those individuals who make unwise choices when they gamble for such high stakes? Do we, through taxes paid to the government, bail someone out of financial trouble when he or she loses heavily in a high-stakes game of craps in a casino in Las Vegas? Building in a floodplain and wagering in a game of craps are both gambling, so what is the difference? Where is personal responsibility? How is one to learn responsibility if one does not have to accept the full measure of the consequences of one's choices?

It is was not always this way, however, said Scott Faber, director of floodplain programs for American Rivers, based in Washington, D.C.[48] According to Faber, "Floods may be acts of God, but flood losses are acts of hubris." Predictable, natural events, such as floods, have turned into natural "disasters" that people try to control with dams and levees because housing and commercial development have "flooded" the floodplains.

"At the turn of the century," writes Faber, "there was virtually no development in floodplains. Over the last 60 years, government programs have assumed responsibility for flood 'control' by building and repairing levees, providing relief, and subsidizing flood insurance. These programs actually put people in harm's way by eliminating incentives for local communities to direct new development away from flood-prone areas."

He goes on to say that levees and dams create a false sense of security, which encourages people to build in flood-prone areas and thus increases the potential for catastrophe when a levee inevitably fails. Thus, thousands of flood-weary Midwesterners decided in 1993 to stop "playing chicken" with the Mississippi and Missouri rivers. They opted instead for a new voluntary program that relocated more than 8,000 homes and businesses, even whole towns, onto the bluffs, so that thousands of people were literally high and dry when floodwaters returned in 1995.

As development continually encroaches on floodplains, says Faber, the rainfall that once was slowly and naturally absorbed by the land now courses rapidly into rivers, which get higher and faster as they flow toward centers of human population. An isolated decision to drain a wetland, till a farm, pave a parking lot, or put in a new street has little measurable effect on flooding by itself, but when combined with thousands of other seemingly unrelated decisions as a cumulative effect, the results can be devastating.

Rather than work together to solve regional problems, Faber says that most communities and rural landowners simply pass the water downstream as fast as possible. More dams and levees cannot eliminate human problems associated with flooding because dams and levees fostered the problem in the first place, and more of the same is hardly the cure. Periodic flooding, at times of mammoth proportions, is one of Nature's nonnegotiable constraints, especially during cool, wet periods in the weather cycle, which heretofore has been another of Nature's nonnegotiable constraints. Hence, a wise community will both recognize and bow to Nature when Nature is beyond its control.

Oregon

This example is about my hometown of Corvallis, Oregon. I have consciously chosen my hometown because it is what I know best, because it is a concrete example of what is actually happening and is a matter of public record, and because it well exemplifies what is taking place all over the United States.

By choosing to discuss my hometown, I am neither vilifying the people for what they have or have not done nor saying that I want things to be different. I live in my hometown by choice; it is a good town with good people who, like me, have all the strengths and frailties of being human, as people do in every other town. My hometown, therefore, is merely a microcosm of the whole.

In 1989, my hometown produced the following "vision statement" titled *Future Focus 2010*:

> We envision that in 2010 Corvallis [Oregon] will be...
> 1. a compact, medium-sized city nestled in a beautiful natural setting
> 2. the historic, civil, cultural, and commercial heart of Benton County
> 3. an economically strong and well-integrated city, fostering local businesses, outside investment, regional cooperation and increased clean industry
> 4. a university town, a regional medical center, a riverfront city
> 5. home...a good place for all kinds of people to live and to lead healthy, happy productive lives
> 6. an environmentally aware community with distinctive open space and natural features, protected habitats, parks, and outdoor recreation
> 7. rich in the arts and celebrating the talents and cultures of the people who live here
> 8. an involved part of the "world community."[49]

This is *not* a statement of vision but rather eight sentences, some with components that even contradict one another, which means there are two potential conflicting statements of vision secreted within the sentences. In ferreting out these two visions, I have necessarily put them into actual statements and have enclosed my personal additions in brackets.

Vision statement one: We envision that in 2010 Corvallis, nestled in a beautiful natural setting, will be a civil, compact, medium-sized, university city that is environmentally aware, a good place for [a diversity] of people to live healthy, happy, productive lives [because it will be surrounded by and interspersed with a] distinctive [network of] open space[s], natural features, protected habitats, and parks, [to provide quality] outdoor recreation [and protect the health of local water catchments]. Economically strong by fostering regional cooperation and local businesses (including a regional medical center), [Corvallis will be socially] integrated [to the point of being the] cultural heart of Benton County, rich in the arts and celebrating the talents and cultures of the people who live here.

Vision statement two: We envision that in 2010 Corvallis will be a compact, medium-sized city that, as the commercial heart of Benton

County, will be economically strong and well integrated by fostering local businesses (including a regional medical center), outside investment, increased clean industry, and involved in the world [society = global market]. [Home of Oregon State University, Corvallis will be the] civil and cultural center of Benton County, a good place for [a diversity of] people to live healthy, happy, productive lives rich in the arts and celebrating the talents and cultures of the people who live here.

Note that in the first vision statement (which features social/environmental sustainability), environmental awareness is both paramount and based on aspects of quality livability (cultural capacity) that are emphasized in such nonnegotiable social constraints as finite open space, natural features, protected habitats, and parks. This statement (based on original sentence number 6) is clearly in conflict with number 3: "an economically strong and well-integrated city, fostering local businesses, *outside investment*, regional cooperation and *increased clean industry*," which is the language of continual—and simultaneous—growth in economics and human population.

The second vision statement (which features a nonsustainable social/environmental outcome) emphasizes continual economic growth (hence continual growth in the human population, which equals carrying capacity) as the social constraint around which development will pivot. The choice is based on number 3 in the original set of sentences: "an economically strong and well-integrated city, fostering local businesses, outside investment, regional cooperation and increased clean industry." This statement is clearly in conflict with number 6: "an environmentally aware community with distinctive open space and natural features, protected habitats, parks, and outdoor recreation" (all of which are finite in existence and limited in possibilities for a lifestyle of environmental quality).

Lifestyle is commonly defined as an internally consistent way of life or style of living that reflects the values and attitudes of an individual or a culture. We in Western society have made lifestyle synonymous with "standard of living," which we practice as a search for ever-increasing material prosperity. If, however, we are to have a viable, sustainable environment as we know it and value it, we must reach beyond the strictly material and see lifestyle as a sense of inner wholeness and harmony derived by living in such a way that the spiritual, environmental, and material aspects of our lives are in balance with the capacity of the land to produce the necessities for that lifestyle.

Whether a given lifestyle is even possible depends on "cultural capacity," a term that is an analogue for "carrying capacity," which is the number of animals that can live in and use a particular landscape without impairing its ability to function in an ecologically specific way. If we want human society (which is the aggregate of local communities) to survive the 21st century in any sort of dignified manner, we must have the humility to view our own population in terms of local, regional, and national carrying capacities, because the quality of life declines in direct proportion to the degree to which local habitats are overpopulated.

If "cultural capacity" is substituted for the idea of "carrying capacity," we have a workable proposition for sustainable community development. Cultural capacity is a chosen quality of life, the quality that can be sustained without endangering the environment's productive ability. The more materially oriented the desired lifestyle of an individual or local community, for example, the more resources are needed to sustain it and the smaller the human population must be per unit area of landscape.

Cultural capacity, then, is a balance between the way local people want to live (the real quality of their lifestyle and of their community) and the number of people an area can support in that lifestyle on a sustainable basis. The cultural capacity of any area will be less than its carrying capacity in the biological sense.

Cultural capacity is a workable idea. People can predetermine the cultural capacity of their local community or their bioregion and adjust the growth of their population accordingly. If they choose not to balance their desires with the land's capabilities, the depletion of the land will determine the quality of their cultural/environmental experiences and the sustainability of their lifestyles.

So far, we the people have chosen not to balance our desires with the capabilities of the land, because we have equated "desire," "need," and "demand" as synonymous with every itch of "want." We have lost sight of ecological reality.

If we desire to maintain a predetermined lifestyle, we must ask new questions: (1) How much of any given resource is necessary for us to use if we are to live in the lifestyle of our choice? (2) How much of any given resource is it necessary to leave intact as a biological reinvestment in the health and continued productivity of the ecosystem? (3) Do sufficient resources remain, after biological reinvestment, to support our lifestyle of choice, or must we modify our lifestyle to meet what the land is capable of sustaining?

Because "necessity" is a proposition very different from the collective "desire, want, need, demand" syndrome, arguments about the proper cultural capacity revolve around not only what people think they want in a materialistic/spiritual sense but also what the land can produce in an environmentally sustainable sense. Cultural capacity is a conservative concept (in the true sense of the word), given finite resources and well-defined values. By first determining what they want in terms of lifestyle, people may be able to determine not only if their local area can support their desired lifestyle but also how they must behave with respect to their environment if they are to maintain their desired lifestyle.

To see how this works, let's examine a few examples of cultural capacity. On September 21, 1989, Hurricane Hugo flattened most of South Carolina's beachfront. Since then, houses have been rebuilt and stand once more "eave to eave" as testimony of American's determination to live by the sea. The result is that so many people are trying to buy so little remaining land that a standard city lot may sell for as much as $500,000.

Today, nearly half the American population lives within an hour's drive of a coast. By the year 2010, predicts the National Oceanographic and Atmospheric Administration, nearly 60%, or 127 million people, will live in the coastal zone, including the shores of the Great Lakes, Puget Sound in the state of Washington, and along the shores of such rivers as the Columbia.

Pollution and destruction of habitats, problems faced in every coastal region of our nation, are fueled by both unchecked growth of the population and an increasing desire on the part of many Americans to live by the sea or some other shore. The Pacific Northwest, just now beginning to feel the pressures of a growing coastal population, which began on the eastern seaboard at the end of World War II, hopes to avoid both the overcrowding and the building in hazardous areas that have plagued such states as South Carolina.

In Oregon, the demographics of the coastal population are changing with the influx of retired persons, many of whom have some environmental awareness. Nevertheless, as people build their dream homes by the sea and along other shores, they fill in wetlands, cut down forests, and cause the erosion of beaches, thus making changes that threaten the very environment that drew them to the coastal areas in the first place. This is a clear example of grossly exceeding the cultural capacity of a chosen area.[50]

The decline of the Hawaiian paradise is another example. The U.S. Fish and Wildlife Service, the Hawaii Department of Land and Natural Resources, and The Nature Conservancy of Hawaii made the decline of

Hawaii's environment the subject of a joint report that took a decade to prepare.

Until people found the Hawaiian Islands, perhaps one new species evolved every 10,000 years. This number is significant because the Hawaiian Islands surpass even the Galapagos Islands, off the coast of South America, in the number of species that evolved from a single ancestor. In Hawaii, at least 50 species have evolved from a common ancestor.

Beginning in the 1700s, the islands became a crossroads for Pacific travel, and early seafarers introduced domestic pigs, goats, horses, and cattle onto the islands as sources of fresh meat. The introduction of foreign species of plants and animals has increased dramatically even within the last 15 years.

In addition to the obvious introductions of domestic animals, less expected imports have affected the islands: bird malaria and bird pox, both of which are carried by mosquitoes, have had a severe impact on native Hawaiian birds. Brown tree snakes, which have devastated the native species of birds on Guam, have been intercepted on flights to Hawaii six times.

The banana poka, a passionflower vine, which is kept in check in its native South America by the feeding of insects, has no such controlling mechanisms in the islands. Consequently, since arriving in Hawaii it has smothered 70,000 acres of forests on two islands and is threatening larger tracts.

To date, nearly two-thirds of Hawaii's original forest cover has been lost, including half the vital rain forests. Ninety percent of the lowland plains, once forested, have been destroyed. Of 140 species of native birds, only 70 remain, and 33 of those are in danger of extinction. Eleven more species are beyond recovery. As of November 1991, 37 species of plants native to Hawaii are listed as federally endangered; within two years, 152 more species will be proposed for federal listing. Among the state's rarest plants are 93 species of trees, shrubs, vines, herbs, and ferns, each of which has only about a hundred known surviving individuals. At least five species have been reduced to just one individual.

The cause of the decline is twofold: (1) the cumulative effect of people's careless, unplanned, unbalanced conversion of the land from Nature's design to society's cultural design in the form of agriculture, ranching, and residential use and (2) human introductions of nonindigenous species of plants, insects, and mammals.

The results include the loss of the forests, which once intercepted and generated rainfall and protected the coral reefs and beaches from siltation caused by the erosion of soil. Forest loss, coupled with the extinction of native plants and animals, affects every level of the islands' economy and cultural heritage, such as the generation of unique materials for clothing, textiles, ornaments, canoes, and scientific study. Because its cultural capacity has been grievously exceeded, Hawaii has become largely a paradise lost.[51]

Thus, when the arguments are over, the people of Corvallis, Oregon—if they want to remain within their "cultural capacity"—must accept that only *one* nonnegotiable social constraint (either protected open space *or* continual growth in economics and human population) can be the dominant focal point for the whole vision. For the first vision statement to be viable, *open space* must be the fixed point (the nonnegotiable social constraint) around which all present and future development revolves, which requires a firm limit to growth (in terms of both economics and human population).

For the second vision statement to be viable, however, *continual economic growth,* which means *continual growth in the human population,* must be the fixed point (the social constraint) around which all present and future development revolves—until there is simply no room left to grow. And then what?

A case in point, the proposed "Annexation A," which is just outside the city limits and is owned by an absentee land development company, has been approved by the City Planning Commission.[52] (Annexation means adding land that will expand the city limits.) It now goes to the city council and, if approved, to the voters. However, since officials for the county wherein the proposed annexation resides have already given the land company permission to subdivide and build on the acreage, the people really have no say, despite any vision statement they may have or the consequences of any deleterious environmental effects from the subdivision.

> The city's planning office has received scores of letters from residents concerned about the proposed development. Most of the letters have opposed the annexation request.
>
> In addressing concerns raised by residents, Commissioner Patrick Lampton said a hearing on one annexation request is not the right time to address complex issues such as how the city should grow.

Those kinds of issues, he said, should be addressed when the city reviews its comprehensive plan, the city's vision of how it wants to grow.[52]

Which vision statement (number one or two) does Commissioner Lampton's comments address? If it is the first vision statement (which features social/environmental sustainability), his comments are out of place because it is vitally important to: (1) plan for and commit to acquiring the most ecologically sound network of open space *prior* to approving annexations, which means that each and every annexation must be studied one at a time to see how it relates to the requirement of available open space in terms of other approved and potential annexations, and (2) study each proposed annexation individually from as many points of view as possible so that each subsequent annexation can be improved in quality with respect to previous ones.

If, on the other hand, Commissioner Lampton's comments refer to the second vision statement, then they are appropriate with respect to continual economic growth as the fixed point around which the vision statement revolves. But there is still a major problem with his point of view, regardless of which vision statement one chooses.

If voters approve "Annexation A," the land development company can build 23 single-family homes and 32 attached townhouses on the 23-acre parcel. If, however, the annexation is not approved by the voters, then the land development company still has the county's permission to construct 32 homes on 173 acres or 1 house per 5 acres, because 5-acre parcels are allowed under the county's rural design code.

The problem is that the 173 acres (which includes the proposed annexation) lie just outside of the current city limits but well within the city's urban growth boundary on which the city's "vision" is based. This means that the county's permission to build 32 homes on the 173 acres and Commissioner Lampton's point of view are both diametrically opposed to the very first adjective of all three vision statements, namely, "*compact*, medium-sized city."

Would you think of 32 homes on 173 acres within an ostensibly finite urban growth boundary as compact? In addition, it will not help solve the number one problem for both the city and the county, which is affordable housing.[52] But what choice do the voters have, especially when employees of the city and county neither cooperate nor coordinate with one another in terms of a vision of social/environmental sustainability?

Now let's examine another problem with respect to the two statements of vision.[53] As early as 1983, a local resident requested that 101 acres west of the town be included within the city limits ("Annexation B") so a research and technology center could be constructed, but the annexation was voted down. In 1984, however, the citizens changed their minds and voted to annex the land for the research and technology center. But the owner of the property failed to seek a building permit within the required three-year deadline, which meant that the land automatically reverted to residential zoning.

What the residents voted for in 1984 is not what they are getting now. The land was purchased in 1996 by an investment company (another absentee land developer) that wants to build 255 single-family houses, 230 apartment units, and 38 townhouses on the property of "Annexation B," which is actually just over 103 acres. The company also says it will build a community recreation center and leave about 25 acres for open space.

Before we even begin to discuss the ramifications of this switch in development, the question is whether the citizens would have voted to annex the land ("Annexation B") to accommodate today's development proposal instead of the original research and technology center. If not, is the current development being done under false pretenses? What choice do the residents really have without the strong organizing context of a vision?

In conjunction with the first vision statement, the residential area of "Annexation B" would be compact, but how would the 25 acres of open space be configured and situated with respect to its connectivity with an open-space network? (As it is, the 25 acres of open space will be severely fragmented within the development.) How would the open space be used? How much open space would there have been under the original proposal? How would that open space have been distributed and used?

Once again, "Annexation B" as a housing development is isolated from the common necessities of life, which would force people to rely on their automobiles—a bad environmental move, one that fragments community and is diametrically opposed to the first vision statement, namely, an *environmentally aware, well-integrated city.* But what are the citizens' real choices?

With respect to the second vision statement, what businesses have been lost by the current plan for "Annexation B"? Is there more land available for these kinds of businesses should they be part of the vision's organizing context for the town's economic diversification and identity? And once again, this type of isolated development flies in the face of a city becoming a *well-integrated city,* which is also part of the second vision statement. But what are the citizens' real choices?

"One of the things [that] makes Corvallis a good place to live is the opportunity for residents to vote on proposed property annexations," says Edward Donnally, a former member of the Corvallis City Council.[54] "The intent of this provision of the law is to allow those affected to control both the rate and nature of the city's growth."

A unique factor in the aforementioned investment company's proposal for its housing development, says Donnally, is that when the people gave limited approval in 1984 to annex the land for a research center, they did not know that a three-year delay in applying for a building permit would cause the tract to revert to residential zoning. Such zoning carries with it a much wider opportunity for development than the voters had intended.

Even though, as Donnally asserts, the letter of the law allows this to happen, he believes that the "intent" of the voters who participated in the process of annexation should be recognized. Such recognition means providing a forum for meaningful public debate *prior* to proposals for development being extended or substantially altered from the intent of the citizens who originally voted for the annexation, which, Donnally says, includes the investment company's current proposal for its housing development.

This may, as Donnally asserts, pose an immediate legal or administrative problem for the city. But the city would be wise not to establish a precedent whereby a developer—with a hidden agenda—can win voter-approved annexation for one purpose and then, by doing nothing for three years, gain an open field for what he or she really had in mind. With this in mind, Donnally recommends the following:

1. Encourage and facilitate public comment as part of the discussion about the investment company's current proposal for its housing development and incorporate those comments into a final decision based on the desires of a majority of the voters.
2. Amend the procedure for annexation so that any land annexed for a specific purpose must be used as it was intended by the voters. This means that no land annexed for one purpose can be used for another without prior approval by the voters. Further, the cost of obtaining such approval is to be borne by the developer who wants the zoning to be changed for his or her benefit.

"If we are to have a truly democratic society," writes Donnally, "we need to enact and amend laws to meet the needs and wishes of the majority of our citizens."

Because choice is the essence of not only our democracy but also sustainable community development, no greater disservice can be rendered by those in power than to unjustly limit the people's power to freely choose. And limiting the people's choice in favor of the traditional short-term economic desires of two special-interest groups is essentially what the Oregon legislature has done.

> A 1995 land-use law could make it harder for the public to comment on residential development requests.
>
> House Bill 3065, pushed through just days before the end of last year's Legislature, cuts the approval process in half and forces comments to focus on a subdivision's legal merit.
>
> "The idea is to get emotions out of land-use decisions," said Drake Butch, of the Home Builders Association of Metropolitan Portland. The lobbying group, along with the Oregon State Home Builders Association, pushed for the bill's passage.
>
> "It's not fair to developers to keep delaying the process with appeals when their proposed developments meet all the legal requirements," Butch said.
>
> He said it's costing developers too much money to go through the approval process because of delays for public comment and appeals.[55]

The effect of this law is to render impotent Oregon municipalities by: (1) stealing choice and self-determining government from the people who live in the area of the proposed development; (2) giving preference to residential developers, an increasing number of whom are absentee, even from out of state; (3) forcing local people to accept absentee interests; (4) limiting—even undermining—the scope of a local people's potential self-determined vision for sustainable community development within the context of their own landscape, especially for the desired future condition of their landscape; and (5) curtailing or even eliminating the ability of local people to actively mourn for the continuing loss of their quality of life and their sense of place as outside choices are forced upon them, often by people who will not have to live with the consequences of their imposed actions.

The whole purpose of choice is for local people to guide the sustainable development of their own community within the mutually sustainable context of their landscape by collectively selecting the self-imposed social constraints necessary to fulfill their vision. After all, the local people and their children must reap the consequences of any decisions that are made. To limit their choices is to force someone else's consequences upon them, often at a great and increasingly negative long-term cost, first socially and then environmentally.

When preferential treatment is given to residential developers, including absentee developers, local people are at a serious disadvantage when it comes to planning for long-term community sustainability within the context of a finite landscape. While the focus of sustainable community development is long term, the interests of residential developers are strictly short term, which usually counteracts long-term planning based on long-term environmental consequences. Further, it is exceedingly unlikely that absentee residential developers are going to have a vested interest in the long-term welfare of the community once they have made their money.

As noted in the above quote, it is the letter of the law that the residential developers want strictly enforced. But the letter of the law lacks moral consciousness, ignores the values of local residents, and discounts long-term planning for sustainable community development, all of which have consequences that are critical to the long-term social/environmental sustainability of a community.

This calls to mind a quote by the British historian Arnold Toynbee: "The history of almost every civilization furnishes examples of geographical expansion coinciding with deterioration in quality." So, long after the residential developer has gone, the community is left to deal with the environmental errors caused by too much haste because the letter of the law was held to be inviolate and shielded from challenge.

Finally, as noted above, the expressed purpose of the law to limit public debate is to "get *emotions* (feelings, human values) out of land-use decisions," which effectively slaughters the quality of human relationships while enforcing the letter of the law for the benefit of residential developers. But emotions, the force behind relationships, are based on personal and collective values, which are the heart and soul of a community.

As if denying the people their right to express how they feel were not enough, developers are now trying to revoke the recently passed measures by which the citizens of several towns in Oregon have granted themselves the legal right to put to a vote all proposed annexations in their respective towns.[56] For 20 years, since 1976, Corvallis has been the only town in Oregon to hold developers on a "short leash" by requiring that all annexations be put to a public vote. In other words, all new developments have to win the blessing of the people in order to receive water lines, sewage lines, and other amenities from the city.

Most developers have taken the extra hurdle in Corvallis in stride. But in 1996, a half-dozen other towns passed measures that require a public vote on annexations (the will of the people for self-determination); the developers are not only staunchly opposed to such measures but also are trying to get them overturned in the state legislature. The developers have conceded the annexation law Corvallis passed 20 years ago and accordingly made their bill retroactive to January 1, 1996.

The annexation law in Corvallis works as follows: A developer takes a proposal to a city planner; from there it goes to the planning commission and the city council. If approved, the proposed annexation is placed on the ballot, brochures are printed, campaign signs are planted in people's lawns, and the annexation is discussed like any other political issue.

If the annexation is approved by the voters, the land is included within the city limits and thus becomes eligible for city services, such as water, sewer, and police protection. "In my view," says Mayor Helen Berg, "the voters in Corvallis are much more aware of planning issues in the community," presumably because they are involved in the process of annexation.

But, according to Joe Chandler, a lobbyist and spokesman for the Oregon Building Industry Association, "this [the voters' recently passed measures to vote on annexations] is basically an undercutting of the entire state land-use system." What the Oregon Building Industry Association is really attempting to foster, however, is industrial control to ensure continual growth in Oregon's population by taking away citizens' voices (which translates into taking away the option of selecting self-imposed social constraints) in deciding how growth is to be managed in their respective towns.

All of the 240 incorporated cities in Oregon are enveloped in "urban growth boundaries," which are invisible lines that were drawn around the cities when the land-use laws were enacted in the 1970s. The purpose of an urban growth boundary is to leave room for growth outside existing city limits but within predetermined bounds that keep developments from spilling over into the countryside.

State Representative Bob Repine, who helped draft the Oregon Building Industry Association's pending legislation, thinks voters should be forbidden to tie the hands of their own elected officials on land-use issues. "It really kind of neuters their decision-making process," the Grants Pass Republican said. "Why don't we play by the rules that we applied 20 years ago?" To this, Chandler adds: "They [the people] should follow the existing process. The answer isn't to hold up land and projects for no good reason."[56]

What is left unsaid, however, is that there is a good reason to rethink land-use projects. Some of the social values of the people in Oregon have changed over the last 20 years, while others have been degraded through unprecedented growth as new industries and people from other states, especially California, have flooded into Oregon.

This tremendous influx of people has driven up not only the price of land but also property taxes and continues to gobble up the countryside, including prime farmland. (A year-long study conducted by the American Farmland Trust, using data from land-use inventories of the U.S. Department of Agriculture, concluded that urban sprawl is destroying 50 acres of prime farmland every hour of every day. In so doing, urban sprawl is threatening land now used to produce 70% of the nation's fruits, 69% of its vegetables, and 52% of its dairy goods.[57]) Without the voters' ability to control the growth of their respective towns, Oregon faces "an overpopulated future and a bleak one," says Jeff Lamb, chairman of the lobbying group that represents the cities with the new annexation laws.

Oregon is not alone in contending with the people's increasing loss of self-determination, which means their ability to select self-imposed social constraints. Natural historian George Monbiot, writing about Southeast Asia, Brazil, East Africa, and his native England, says that rural communities are forced to take seriously the welfare of their land because its resources are all they have to meet their diverse requirements. When the land is privatized, that which had been the people's communal commons passes into the hands of people whose priority is to make money, and the most efficient way to do that is to select the most profitable product and concentrate on producing it.[58]

Without the security of land tenure and autonomy of decision making, writes Monbiot, people have no chance of defending the environment that provides their livelihoods. Brazil needs land reform; Kenya and Indonesia need to recognize and protect the traditional land rights of the indigenous peoples. By themselves, these policies will not guarantee environmental protection, but without them, environmental destruction is guaranteed.

If a land-use decision arises from an informed consensus of the local people, including everyone a given development might affect, says Monbiot, we are likely to see, reflected in that decision, the people's interests become vested in the quality of their surroundings and hence in the quality of their lives. If, on the other hand, a decision emerges from an impenetrable cabal of landowners, developers, and government officials, accountable to no one but the corporate/political elite, none of whom has to suffer the adverse consequences of their land-use choices, the forthcoming decision is likely to have a far more negative effect on both the environment and its inhabitants.

Concerning England, Monbiot offers the following commentary: The developers have "the most extraordinary legal powers to subvert the democratic process and impose their projects on even the most reluctant population." If ordinary people do not like a local authority's decision to approve a particular development, there is nothing they can do about it. But if a developer does not like the local council's decision to reject his or her proposed development, he or she can appeal to the secretary of state for the environment; in other words, the central government.

The developer knows that such an appeal will cost the local council hundreds of thousands of pounds to contest. So time and again, developers use the threat of an appeal to blackmail a local council into compliance with their wishes.

If, however, a local council has sufficient funds to fight the appeal, and if the secretary of state rejects the developer's plans during the appeal, all the developer needs to do is submit another, almost identical planning application, and the whole process begins again. This cycle can go on until both the money and the willpower of the local council and local citizens are exhausted, assuming the developer has the financial wherewithal to outlast them. Thus developers get what they want. Does the dilemma in England ring a familiar note in your own city?

"The results of this democratic deficit are visible all over our cities," writes Monbiot. "Where we need affordable, inclusive housing, we get luxury, exclusive estates; where we need open spaces, we get more and more empty office blocks; where we need local trade, we get superstores...." In addition, traffic becomes increasingly congested, affordable housing is relegated to the countryside, and communities lose the resources that held them together.

If this suspension of accountability is onerous in the town, it is worse in the countryside, where the message, with few exceptions, clearly is: "It's my land and I can do what I want with it." It was not always this way, says Monbiot, but the concept of property has changed dramatically over the centuries.

Property used to be a matter of possessing the right to use land and its resources, and most areas had some kind of shared rights. Today, the land itself is considered to be property, and the words for the British rights of old have all but disappeared: "estovers" (the *right* to collect firewood), "pannage" (the *right* to put one's pigs in the woods), "turbary" (the *right* to cut turf), and "pescary" (the commoner's *right* to catch fish) are no longer in the British vocabulary. Now, while the landowner's rights are almost absolute, the common people no longer have the right of access to most lands in England. The people's rights are effectively nonexistent.

There was a similar kind of shared rights among the indigenous Cherokee peoples of North America.[59] In the traditional Cherokee economic system, both the land and its abundance would be shared among clans. One clan could gather, another could camp, while yet a third could hunt on the same land. There was a fluid and common right of usage rather than an individual right to private property. The value was thus placed on sharing and reciprocity, on the widest distribution of wealth, and on limiting the inequalities within the economic system.

The Cherokee notion of the common right of shared usage fits nicely into Monbiot's commentary, the upshot of which can be stated as follows: The exclusive right to do with a piece of land as one will to the exclusion of other people (present and future) is perhaps the most obvious of class barriers. "We [the common people] are, quite literally, pushed to the margins of society," laments Monbiot. "If we enter the countryside, we must sneak around it like fugitives, outlaws in the nation in which we all once had a stake. It is, in truth, not we who are the trespassers but the landlords. They are trespassing against our right to enjoy the gifts that Nature bequeathed to all of us."

First Nations People of Canada

Although the foregoing constraints were fairly simple, the forthcoming ones are not. Let's examine two previously mentioned scenarios concerning the First Nation peoples of Canada, with constraints in mind. To keep the discussion as relevant as possible, the scenarios, with some modification, are restated, and observations about the role of social constraints have been added. The purpose of presenting the material in this way is to clarify how constraints work.

Example 1

In 1993, I was asked to review an ecological brief for a First Nation in western British Columbia, Canada, whose reservation is located between the sea and land immediately downslope from that which a timber company wanted to cut. The problem lay in the fact that the timber company could only reach the timber it wanted to cut by obtaining an easement through the reservation, which gave the First Nation some control over the behavior of the timber company. The First Nation wanted this control to have an active voice in how the timber company would log the upper-slope forest, because the outcome would for many years affect the reservation, which is immediately below the area to be cut.

By virtue of the company's required easement through the First Nation's land, the First Nation was the strong organizing context that would control the behavior of the timber company as it logged the upper-slope forest. If, however, the timber company had not been required to pass through the First Nation's land, it could, through self-serving logging practices, easily have become an uncontrollable factor that would have destroyed the cultural values of the First Nation's land for many generations.

Before meeting with the timber company, the First Nation's chief asked for some counsel. My reply was as follows, with a discussion of the constraints added in italics:

> Before I discuss the ecological brief I've been asked to review, there are three points that must be taken into account if what I say is to have any value to the First Nation. What I'm about to say may be difficult to hear, but I say it with the utmost respect.
>
> **Point 1:** Who are you, the First Nation, in a cultural sense? You are not your old culture because you have—against your will—been forced to adopt some white ways, which means you have given up or lost ancestral ways. *Ancestral social constraints have been forcibly removed, which in and of itself changed the people's cultural norms and thus their sense of identity.*
>
> The questions you must ask and answer are: Which of our ancestral ways still have sufficient value that we want to keep them? Which of the white ways do we want to or are we willing to adopt? *Which ancestral social constraints retain sufficient cultural value that you want to perpetuate them? Which social constraints pertaining to white Canadian culture are you willing to accept?*

How do we put the chosen elements of both cultures to-gether in such a way that we can today define who we are as a culture? *The answer to this question not only will determine the array of and the negotiability of the adopted constraints but also will define the people as a culture in today's world.*

Point 2: What do you want your children to have as a legacy from your decisions and dealings with the timber company? *Which social constraints, with what degree of negotiability, are you bequeathing to the children as the circumstances they will inherit?* Whatever you decide is what you are committing your children, their children, and their children's children to pay for as the effects of your decisions unto the seventh generation and beyond. This, of course, is solely your choice and that is as it should be. But whatever you choose will partly answer Point 3.

Point 3: What do you want your reservation to look like and act like during and after logging by the timber company? *Which social constraints are you going to impose on the timber com-pany, and how stringent (= negotiable) will they have to be for you to protect your reservation?* How you define yourselves culturally, what choices you make for your children, and the conscious decisions you make about the condition of your land (*as well as the degree of negotiability of the constraints to achieve that condition*) will determine what you end up with. In all of these things, the choice is yours. The consequences belong to both you and your children.

Now to my comments: This is a difficult task at best. As with any definition, it is a human invention and has no meaning to Nature. Therefore, you must tell the timber company, clearly and concisely, what the terms in this ecological brief mean to you and how you interpret them with respect to the company's actions that will affect your reservation.

1. Every ecosystem functions fully within the limits (*con-straints*) imposed on it by Nature and/or humans. Therefore, it is the type, scale, and duration of the alterations to the system—the imposed limits—that you need to be concerned with.

If your reservation looks the way you want it to and functions the way you want it to, then the question becomes: How must we and the timber company behave (*one set of social con-straints with respect to the ecosystem*) to keep it looking and functioning the way it is? If, on the other hand, your reservation does not look the way you want it to and does not function the way you want it to, then the question becomes: How must we and the timber company behave (*an alternative set of social constraints with respect to the ecosystem*) to make it look and function the way we want it to?

But regardless of your decisions or the company's actions, your reservation will always function to its greatest capacity under the circumstances (*constraints*) Nature, you, and the company impose on it. The point is that your decisions and the company's actions (*social constraints*), excluding what Nature may do (*environmental constraints*), will determine how your reservation both looks and functions. This reflects the importance of the preceding Point 3, which is what you want your reservation to look like and how you want it to function *after* the timber company has left. It also reflects the importance of what you decide.

2. If you want the landscape of your reservation to look and function in a certain way, then how must the timber company's landscape look and function to help make your reservation be what you want it to be? Keep in mind that the landscape of your reservation and the company's timber holdings are both made up of the collective performance of individual stands of trees or "habitat patches" (a stand is a delineated group of standing trees). Therefore, how the stands look and function will determine how the collective landscape looks and functions (= *result or effect of type of social constraints that created the habitat patches*).

3. Remember that any undesirable ecological effects (*a result of poorly chosen social constraints, which in turn may impose a set of environmental constraints as reciprocity in the future*) are also undesirable economic effects over time (*which will impose a set of future social constraints*). Your interest in your reservation (*social constraints based on culture*) will be there for many, many years—generations perhaps—but the company's interest in the forest (*social constraints based on economics*) may well disappear just as soon as the trees are cut. So, the company's short-term economic decisions may be good for them immediately but may at the same time be a bad long-term ecological decision and thus a bad long-term economic decision for you.

4. To maintain ecological functions means that you must maintain the characteristics of the ecosystem in such a way that its processes are sustainable. The characteristics you must be concerned about are: (1) composition, (2) structure, (3) function, and (4) Nature's disturbance regimes, which periodically alter the ecosystem's composition, structure, and function.

Nature's disturbance regimes tend to be environmental constraints. True, we can tinker with them, such as the suppression of fire in forests and grasslands, but in the end our tinkering catches up with us and we pay the price.

We can, for example, change the composition of an ecosystem, such as a forest, which means that composition is negotiable. In this case, composition is the determiner of the structure and function in that composition is the cause of the structure and function rather than the effect of the structure and function.

Composition determines the structure, and structure determines the function. Thus, by negotiating the composition, one simultaneously negotiates both the structure and function. Once the composition is in place, however, the structure and function are set—unless, of course, the composition is altered, at which time both the structure and function are altered accordingly.

The composition or kinds of plants and their age classes within a plant community create a certain structure that is characteristic of the plant community at any given age. It is the structure of the plant community that in turn creates and maintains certain functions. In addition, it is the composition, structure, and function of a plant community that determine what kinds of animals can live there, how many, and for how long.

If you change the composition of your forest, you change the structure, hence the function, and you affect the animals. The animals in general are thus ultimately constrained by the composition.

If, therefore, you want (as part of your vision) a particular animal or group of animals in the forest, you have to work backward by determining what kind of function to create, which means you must know what kind of structure to create, which means you must know what type of composition is necessary to produce the required habitat(s) for the animal(s) you want. Thus, once the composition is ensconced, the structure and its attendant functions operate as a unit in terms of the habitats required for the animal(s).

People and Nature are continually changing a plant community's structure and function, which subsequently changes the composition of the animal community dependent on it. People and Nature do this by altering the composition of the plant community, which in turn alters its structure, which in turn affects how it functions.

For example, the timber company wants to change the forest's structure by cutting the trees, which in turn will change the plant community's composition, which in turn will change how the community functions, which in turn will change the kinds and numbers of animals that can live there. These are the key elements with which you must be concerned, because an effect on one area can—and usually does—affect the entire landscape.

Composition, structure, and function go together to create and maintain ecological processes both in time and across space, and it is the health of the processes that in the end creates the forest. Your forest is a living organism, not just a collection of trees—as the timber industry usually thinks of it.

5. Scale is an often-forgotten component of healthy forests and landscapes. The treatment of every stand of timber is critically important to the health of the whole landscape, which is a collection of the interrelated stands.

Thus, when you deal only with a stand, you are ignoring the relationship of that particular stand to other stands, to the rest of the drainage, and to the landscape. It's like a jigsaw puzzle where each piece is a stand. The relationship of certain pieces (stands) makes a picture (drainage). The relationship of the pictures (drainages) makes a whole puzzle (landscape). Thus, the relationships of all the stands within a particular area make a drainage and the relationships of all the drainages within a particular area make the landscape.

If one piece is left out of the puzzle, it is not complete. If one critical piece is missing, it may be very difficult to figure out what the picture is. So each piece (stand) is critically important in its relationship to the completion of the whole puzzle (landscape). Therefore, the way each stand is defined and treated by the timber company is critically important to how the landscape, encompassing both the company's land and your reservation, looks and functions over time.

6. Degrading an ecosystem is a human concept based on human values and has nothing to do with Nature. Nature places no extrinsic value on anything. Everything just is, and in its being it is perfect (intrinsic value). Therefore, when considering intrinsic value, if something in Nature changes, it simply changes—no value is either added or subtracted. But superimposing the extrinsic value of human desires on Nature's intrinsic value creates a different proposition. Thus, whether or not your reservation becomes degraded depends on what you want it to be like, what value or values you have placed on its being in a certain condition, to produce certain things for you. If your desired condition is negatively affected by the company's actions, then your reservation becomes degraded. If your desired condition is positively affected by the company's actions, then your reservation is improved. Remember, your own actions can also degrade or improve your reservation.

   7. It is important that you know—as clearly as possible— what the definitions in this brief really mean to you and your choices for your children and your reservation. (*In other words, which constraints are important to you socially and how negotiable are they?*) Only when you fully understand what these definitions mean to you (*and how their implications affect social and potential environmental constraints*) can you negotiate successfully with the timber company.

Example 2

Now let's revisit the example from the Northwest Territories of Canada, where the First Canadians wanted to create a vision for 800 square kilometers of forest so they could draft a management plan. But this time, we will deal only with those areas of the example to which constraints apply—the part in which I helped them reframe their negative statements into positive ones. (If you want to refresh your memory about this example, see page 94.) A discussion of the constraints is added in italics.

   I helped them reframe the negative into a positive by asking a series of questions.

   "What is your staple diet?"

   "Moose" (*a social constraint with respect to moose*).

   "What kind of habitat do moose need?"

   "Willow and birch thickets" (*an environmental constraint with respect to moose*).

   "When do you hunt moose?"

   "In the late summer and autumn."

   "Do you have any medicinal plants that are important to you?"

   "Yes, such and such" (*a set of social constraints with respect to the medicinal plants*).

"Where do they grow?"

"In this kind of place and that kind of place" (*a set of environmental constraints with respect to the medicinal plants*).

"I notice that birch bark is used to make various domestic objects. Are birch trees important to you?"

"Yes" (*again, a social constraint with respect to the birch tree*).

"What is the habitat for birch?"

"Such and such a place" (*again, an environmental constraint with respect to the birch trees*).

Because a community's visioning process is a public one, it gives the people the right to comment on all aspects of the process (from creating the vision itself through its implementation and monitoring), which in effect places control of the process directly in the hands of the people, should they choose to accept responsibility for the outcome. It is the responsibility for the outcome that demands an understanding of and exacts the accountability for how people accept the social constraints dictated by the vision. And because people are ultimately responsible for their own behavior, they require a mechanism through which they can measure the appropriateness of their performance, which is the express purpose of monitoring.

MONITORING TESTS THE EFFECTIVENESS OF CONSTRAINTS

Although the word "monitor" is variously construed, its meaning here is to scrutinize or check systematically with a view to collecting specific kinds of data that indicate whether one is moving in the direction one wishes. Monitor has the same origin as monition, which means a warning or caution, and is derived from the Latin *monitio* for a reminder.

With respect to social/environmental sustainability, monitoring means to keep watch over and warn in case of danger, such as straying from a desired course. Monitoring is to remind us of activities that we already know are too harsh and could offend the system; on the other hand, it is to help us conserve the options embodied within the system for ourselves and future generations, but this requires the ability to ask relevant questions because monitoring is dependent on questions.

The Questions We Ask

Learning how to frame good and effective questions is paramount not only for crafting a collective vision for the future but also for the process of monitoring what is necessary to achieve the vision. A question is a powerful tool when used wisely, because questions open the door of possibility. For example, it was not possible to go to the moon until someone asked, "Is it possible to go to the moon?" At that moment, going to the moon became possible. To be effective, each question must: (1) have a specific purpose, (2) contain a single idea, (3) be clear in meaning, (4) stimulate thought, (5) require a definite answer to bring closure to the human relationship induced by the question, and (6) explicitly relate to previous information.

In a discussion about going to the moon, one might therefore ask, "Do you know what the moon is?" The specific purpose is to find out if one knows what the moon is. Knowledge of the moon is the single idea contained in the question. The meaning of the question is clear: Do you or do you not know what the moon is? The question stimulates thought about what the moon is and may spark an idea of how one relates to it; if not, that can be addressed in a second question. The question as asked requires a definite answer, and the question relates to previous information.

A question that focuses on "right" versus "wrong" is thus a hopeless exercise because it calls for human moral judgment, and that is not a valid question to ask of either an ecosystem or science. If, however, one were to ask if a proposed action was good or bad in terms of a community's collective vision, that is a good question.

For example, a good short-term economic decision may simultaneously be a bad long-term ecological decision and thus a bad long-term economic decision. To find out, however, one must ask: Although this is a good short-term economic decision, is it also a good long-term ecological decision and hence a good long-term economic decision? An answer to anything is possible only when the question has been asked.

In essence, questions lead to the array of options from which one can choose. Conversely, without a question, one is blind to the options. Learning about the options is the purpose of monitoring. In turn, to know what to monitor and how to go about it, one must know what questions to ask because an answer is only meaningful if it is in response to the right question.

Five Steps of Monitoring

Because of the uncertainties of the future, the best monitoring and the best adjustments (target corrections) based on that monitoring provide several preplanned actions, such as: "If A happens, I will do B; if C happens, I will do D;" and so on. Otherwise, we monitor only outcomes and merely hope corrective actions will be found in time, if the outcomes are undesirable.

An example might be the assumption that placing fish ladders in dams will sustain the migration of salmon and perpetuate their survival. Over time, however, we learn that the reservoirs created by the dams (in addition to a host of other human activities) also affect the survival and migration of the salmon. Therefore, monitoring a single variable, even a seemingly reasonable one, such as counting fish, may do nothing to clarify the issue or save the fish, which was the purpose of the fish ladders. We must therefore accept and remember that things are inevitably more complex than we are able to foresee, which is the very reason we need to monitor in the first place.

Good monitoring has five steps: (1) crafting a vision, goals, and objectives; (2) preliminary monitoring or inventory; (3) monitoring implementation; (4) monitoring effectiveness; and (5) monitoring to validate the outcome.

Step 1: Crafting a vision, goals, and objectives—Crafting a carefully worded vision and attendant goals and objectives that state clearly and concisely your desired future condition and how you propose to get there within some scale of time is the necessary first step in monitoring so that you know what you want, where you want to go, and what you think the journey will be like. The vision and its goals and their objectives form the context of the journey against which you measure (monitor) all decisions, actions, and consequences to see if in fact your journey is even possible as you imagined it and what the consequences of the journey might be.

Once you have completed your statements of vision, goals, and objectives, you not only will be able to but also must answer the following questions concisely: (1) What do I want? (2) Why do I want it? (3) Where do I want it? (4) When do I want it? (5) From whom do I want it? (6) How much (or how many) do I want? (7) For how long do I want it (or them)? If a component is missing, you may achieve your desire by default, but not by design.

Only when you can answer all of these questions concisely do you know where you want to go and the value of going there, and only then can you calculate the probability of arrival. Next you must determine the cost, make the commitment to bear it, and then commit yourself to keeping your commitment. Only then are you ready for the next steps in monitoring.

Step 2: Preliminary monitoring or inventory—Preliminary monitoring is to carefully observe and understand the circumstances with which one begins, which means taking "inventory" of what is available in the present. Taking inventory requires the following questions: What exists now, before anything is purposefully altered? What condition is it in, and what is its prognosis for the future? Even though preliminary monitoring may require multiple questions, the outcome is still a single realization.

If, for example, you go to your doctor for an annual checkup, the doctor not only would have to take a series of measurements, such as your blood pressure and blood tests, but also would have to know what a healthy person is (including, if possible, you as a healthy person) as a benchmark against which to judge your current condition. If you are indeed healthy, then all is well; if not, your doctor would presumably prescribe tests to pinpoint what is wrong and ultimately prescribe medicine to correct your ailment and make a prognosis for your future.

If you go to your doctor but only allow him or her to take your blood pressure without checking the level of your cholesterol, your doctor cannot deal with your health as a systemic whole, and thus loses the ability to see the various components as parts of an interactive, interconnected, interdependent system. In this, your body is similar in principle and function to your family, the community in which your family resides, the landscape in which your community rests, and the landscape within the bioregion.

Step 3: Monitoring implementation—Monitoring the implementation of projects on the ground asks the following question: Did we do what we said we were going to do? Although this type of monitoring is really just documentation of what was done, it is critical documentation because without it, it may not be possible to figure out what when awry (if anything did), how or why it went awry, or how to remedy it. Thus, to continue the doctor analogy, it is important to document whether your doctor really did the test he or she deemed necessary because doubt as to the performance of one test can seriously obscure the results and failure to perform a test can alter completely (and perhaps disastrously) the doctor's interpretation of the outcome.

Step 4: Monitoring effectiveness—Monitoring to assess effectiveness means monitoring to assess the implementation of your objectives, not the goals or vision. Recall from our earlier discussion that a vision and its attendant goals describe the desired future condition for which you are aiming. They are qualitative and thus not designed to be quantified. An objective, on the other hand, is quantitative and so is specifically designed to be quantifiable.

Monitoring to assess effectiveness of an objective requires asking: Is the objective specific enough? Are the results clearly quantifiable and within specified scales of time? Monitoring the effectiveness of your project with the aid of indicators provides information (feedback) with which to assess whether you are in fact headed toward the attainment of your desired future condition (the condition of your collective vision), maintaining your current condition, or moving away from your desired future condition.

Monitoring for effectiveness means the systematic monitoring of indicators that are relevant to achieving your vision. A good indicator helps a community recognize potential problems and provides insight into possible solutions. What a community chooses to measure, how it chooses to measure it, and how it chooses to interpret the outcome will have a tremendous effect on the quality of life in the long term.

Indicators close the circle of action by both allowing and demanding that you come back to your beginning premise and ask (reflect on) whether, through your actions, you are better off now than when you started: if so, how; if not, why not; if not, can the situation be remedied; if so, how; if not, why not; and so on.

Here a caution is necessary. Traditional unidimensional indicators, which measure the health of one condition (say, the economy), ignore the complex relationships among economy, community, environment, neighboring communities, and the bioregion. When each component is viewed as a separate issue and thus monitored in isolation, measurements tend to become skewed and lead to ineffective policies, which in turn can lead to a deteriorating quality of life. Indicators must therefore be multidimensional and must measure the quality of relationships among the components of the system being monitored if a community is to have any kind of accurate assessment of its sustainable well-being.

Only with relevant indicators and a systematic way of tracking them is it possible to make a prognosis for the future based on your vision, goals, and objectives, which states a desired future condition within some scale of time and a plan to achieve it. Only with relevant indicators and a systematic way of tracking them is it possible to make the necessary target corrections to achieve your vision because only now can you know which corrections to make.

Returning to the doctor analogy, assessing effectiveness asks: Was the right test used (was it relevant to your condition)? Was the test effective (if it was the right test, did it perform as it was supposed to)? These are important questions, because if the wrong test was used or the test was ineffective, the results can be very different from those you were led to expect and the outcome could be unexpectedly life-threatening.

Step 5: Monitoring to validate the outcome—Monitoring for validation of the outcome is considered by many to be research. This type of monitoring involves testing the assumptions that went into the development of your objectives and the models on which they are based.

Monitoring for validation may require asking such questions as: Why didn't the results come out as expected? What does this mean with respect to our conceptual model of how we think the system works versus how the system actually works? Will altering our approach make any difference in the outcome? If not, why not? If so, how and why? What target corrections do we need to make to bring our model in line with how the system really works?

Validation is a necessary component of any monitoring plan because this is where you learn about the array of possible target corrections. In addition, monitoring for validation may have wide application for other projects.

Visiting once again the doctor analogy, suppose your doctor says, "The results of your tests show that you may have an unusual form of 'Highfalutin Disease.' Let me check with my colleagues and the literature to see what is known about it."

Three weeks later, your doctor calls you into the office and says, "Your particular form of 'Highfalutin Disease' is indeed unusual, and I can find no common cure. But there is a drug called 'Dumpin Highfalutin,' which shows promise in laboratory tests. It is now ready for human trials to see how well they corroborate laboratory results. If you are willing to become part of a controlled medical experiment, I think you may qualify for the drug. It's your best chance at the moment to regain your health."

You take part in the drug experiment because you are assured that it will be carefully monitored under strictly controlled conditions, and you have faith in what you are told.

Here, one must keep in mind that dealing with a medical issue on a personal basis is simpler in many ways (except perhaps to the individual and immediate family and friends) than an entire community dealing with a collective vision—even though both have unknowable outcomes that are projected into an unknowable future.

Information Feedback: The Achilles' Heel of Monitoring

Although monitoring may or may not be the weakest point in a medical experiment, it seems inevitably to be the weakest point in how a community deals with its shared vision for a sustainable future. To illustrate this, I draw on the excellent paper by ecologists W.H. Moir and W.M. Block.[60]

The crux of making a shared vision work lies in monitoring, which at the same time is the weakest point in the process. A shared vision for a sustainable future must be considered a working hypothesis because it is applied to ongoing and proposed human activities within a dynamic ecosystem whose multiple interactions and self-reinforcing feedback loops are largely unknown and whose outcomes, therefore, are uncertain.

Because outcomes of a shared vision are uncertain, human activities encompassed by a vision can be thought of as tentative probings into various aspects of Nature and are best taken one step at a time and tested at each step. Through such testing, one hopes to detect potentially adverse and unpredicted effects at an early stage so that deleterious activity can be corrected to the best of one's ability *before* serious, widespread, or irreversible damage occurs.

Although Moir and Block liken adaptive management to a weak flashlight beam guiding us through the inky dark night, the same can be said of a shared vision projected into a hoped-for future in which the weakest part of the beam is the information feedback system. Clearly, it is one thing to promise a complicated, expensive, and continual activity, such as repetitious monitoring to create a continual flow of information (particularly for effectiveness of actions and causative trends) between the people of a community and their immediate environment, but it is quite another to actually implement it as promised.

Putting Time in Perspective

Beyond the time and money committed to doing the visioning process correctly, communities spend the preponderance of their time, energy, and money in planning, which is carried out in the sociopolitical–economic arena, where many of the basic dimensions of monitoring are formulated. At this time, the scientific basis for planned actions is reviewed, and the unknown effects of the planned actions on the environment elucidate the often controversial nature of a community's proposed activities, despite the fact that the character, importance, and probability of unwanted ecological surprises in the future are seldom explored or made explicit.

Be that as it may, to garner the support of skeptical or downright hostile members of a community, people are told, usually by planners, that an activity will either be modified or stopped (if scientific information warrants it) either at the earliest sign of an adverse effect or when it becomes clear that the specified objectives will not be met. "But when," ask Moir and Block, "does this become clear?"

One of the major faults associated with the implementation of a shared vision is that it is based on short-term or high-frequency responses from the environment, whereas the effects of human behavior ripple into the distant future, often beyond the ability of short-term corrective actions to be of value. In the mere instant of short-term monitoring, we find no viable answer to Garrett Hardin's question: "And then what?"[61]

Surprises (usually unwelcome ones) are inevitable, and their seeds may or may not be entrained in the stream of data from monitoring and may or may not be discovered by those who observe the data because most monitoring programs are scaled to the immediate future and thus are poorly scaled to the slower, longer-term responses of the environment. Planners who want quick feedback promise corrective actions only in the near term or not so distant future. In practice, however, planners react from crisis to crisis (from ecological surprise to ecological surprise) in part because they do not see the correlation between information that occurs frequently and events at the next magnitude of scale that occur less frequently than the information would indicate.

This is not to say that monitoring for short-term events is unimportant; it is only to say that in ecosystems with long-term feedback loops and/or high degrees of environmental variability, monitoring only for the short term will likely prove to be a disastrously myopic choice. But monitoring for the long-term ecological effects of human activities fails, if it gets started at all, because humans have a tragically short attention span, which leads to broken feedback loops of information.

The Danger of Interrupting Information Feedback

The most important feedback of environmental information occurs when planners decide whether they should change the direction or intensity of a particular activity. Because this decision requires the longest environmental feedback loop, it is the loop most likely to be broken without a firm and serious commitment by the planners to the citizens of a community and by the citizens of a community to themselves, which means a commitment of adequate funding to complete the task of long-term monitoring.

It is here, in the arena of broken feedback loops, that Moir and Block share their experiences of failure in monitoring:

1. Planners, members of the city council, the mayor, and/or county commissioners lose interest and hope the issue will fade or the crisis wane.
2. Monitoring (especially long term) is too expensive and either loses or never had adequate funding. Diminishing both the level of funding and the number of trained personnel is perhaps the most frequent cause of failure.
3. The lag time between implementing an activity and the environment's response is so long that a planner gets no data, stale data, messy data, or data that are inappropriate for timely decisions or actions.
4. The issue(s) driving the monitoring program is no longer relevant to the future citizens of the community.
5. The system of monitoring apparatus (such as photosites, corner stakes, and other markers identifying permanent sampling plots) is not maintained, even though interest in the issue may rekindle. The most serious loss to effective monitoring is the inability to return to the *exact* field locations for repeat measurements.
6. There are too many issues to monitor every one, so priorities are established (triage), and this or that monitoring program fades into history.
7. Because an issue is too hot to handle, no action is better than potentially placing oneself in a losing situation. People can disagree about an issue, and if the numbers are fragmentary or incomplete, both can be right. But when good numbers are avail-

able, someone is likely to be held accountable and suffer the righteous indignation of the public. Furthermore, the situation is almost always lose–lose when that which is to be monitored was already degraded irreparably prior to the onset of monitoring. In highly controversial situations, the planner, city councilor, mayor, or county commissioner can always be replaced.

8. There is reluctance on the part of present planners, city councilors, mayors, and county commissioners to commit their future replacements to present obligations, which they see as an act of arrogance. But are the present questions really crimping the generations of the future who will benefit by continuing to collect the data we have bequeathed them as an unconditional gift of potential knowledge? Will they not have the opportunity to find better ways of addressing the issue(s)? Will today's issues even be relevant in that distant time?

Any of these eight circumstances weakens the level of commitment and severs the flow of information, which once severed cannot be repaired. Bear in mind that the maladies discussed above are at least partly related to who funds the monitoring; who develops, conducts, analyzes, and interprets the data; and who makes the decisions about subsequent adjustments in activities.

In the end, it is through the questions we ask that we derive our vision, goals, and objectives. It is the questions we ask that frame our perceptions and direct our actions, which require monitoring. And it is the questions we ask that determine what and how we monitor. Therefore, social/environmental sustainability depends first and foremost on the relevance of the questions we ask, for they become our compass and map into the future.

As community leaders, let us facilitate group processes that transform a collection of people into a healthy, sustainable community within the context of a healthy, sustainable environment in the present for the future. Let this be our personal legacy to our children and theirs. After all, "the care of the earth is our most ancient and most worthy and…our most pleasing responsibility," says Wendell Berry. "To cherish what remains of it, and to foster its renewal, is our only legitimate hope." But this hope depends on, hinges on, wise leadership.

PART II

THE ESSENCE
OF LEADERSHIP

*I have met a few people with much wisdom
and little knowledge. I have met many people
with much knowledge and little wisdom.*

Although the best leaders may lead unintentionally, an effective leader, one who leads intentionally, must have the same characteristics as one who leads intuitively. What are these characteristics?

I must preface the following discussion by saying that in dealing with the characteristics of an effective leader, I find that psychotherapy and leadership are very similar because they both deal with the care of people's emotions. I believe the personal qualities that make a good and true leader are very similar to, if not the same as, the qualities that make a good and true psychotherapist because both people must be as clear and healed themselves as personally possible if they are to be a model worth emulating, even temporarily.

In fact, the only real difference I find between them is the end toward which the principles and human qualities are applied. A psychotherapist helps people to reenvision and heal their lives on an individual basis (but also as individuals in a group dynamic), whereas a leader helps people to envision or reenvision their future and heal their lives through transforming collective relationships.

To discuss the outer mechanics of leadership without having discussed the inner essence of leadership achieves little in the end but yet another intellectual treatise written in a technically appropriate manner. True leadership, however, is a balancing act between the emotional and intellectual components of the human psyche, which are equally important. What I attempt to do, therefore, is blend the heart and the head, which elevates both components of a leader to a higher level of ability, clarity, authenticity, and consciousness.

TRUE LEADERSHIP

6

As we evolve," notes Sufi teacher Pir Vilayat Inayat Khan, "we're able to transform the situation and the people around us by helping them to fulfill their purpose. Our purpose is to enlist the purpose of other people. That is really the secret of leadership." Why, then, are most shared visions not implemented? Corvallis, Oregon, my hometown, is a typical example:

> ...Corvallis, a city of about 43,000 people in the heart of the Willamette Valley,...completed one of the first and most successful community visioning projects in Oregon [Future Focus 2010]: "Charting a Course for Corvallis"...."[But] we didn't prepare a formal action plan," said Cynthia Solie, who directed the Corvallis project. "What was most important to us was building consensus, reflecting the community's values, and communicating the vision so that citizens and community leaders would have this picture in their heads to guide their daily activities."[62]

That was in 1989, and the vision (which is not a vision but rather a collection of contradictory statements) has yet to be acted upon almost ten years later. And that exercise is touted as a success story.[62] Why was it touted as a success story? The "vision" was never implemented even though a community can, through a visioning process: (1) better understand the core values of its citizenry and use them as a basis for planning, (2) identify the trends and forces affecting the community, and (3) articulate a wide-angle picture in time and space to guide short-term decisions in relationship to long-term outcomes and initiatives.

Why was no action taken? Did people know they were going to all that trouble and expense just for an exercise on paper? Were the personal behavioral constraints necessary to accomplish the goals too frightening socially, too restrictive ecologically, and hence too expensive economically in the short term?

What happened to the sense of urgency that promulgated the vision in the first place? Were there too many self-centered special-interest groups with enough political clout to render the vision impotent? Did too many people commute to Corvallis to work but choose to live somewhere else and therefore were not interested in a vision for the city? Were too many of the business leaders, such as home builders and developers, more interested in making all the money they could immediately, so they could retire somewhere else and not live with the consequences of their actions? Were there no leaders of sufficient moral courage and political will to shepherd the vision through the maelstrom of change and its requirement of self-restraint?

If the reason for inaction was none of the above, could it be that the people simply lacked the conceptual framework that would allow them to understand the positive consequences of a shared vision for the present generation as well as the future? Consider that after Galileo had invented the telescope to study the heavens, he invited his contemporaries to peer through it and see for themselves the evidence that would overturn the conventional wisdom concerning the planets and stars. Many declined, however, because in their closed minds what Galileo was saying was impossible; so they refused to look, which, unfortunately, too often validates a comment by English statesman David Lloyd George: "It is always too late, or too little, or both. And that is the road to disaster."

If this is the mindset of our local political leaders, what is the point of going through the pain and expense of giving birth to a vision if it is simply left to gather dust in some city, county, or state office, which says nothing about betraying the time the citizens donated, the expenditure of their tax dollars, their trust in the process, and their expectations for the outcome. Would they have been willing to pay for the process and participate in it if they had known nothing would come of it? Probably not. The critical question is: Where was the leadership?

The lack of civic leadership is a problem not unique to the city of Corvallis; consider New Zealand. "While our citizens cry out for government action to make their cities and lives livable, for an imaginative assault on the new social ills that are eroding the quality of their lives, the national leadership continues to over-emphasize economic growth at the expense of both the environment and a more natural pace of life, increasing productivity at the expense of job satisfaction, technology at the expense of human spirit, bureaucracy at the expense of more imagination and more public participation in government, and individualism at the expense of a sense of community."[63]

Is it surprising, therefore, that the single most common criticism of the community visioning processes is the lack of successful follow-through? This reticence to deal honestly with a shared vision makes it worth repeating part of Winston Churchill's speech to the British Parliament in 1935, as he saw with clear foreboding the onrushing threat of Nazi Germany to international peace:[5]

> When the situation was manageable it was neglected, and now that it is thoroughly out of hand we apply too late the remedies which then might have effected a cure. There is nothing new in the story....It falls into that long, dismal catalogue of the fruitlessness of experience and the confirmed unteachability of mankind. Want of foresight, unwillingness to act when action would be simple and effective, lack of clear thinking, confusion of counsel until the emergency comes, until self-preservation strikes its jarring gong—these are the features which constitute the endless repetition of history.

"If you build castles in the air," wrote Henry David Thoreau, "your work need not be lost. That is where they should be. Now put the foundations under them." To this, Franklin Delano Roosevelt would no doubt have added: "The only limit to our realization of tomorrow will be our doubts of today." The problem faced by Corvallis and other communities is one of foundations and, as such, often resides not only with the visioning process itself but also with a lack of leadership to ensure a true, freely participatory visioning process and adequate follow-through into the implementation phase and beyond.

If implementation is not actively linked with completion of the visioning process itself, the chances of achieving the vision are slim at best for the following reasons: (1) a community, such as Corvallis, never develops an action plan; (2) a community develops an action plan but omits important interested parties; (3) a community never implements its action plan; and (4) a community fails to monitor progress in implementing its action plan.[61] Again, leadership is the key not only to a successful visioning process but also to the successful implementation of the vision, because, as Will Rogers noted: "Even if you're on the right track, you'll get run over if you just sit there."

PERSONAL VALUES AND PHILOSOPHY OF LIFE

A leader cannot keep personal values and beliefs out of the relationship with those he or she would lead; if one does, then leadership is vague and hollow.[64] Although a leader must be willing to openly discuss the issue of values, to do so implies that one's own philosophy and core values will at times be revealed, which must be done with total honesty and grace. I believe that while a leader has an obligation to expose his or her values in a dignified manner, that same leader has an ethical obligation to refrain from imposing them on others.

Leadership is not meant to be a form of indoctrination whereby the leader manipulates the people at large to act or feel in the "right" or "politically correct" way. Each person's truth is just that: each person's individual sense of truth. But no one knows what is right or true for anyone else. Good leadership therefore requires a great deal of humility because, as George Bernard Shaw instructs us, "We are made wise not by the recollection of our past but by the responsibility of our future."

Unfortunately, there are many well-intentioned leaders who are overzealous in "straightening people out," which implies that, by virtue of their greater wisdom, they will provide the answers to the troubled populace. But leadership is not synonymous with preaching, which is not to say that a leader should simply accept whatever the people say by remaining passive and silent.

One of a leader's duties is to challenge the values of the citizenry. When a leader senses that certain behavior is unwise or destructive, that it is stealing freedom of choice from generations of the future, it becomes the leader's duty to confront the people and invite them to examine the payoffs and consequences of their choices and actions, because those choices and actions affect not only themselves but also their children and grandchildren in the present and the children as yet unborn.

A core issue in leadership is the degree to which and the way in which a leader's values should enter into her or his relationship with the public. Although a leader clearly has personal values and goals, it is totally inappropriate to foist them off on the public. Leadership is about accepting and giving counsel in order to arrive at mutually acceptable and sustainable decisions; it is not about dictatorship, which is no more than blatant power mongering.

An ethically sensitive leader is aware of her or his own values and encourages her or his followers to develop their own. A leader, however, must challenge the values of her or his followers and help them decide whether they are truly living by their professed values or are merely espousing perceived parental and societal values without consciously evaluating them. Leaders must also be alert to the possibility of manipulating the citizenry into uncritically accepting values wholesale and thereby simply becoming a substitute for a parent, something too many people today already expect their leaders and government to be.

At this juncture, it is important to emphasize that no person can hold in his or her mind a neutral thought. Hence, no person can be truly objective. Because a leader's personal values do in fact influence his or her relationships with the people at large, it is crucial for a leader to be absolutely clear about his or her values and how they influence both his or her work and the future into which he or she would lead the people.

People both need to and have a right to know where their leaders stand on values and issues in order to test their own thinking. People deserve forthright and honest involvement on the part of their leaders. Because leaders themselves do not have all of the answers, leadership must be a process whereby the people are challenged to honestly evaluate their own values and then decide for themselves which direction they want their future to take, albeit the will of the majority rules in a free democracy. "But how," you might ask, "in all of this does a leader deal with personal needs?"

Just as leaders cannot exclude their own values from their relationships with the people at large, neither can they hope to keep their personal needs, and thus their personalities, separate from those whom they lead. Leaders must recognize the supreme importance of becoming consciously aware of their own personal needs; areas of unfinished emotional business, most often related to their upbringing; potential personal conflicts; defensive coping mechanisms; and their sense of vulnerability. They must realize how these personal realities might prevent their followers from freely and fully exploring certain dimension of themselves.

Unless a leader develops this conscious self-awareness, she or he will obstruct the ways in which followers can change or will use followers to satisfy personal needs. Leadership then shifts from what is best for the people to what is best for the leader. The crux of the matter is to avoid exploiting the people for the sake of meeting the personal needs of the leader.

Here one might ask what kind of personal awareness is crucial. We all have blind spots and distortions of reality. It is therefore a leader's responsibility, both personally and to the people whom he or she serves, to work continually toward expanding self-awareness with the aim of recognizing areas of personal distortion, bias, prejudice, and vulnerability. It is particularly important that a leader become increasingly aware of the nature of unfinished emotional business that might come to the fore in his or her relationship with those who follow. To accomplish this, one must consciously, purposefully do what Carl Jung called one's "inner work."

A leader must develop a sensitivity to unmet personal needs so that leadership is not used as a means to satisfy those needs. If a leader both recognizes and works through his or her own personality problems, there is less chance of projecting them onto the ordinary citizenry with whom he or she works. A good leader must recognize that one's effectiveness depends on one's ability to create and maintain sound personal relationships and that personal problems may interfere with those relationships.

As Gerald Corey says of psychotherapists,[64] leaders have other aspects of their personalities that must be examined if they hope to be instrumental in using themselves to create healing relationships. These aspects include the need for control and power; the need to be nurturing and helpful; the need to change others in the direction of their own values; the need to teach, preach, persuade, and suggest; the need to feel adequate, particularly when it becomes overly important that the people confirm one's competence as a leader; and the need to be respected and appreciated.

Such needs are neither neurotic nor necessarily destructive, asserts Corey, but they must be kept in a healthy perspective if one's needs are to be met by helping others find satisfaction in their own lives. Many of one's needs for dignity, self-worth, and respect come from the quality of one's relationships with those with whom one works. If one does not derive deep satisfaction from one's work, then it is likely one is in the wrong profession.

For this reason, ethical leadership demands that a leader recognize the central importance of continuously probing one's own depths to determine in which direction one's personality is leading one's constituency—toward betterment or stagnation.

CHARACTERISTICS OF AN EFFECTIVE LEADER

"The true test of character," according to John Holt, "is not how much we know how to do, but how we behave when we don't know what to do." Too often, people who lack within themselves the inner spiritual authority of true leaders find themselves in positions of power, which they confuse with leadership and thus abuse the limited authority of the position. Such people are smitten with power and are loath to relinquish it, even momentarily, for fear of losing it altogether. These people cannot lead because leadership requires a great deal of trust, a clear sense of interdependence, a clear sense of high principle, and the courage to stick with it despite any and all personal costs.

To wit, in December 1783, General George Washington rode to Annapolis, Maryland, where the Continental Congress was meeting.[65] Although he learned that only seven states had sent delegates, he wanted to affirm what Congress stood for, even if the present was but a shadow of the formative days of 1776.

Around noon on the 23rd of December, General Washington strode to the statehouse, where he was met at the door by a solemn Charles Thomson, the Irish-born Philadelphian who had served as secretary of Congress since 1774. Thomson escorted General Washington into the chamber, where 20 congressmen and the current president, Thomas Mifflin of Pennsylvania, awaited him amidst aisles and galleries packed with spectators.

"Sir," said Mifflin, "the United States in Congress assembled are prepared to receive your communications."

Washington rose and bowed; the congressmen in turn raised their hats as a sign of respect but without bowing. By withholding their bows, the congressmen affirmed the civil superiority over the power of the military.

Washington, with trembling hands, began his statement by conveying his happiness that the United States was now a "respectable nation," enabling him to resign "with satisfaction" the commission he had accepted "with diffidence." He overcame his diffidence, he said, because he had been confident of "the rectitude of our Cause," the support of Congress, and "the patronage of Heaven."

Although it is said that he could not read the close of his speech because he was so choked with emotion, this is what he had written: "I consider it an indispensable duty to close this last solemn act of my official life, by commending the interests of our dearest country to the protection of Almighty God, and those who have the superintendence of them, to his holy keeping."

"The whole house felt his agitations," wrote one congressman to his fiancée. "The spectators all wept and there was hardly a member of Congress who did not."

Struggling with the final words, Washington said: "Having now finished the work assigned me, I retire from the great theatre of action, and bidding an affectionate farewell to this august body under whose orders I have so long acted, I here offer my commission, and take my leave of all the employments of public life."

"What," you might ask, "is the significance of this story?" The significance is that liberty is always expensive. True liberty demands that each and every leader know not only when his or her duty to history has been completed but also when to step down with dignity and grace so that the pivotal idea of a free democracy as the central pillar of our nation can deepen in the centuries to come.

With this in mind, it seems clear that today's means of exercising power and authority must give way to new forms of leadership. Our concept of leadership must be recast to include the ability to foster collective decision making and collective action. If leadership is to find its highest expression in service to the community as a whole, we must increasingly choose leaders who are truly motivated by the desire to serve.

It is, after all, a leader's duty to create a response from the followership, not the followership's duty to respond to the leader. While we unfortunately hear most often of the abuses of power, power can be a good thing when used constructively and toward a positive end, which means that leadership must never be handled carelessly or selfishly.

Other-Centered and Authentic

A true leader is other-centered and is therefore concerned primarily with facilitating someone else's ability to reach his or her potential as a human being by helping that person develop his or her talents and skills and value his or her experiences. Authentic leadership thus comes from the heart and deals intimately with human values and human dignity.

Authenticity is the condition or quality of being trustworthy or genuine. Beyond the dictionary definition, authenticity is the harmony among what one thinks, says, and does and what one really feels—the motive in the deepest recesses of one's heart. The adage "deeds speak louder than words" is true as far as it goes, but what is left unsaid is that "motives speak louder than deeds." One is authentic only when one's motives, words, and deeds are in harmony with one's attitude.

Ralph Waldo Emerson wrote: "Your attitude thunders so loudly that I can't hear what you say." One's attitude is the visible part of one's behavior, but one's motive is often hidden from view. When one's visible behavior is out of harmony with one's motive, that attitude points to a hidden agenda. Therefore, an authentic person is one who is willing to risk shedding stereotypical roles and being a real person in a relationship.

There is, however, a current lack of public trust in leaders—a lack of trust based on a perceived lack of authenticity. Consider the following observations of columnist Leonard Pitts, Jr.[66] "I'm hard put," writes Pitts, "to remember the last time a public figure expressed remorse and made me believe there was really any there." It is not a shortage of wrongdoing, he continues, but rather the apologies we have seen, which are "slickly crafted written statements often followed by carefully orchestrated acts of contrition." What we have not seen is real regret from people who are genuinely sorry for their misdeeds.

Public penitence, contends Pitts, is today a stage-managed process choreographed by media consultants who always give the same advice: "Admit the wrongdoing, express contrition, and move on—preferably all in one breath." There is no apparent need to feel sorry.

"The buck stops here," read the sign on President Harry S. Truman's desk. The buck today is "passed around like the common cold." When, however, there must be some accountability, the apologies come with a footnote of "self-justification and outright insincerity."

President Clinton, for example, in responding to allegations of irregularities in campaign financing, said, "Mistakes were made." But he never said by whom they were made, leaving us, quips Pitts, to assume the mistakes occurred under their own volition. When the president of the United States, ostensibly the single most powerful person in the world today, either cannot or will not stand up and forthrightly admit that he "screwed up royally," why should we as a society expect any better from lesser figures in the parade of world leaders? If this is the fare our leaders expect us to swallow, why even bother listening?

"They pretend to be remorseful and we pretend to believe them," concludes Pitts. We are, he says, grateful for at least the appearance of propriety, even though we know that something necessary is missing—authentic humility and penitence.

This current lack of public trust in leaders today may, in a narrow sense, be brought about by a leader's dishonest behavior or, in a broader sense, by a leader's perceived self-centeredness. But it may also be caused (through no fault of the leader) by unrecognized cultural evolution.

Consider what has happened recently in present-day Serbia under the dictatorial rule of President Slobodan Milosevic (a former Communist turned Socialist).[67] When President Milosevic nullified the November 17, 1996 elections that gave victories to his opposition (composed of three political parties that form the Zajedno [Together] coalition) in 14 cities across Serbia, he clearly demonstrated that he was not a leader in the true sense. Fearing his apparent loss of power, his act was both illegal and self-centered.

Opposition leaders such as Zoran Djindjic and Vuk Draskovic, on the other hand, were true leaders and led peaceful demonstrations with thousands of Serbian citizens in Belgrade in protest of President Milosevic's tyranny. Milosevic's tyranny, which began a decade ago with the disappearance of everyday civil niceties, put the country (then Yugoslavia) into an economic tailspin and produced years of mind-numbing propaganda. The result was that Belgrade became a surly city, where few people bothered to excuse themselves, shopkeepers either snapped at or ignored customers, and no one would give up a seat on a crowded bus.

One unexpected consequence of nearly three months of such leadership and peaceful anti-dictatorial protests has been a return of civility and even a reborn sense of humor. Going about her errands on a clear morning in Belgrade, 71-year-old Radmila Jovanovic, a retired engineer, was shocked at the way her native city was changing: people were being polite. "Within five minutes," said Radmila, "people had bumped into me three times. All of them excused themselves. I was so surprised. I went into a shop, and the saleswoman wished me a good day and asked what she could do for me. I was in shock."

"Until now, I felt that the city had been dead for years," said Ljubica Simovic, a 42-year-old art historian who now works in a store. "But now our lives have been changed. This great spirit we used to have is back, and the students are really full of humor."

Dusan Trifunovic, a 43-year-old engineer, rarely misses a protest. "The atmosphere is great. For the first time in many years," he said, "people are smiling here. I see friends that I haven't seen since school days. We march together and are rediscovering our sense of humor."

The protesters, united in their contempt for Milosevic's Socialists, have supplanted anger with satire and mockery as one of their main weapons in this capital of 1.5 million people. The humor is reminiscent of Belgrade's cosmopolitan past, when sharp-witted artists found ways to poke fun at their Communist rulers. Today, for example, pro-democracy supporters carry signs that read: "I think, therefore I walk," referring to their daily protests as "walks" to circumvent an official, but not strictly enforced, ban on demonstrations.

In addition to protesting Milosevic's tyranny, social values are changing. The attitude of the young people provides hope for the future, says historian Latinka Perovic: "In the shadow of war and general degradation, cut off from the world, a generation has grown up...that has mocked the hypocrisy and lies and refused to take them as a principle on which society and its institutions function."

Cultural evolution expresses itself through changing values. Culture is not genetically inherited; it can only be learned from the past, modified in the present, and passed on to future generations. The notion of culture poses two questions: (1) What happens when the evolution of culture and the resulting shift in values in one part of a society tear the social fabric with great force? and (2) How do we heal the social rupture that results from this shift in cultural values?

If society has learned anything from the decade of the 1960s, it must be that one cannot unilaterally destroy "the establishment" without offering a viable alternative with which to replace it. Before an old paradigm can be cast out, there must be a new one to take its place.

How do we know a new paradigm is at hand? We know because we are suddenly faced with a crisis that tells us that our old belief system is no longer as functional as it once was. There is a point at which we must break free of our habitual belief systems and choose to change or stagnate. The frightening thing about change is that it inevitably means letting go of familiar people and places as we move to another stage in life. Each new paradigm is built on a shift of insight, a quantum leap of intuition.

On the collective level, this means that cultural evolution takes place with only a modicum of hard, scientific data. Those who cling to the old way may demand irrefutable proof that change is needed, but such proof most often is not readily available. The irony is that the old way also began as the new and also was challenged to prove change was necessary or even desirable.

Time and human effort have proven the old paradigm to have been more "right" than its predecessor but still only partially "right." So it is with the new; it too will be more "right" than the old and eventually will be proven to be only partially correct and in need of change.

The personal trap is that any paradigm that has become comfortable also has become self-limiting. New data cannot fit into the old way of thinking, which has grown rigid with tradition and hardened with age. It is therefore necessary periodically to crack open the old if a new thought form is to enter and grow, moving the individual forward in a renewed sense of authenticity.

That new data cannot fit into an old way of thinking was forcibly brought home to me some 20 years ago by an old logger. I was asked to give a speech on new ways to practice forestry, ways that were deemed to be ecologically sound. Accordingly, I spent much time explaining the necessary changes in the techniques of logging if we were to have ecologically sustainable forests. I finished the session feeling that I had done a good job and basking in the warm afterglow, when an old logger came up to me.

"Sonny," he said, his bright blue eyes snapping under his thinning silvery hair, "I'm sure you have a good point there, but I just can't find it. Mostly," he continued with a broad grin, "I think you're just full of shit."

Taken aback, I asked him why he thought that.

"Well," he replied, "the way I think of a forest, you just don't make no sense nohow." Having said that, he winked at me and left.

As though struck by a bolt of lightening, I realized that he was absolutely correct. Without a dramatic shift in the philosophical under-pinnings of our belief systems, new data simply have nowhere to go.

Moving forward may be difficult for those whose belief system and personal identity are totally invested in the old paradigm because, in their perception at least, there is no reason to change. For those who subscribe to a new paradigm, on the other hand, moving forward is easier, because there is something toward which to move—a new view that hints at a sustainable future, a view more in tune with today's ecological understanding. Yet those who harbor new ideas are no better or more "right" than those who cling to the old ways; the two views are only different.

Historian Arnold Toynbee asked the critical question of why 26 great civilizations fell. The answer, he concluded, was that the people would not, or believed they could not, change their way of thinking to meet the changing conditions of their world.

Thus, communities can move forward, evolve, if you will, only to the extent that individuals within those communities are ready and willing to grow personally and accept new philosophies and methods of doing business demanded by a rapidly changing culture. Communities cannot and will not remain the same, despite those who attempt to thwart change, so those who feel they cannot or those who will not accept new ideas must fall by the wayside. Nevertheless, most people seem to resist change, even that which they understand to be good in the long term and for the generations of the future, if it means they must forego their immediate desires and pleasures, which they interpret as part and parcel of their personal well-being and security.

The crux of the issue is that cultural evolution (changing times, if you will) is really about changes in how we humans relate to ourselves, one another, and the world around us. And it is precisely within the context of these changing relationships that people at large can experience growth from the authenticity of a true leader who, in turn, may be able to speed up the rate of cultural evolution for the good of the whole.

If, however, a leader hides behind the safety of political correctness or within the rigid walls of his or her position and refuses to accept responsibility or risk change, the citizens will keep themselves hidden from that leader. If a leader is merely a technical expert who leaves his or her own reactions, values, and self out of the equation, the result will be sterile, hollow leadership. It is through his or her own realness and aliveness that a leader can significantly touch the citizenry.

If a leader makes life-oriented choices, radiates a zest for living, is real in her or his relationships with the citizenry, and lets herself or himself be known to them, despite personal problems and errors, which we all have and make, she or he can inspire and teach the people in the best sense of the word—through example. Witness the late Diana, Princess of Wales. This does not imply that a leader has all the answers or is without personal problems, but it does mean that a leader must be willing to look at her or his own life and have the courage and willingness to make the same kinds of adjustments she or he wants the people at large to make.

A leader who "walks his or her talk" can inspire a sense of hope that people can change and that change is worth the risks and the effort. Such a leader can extend hope to the people and by example can inspire them to strive mightily in the face of all the uncertainties embodied in the risks of change. Hope, after all, is seeing the opportunities in an uncertain future and mapping one's course toward them.

In short, a leader is a model for the people. If a leader models incongruent behavior, low-risk activity, deceit through vagueness and duplicity, one of two things will happen. First, he or she will not be trusted, and second, people of like mind will take the example as permission to follow the lead and act accordingly.

If, on the other hand, a leader models realness by engaging in appropriate self-disclosure, he or she can anticipate that such authenticity will inspire a greater following based on trust and emulation than would otherwise be possible. In the end, the degree of aliveness, commitment, and psychological health of a leader (who has worked through his or her own personal issues) is the crucial variable that determines the outcome of leadership. To accomplish this, however, one must have honor.

An Honorable Person

Personal honor is a gift a person gives to himself or herself; it is a code of ethics by which one lives and conducts oneself. One's honor is one's personal integrity, which is maintained without legal or other obligation. At this juncture, a leader must understand that personal integrity includes each commitment one makes to oneself and that such personal commitments are every bit as important to keep as those made to one's constituents. It is that inner essence, the spiritually backed standard, that makes one what one is.

A leader must have an inner sense of honor, such that one's word is one's bond. In olden days, a contract between two people was sealed with a handshake and each party's word was at least as sound as a legal document—or even sounder.

Israeli Prime Minister Yitzhak Rabin was a shining example of a man with personal honor because he was through and through a warrior, but one who had the courage and wisdom to see that peace was the only road to the security of his country—and he chose to take that road, no matter how difficult. While honor is normally thought of in terms of men, it is an attribute shared equally between men and women, which brings us to the subject of balance between a leader's masculine and feminine aspects.

Balancing the Masculine and Feminine

Although a leader can lead someone from here to there in the outer, physical–spatial landscape without actually having been there before, psychologically, a leader can only lead someone to a given place of consciousness in the inner landscape if the leader has in fact been there before himself or herself. For example, linear, left-brain thinking, which is a masculine trait, is more prevalent and comfortable in our society than is right-brain thinking, which is a feminine trait.[68]

While tapping into the right side of the brain is more powerful than using the left side, it is difficult to appeal to the right side because it is so often dormant in our society where relationship and creativity are by and large dashed upon the social rocks of patriarchal conformity. Therefore, to appeal to the right side of the brain, the conceptual side, a leader must either have a strong innate balance or must consciously develop it before being able to stimulate it in others.

It is a necessity for a good leader to be well balanced between the right and left brain, the feminine and masculine aspects of the self, because a truly effective leader must be able to make an emotional connection with those who follow. I say this because a leader cannot change people's minds but can bring their convictions and values to the surface. Before this is possible, however, an emotional connection must be made, and that lies within the realm of the right side of the brain.

A common human trait is to make decisions based on emotion and justify them with "fact." Although you may disagree with this statement, believing yourself to be totally rational and objective because you do thorough research before you make a decision, think back to your last major decision, your last big purchase—a car, house, an important article of clothing. Why did you select the one you did? Was it color, size, how it made you feel, or what you thought it might do for your social standing that caused you to select it? After your initial reaction, did you feel that you needed to justify the price? This same principle applies to concepts and ideas; we buy the emotion before we accept the "facts," which lends credence to the observation by American author Charlotte P. Gilman that "a concept is stronger than a fact."

Therefore, leaders who appeal to the right side of their followers' brains, who touch them emotionally, make a lasting connection. Such leaders not only create experiences for their constituency or cause a long-dormant memory to be vividly recalled but also make a memorable connection that has the power to motivate.

But before any of this can happen, before a new idea will be accepted, the leader must be likable as a person. Do we feel good about him or her? Is he or she authentic and trustworthy? This is critical, because genuine passion is not only rare but also the way to the emotions and the soul. Passionate leaders are often described as dynamic, charismatic, riveting, or engaging because the authenticity of their message, their vision, is palpable, especially if it is one in which their constituency can also believe.

Such a leader makes people feel good about themselves, which, in turn, makes them want to follow if for no other reason than to be around the leader. Although a powerful leader can leave people on a natural high, to be genuine, he or she must also be therapeutic as a person, such as Mahatma Gandhi.

A Therapeutic Person

A therapeutic person is one who has healing powers, for, as Carl Jung said, it is the personality of the doctor that has the curative effect.[4] "But why," you might ask, "do you use the term therapeutic?" I use the term therapeutic because a good leader not only must bear the uncertainties and fears of those who follow but also must help them reach beyond where they thought they could go.

In this sense, an effective leader treads, albeit lightly, in the realm of psychotherapy. Hence, because a leader is asking people to risk a greater personal honesty by looking within, it is critical that the leader exhibit the courage to search within and hold his or her own life open to the same kind of scrutiny that is being asked of his or her constituents, all the while knowing that, in moments of weakness, we have all done things of which we may be ashamed.

Professor Gerald Corey has provided an excellent synopsis of a therapeutic person in terms of being a psychotherapist.[64] It is with gratitude and humility that I adapt his synopsis to the realm of leadership, for they are in many ways one and the same. In this sense, as Corey says of psychotherapists, leaders must continually ask themselves: What do I personally have to offer those who are struggling to find their way? Am I living my life honestly, freely, and boldly as I am urging others to do?

There are two central questions tied to a leader's personhood: (1) How can a leader be a therapeutic person? and (2) How can a leader be an instrument of awareness and growth for those who follow? Here I return to the notion of a leader as a public example whose life, as Mahatma Gandhi once said of his own life, is his or her message.

Leaders can acquire extensive theoretical and practical knowledge and make that knowledge available to their constituents. But until that knowledge is integrated into one's real life as a leader, it is seldom, if ever, inspirational because, in the end, one always brings oneself as an example before one's constituents in one's own unique human qualities and the experiences in life that have molded him or her. This is a critical concept because a true leader must, above all else, inspire others to follow the noble path of service to *all* citizens, present and future.

If, therefore, leaders are going to promote inner growth and change in their constituents, they must be at least equally willing to grow and change within by exploring their own choices and decisions and by striving to always be aware of, accept, and act on their own potential for growth. Their willingness to live in accordance with their own truths and to set an example of those truths by how they live is the positive model that makes effective leaders "therapeutic persons" for their followers.

As Corey stated, and I emphasize, the following list is *not* proposed as a model of perfection. Rather, the importance lies in a person's continuing struggle to attain these dimensions, albeit he or she may repeatedly miss the mark. It is the willingness to remain open to the struggle of continual personal growth that is crucial for a vital leader, not only for the leader himself or herself but also for the experience of those who follow.

I propose this evolving list of characteristics of a therapeutic person in the same vein as Corey did for psychotherapists, not as some dogmatic itemization of what is "right," but rather to provide a foundation from which to examine your own concepts of a therapeutic leader. I also recommend that you add to this list any characteristics that you feel are missing. To better allow you to *feel* the list, it is presented in the first person.

1. I must find my own way in that I can only lead effectively where I have personally traveled. In so doing, I am in the process of developing a style of leadership that is uniquely mine and consciously reflects both my philosophy of life and style of living. Although I must of necessity be a sifter who borrows ideas from others, I remain true to myself in how I apply that which I borrow.

2. I respect myself and appreciate both what I am and what I am consciously becoming. I can give out of my own authenticity, rather than seeking a false sense of fulfillment from others. I have the humility to ask of, to be needed by, and to receive from others without isolating myself as a means of control.

3. I am comfortable with my own sense of personal power and am secure enough to allow other people to also be comfortable with their own sense of power. Hence, there is no need for me to diminish others or encourage them to maintain a subordinate stance. I consciously use my power with respect as a healthy model for those who follow.

4. I not only am in touch with myself and open to change but also am willing to take calculated risks. Rather than settling for less or that which is comfortable, I am willing to plunge into the unknown, where I find within my uncertainties my own untapped potentials.

5. I strive continuously to expand my awareness of myself and others, realizing that limited freedom comes with limited awareness and vice versa. To enrich my own life and thus the lives of others, I direct my energy toward new experiences that will in turn expand my awareness of cause and effect and hence improve all of my myriad relationships.

6. I am both willing and able to accept ambiguity because personal growth means leaving the perceived safety of the familiar for the uncertainty of the unknown. I know that the price of entering an unknown territory is a degree of ambiguity in life. But instead of perceiving it as a threat to my existence, I view it as a hidden potential to which I am inextricably drawn. And as I learn increasingly to trust myself and my intuition, I become increasingly trustworthy to others.

7. I have a personal identity in that I know what I am, what I am capable of becoming, what I want from life, and what is essential. I am willing to continuously and consciously reexamine my values and strive to get in touch and stay in touch with my inner core and live from the authenticity of my own center. My standards are internalized, and I have the courage to act in a way that is consistent with my own belief. I know the only way to communicate my inner truth is to live that truth.

8. I am consciously aware of my own struggles and pain from which I gain a frame of reference that allows me to identify with

others while maintaining my own identity. Put differently, I do not get mired in someone else's emotional quicksand.

9. I am committed to living life to the fullest and best, and I refuse to settle for mere existence. As Winston Churchill once said about the road to success, I go from "failure to failure with enthusiasm."

10. I am authentic and refuse to hide behind masks of persona, sterile roles, or facades. I will risk instead to be genuine.

11. I am able to give and receive love from the fullness of my soul. I am thus vulnerable to those I love and have the capacity to care for others.

12. Recognizing that shame can only live in the past and fear can only live in the future, I choose to live in the present, where there is neither shame nor fear. I choose the eternal now and invite others to join me.

13. Although I make mistakes like everyone else, I willingly admit them. I do not lightly dismiss my errors, but choose instead to learn from them rather than be encumbered with pointless misery.

14. My "work" is a labor of love and a way of living. Although I find deep, spiritual meaning in the work I do, I am not enslaved by it for my identity. My work is coupled with other dimensions in life, which collectively provide me with a sense of purpose and fulfillment.

15. Unbound by my past ways of being, I am constantly changing as I struggle to become that which I want to be. In so doing, I am constantly revitalizing and recreating significant relationships.

16. Being open to my own emotional experiences, I can be emotionally present for others in their pain or joy.

17. Aware that I have no choice but to make choices that shape my life, I am not a victim of my past decisions because I know that if I err, I can always choose to choose again and yet again if need be.

18. I openly challenge unreasonable assumptions and self-destructive beliefs and attitudes, rather than submit to them. Being thus engaged, I do not needlessly limit myself with negative self-talk.

19. I know that in the end all I have to give of real value is my love, trust, respect, and the benefit of my experiences. I am also aware that people do not care about how much I know as a leader until they know how much I care about them. Someone

once said that soldiers will follow a leader whom they know is willing to die for them if need be. This is the kind of caring that really counts.

20. I know that choice is the root of all human relationships and that choice (both conscious and unconscious) directs the outcome of all such relationships. I understand that choice is the cause of an effect and am thus careful to choose wisely for all concerned—present and future.

As Corey himself indicated, this snapshot of a leader might appear unrealistic. After all, who can be all these things? Again, I point out that these are characteristics of leadership to *strive* for as you reach to become more of your potential self. As a Chinese proverb points out, even the journey of a thousand miles must begin with a single step.

I emphasize the word "strive" because, as Jungian analyst Eleanor Bertine says of human relationships, "Acceptance means taking the other person as he [or she] is, without reservation," which includes one's own relationship with oneself. She goes on to say that people often remark they like this but not that about so-and-so. Such an attitude reflects one's biases concerning the "assets and liabilities" of the other person, which, according to Bertine, is not love. Love is unconditional acceptance of all faults and virtues.

"Why," you might ask, "should I struggle so hard to achieve these aspects of leadership?" Sociologist and minister Marvin Layman offers what I think is a compelling reason. Layman writes that religion, psychology, and medicine all have a healing role—that of making whole the individual. I include leadership in this group.

"Never before," says Layman, "has there been a greater need for such 'physicians of the soul.' For in our corrupt and spiritually bereft society, those…[with] psychic wholeness are desperately needed bastions of strength for many others." A truly competent leader, according to Layman, must be more than just technically proficient; he or she must have a genuine feeling for, even a love of, people, a considerable degree of psychological maturity, and some degree of wisdom and "inner soul quality."

I present this view of leadership in the hope that you not only will examine it but also will develop your own concept of leadership, that which you deem essential to those people whom you would lead so that one day you would be comfortable following them.

Detachment and Equanimity

Detachment from an outcome is total acceptance of what is without any desire to have something else, which is a critical concept in true leadership. Detachment is checking one's ego at the door as one comes into the room. This is, at best, difficult to learn, and I have consciously struggled with it for over two decades.

When I was younger, I was deeply upset by the clear-cut logging of the old-growth forests in the Pacific Northwest, where I grew up. I would argue long and loudly about the need to save them and the greed and stupidity of those whose actions would liquidate them. I tried to convince anyone and everyone that the forests needed to be saved. I was so rabid in presenting my point of view as the right one that few people cared to listen, unless they already agreed with me. Consequently, I became frustrated, cynical, and self-righteous, all of which only made matters worse. I became enraged at the "greedy bastards who were clear-cutting my forest," but I never thought to ask them how they felt about the forests they were liquidating.

One day, as I was giving a passionate speech on the need to "preserve" the ancient forests of the Pacific Northwest, I suddenly felt the sword taken from my hand and a sense of peace come over me, a sense that was immediately reflected in the audience. Several people came up to me later and said they had never thought about it that way and that what I said made sense. It was then I realized that to speak for the forests or for anything else, I had to change—not the people in the audience, but me! If I wanted people to listen, it was incumbent upon me to change, to say what I had to say in a way that would allow them to hear. But how? I did not know how.

A few weeks later, I saw the movie *Gandhi*. Then I read a couple of biographies about Gandhi in which he was often quoted, and through his writings he gave me the answer. I had to detach myself from the outcome, a truly difficult task.

If Gandhi was correct, in detachment lay acceptance of the outcome. Expectation is the attachment, the vested interest in the outcome, because the person with the expectation sees himself or herself as possessing the means to achieve the right and justifiable result. If, on the other hand, one acts willingly out of duty to a Higher Authority, one can act with detachment, because the Higher Authority is acknowledged as possessing the wisdom to justly govern the outcome. Detachment here does *not* mean that one acts without commitment; quite to the contrary, while one is firmly committed to the principle that serves all people in the greatest good, one is detached from an outcome that would serve only the desires of one's own ego.

If I am detached, I have no vested interest in the results of a given process as they might affect my personally desired outcome. This means that I can treat all sides, all points of view, and all possible outcomes with equanimity only to the extent that I can set aside my own ego-desires. Equanimity is the kernel of peace in detachment just as surely as anxiety is the kernel of agitation in attachment.

For example, a person who has worked passionately for a cause may suddenly have the insight that passion placed before principle is a house divided against itself that cannot long stand. Because of this new understanding, he or she now becomes focused on the principle as a process and becomes detached from the passion—the desired result. The reaction of his or her peers most often is: "How can you give up the cause? We've believed in it for so long."

For these people, attachment to the cause has become life itself, their very identity. Therefore, even as they ostensibly fight to "win," they cannot afford to win because if they were to actually resolve the issue at the heart of their cause, they would have to find a new identity, something most people are loath to do.

If one, as a leader, is truly detached from the outcome, one will find equanimity to be one's touchstone. Equanimity, the outworking of detachment, is reflected in the calm, even-tempered, and serene personality of one who is simply open to accepting what is. Such a person can lead without wasting energy through either the need for or the expectation of approval or a predetermined outcome. Such a person acts out of peace.

In turn, the peaceful action allows others to see an alternative way of perceiving something, because no one is trying to convince them of anything. They are given the ideas and the space to consider them. Then, if they so choose, they can change their minds in privacy while retaining their dignity intact.

The leader who is detached from the outcome is part of the principle for which he or she stands and is therefore part of the resolution or transcendence of the problem. On the other hand, a leader becomes part of the problem when attached to a point of view and its *necessary* outcome. A leader's detachment and equanimity serve to make followership an exciting prospective because people feel safe in the care of one with equipoise of character.

A Good Follower

I must follow the people.
Am I not their leader?

Benjamin Disraeli
19th century British prime minister

You must learn to follow before you can learn to lead. Learning to be a good leader means starting at the bottom of the ladder as a simple follower and learning about each individual rung and its relationship to every other rung as you climb the ladder to the top. President Theodore Roosevelt once said: "To me there is something fine in the American theory that a private citizen can be chosen by the people to occupy a position as great as that of the mightiest monarch...and that...after having filled this position, the man [person]...goes back into the ranks of his fellow citizens." Back into the ranks from which one rose. Down from the pinnacle of power to the status of a private individual.

Elizabeth Sherrill gives an excellent example of a man who rose from followership to leadership and then went back to followership with grace.[69] As roving editor for *Guideposts* magazine, she once interviewed Harry Truman at his home in Independence, Missouri. As she and her family left the Truman home, her five-year-old son, Donn, began to cry in the back seat of the car.

"What's the matter?" she asked Donn.

"I wanted to see the president!" he wailed.

"You did. You met Mr. Truman," she replied.

"No." He shook his head. "He wasn't a *president*. He was just a man."

"Just a man," mused Sherrill. "Just a man who for a time had wielded more power than anyone else on earth. Just, Theodore Roosevelt would have said approvingly, an American president."

Beginning as a follower at the bottom of the leadership ladder is critical, because you as leader must never ask a follower to do something that you yourself are not willing to do—and one does not lead forever. It is therefore imperative that you know what it feels like to be a follower.

You can get a good sense of what I am talking about by watching the movie *The Doctor*. William Hurt plays the part of a good but insensitive surgeon who is diagnosed with cancer of the throat and suddenly learns what it feels like to be treated as a patient. As a patient, he must fill out seemingly endless forms and wait interminably to be seen by the doctor. His privileged status as a doctor is moot because he must go to a doctor whose specialty not only is different than his own but who also is a woman. And finally, he must face all the uncertainties of the doctor's answers to his frightened questions.

Having seen himself as a doctor through his own eyes as a patient, he makes all the interns with whom he subsequently works spend time as patients so they will understand—with a great deal of humility—what it feels like to be on the receiving end of their services. This is why one must learn to follow before one can learn to lead.

A good leader always searches for signs of leadership talent among his or her followers and in so doing looks for certain characteristics that help identify a potential leader to encourage. These characteristics include (1) authenticity, (2) other-centeredness, (3) using adversity to advantage, (4) persistence, (5) learning from one's mistakes, (6) focusing on positive thoughts, and (7) seeing, recognizing, and seizing an opportunity.[70]

Authenticity can be simply characterized as "what you see is what you get." In other words, a person is simply who he or she is without any hidden agenda or put-on persona.

The person is other-centered as opposed to self-centered, which means the person is interested in serving rather than garnering power.

A potential leader has her or his share of failures and frustrations, but knows how to take advantage of such adversity. What might be an obstacle to an average follower is a glorious opportunity to a ripening leader.

Persistence, which is the relentless pursuit of a goal, is a sure sign of a potential leader because perseverance is a prime ingredient for success in anything. William Penn observed: "Patience and diligence, like faith, can remove mountains." And all leaders must, through sheer persistence, overcome mountains of rejection, dismissal, and repudiation to achieve the vision of their ideas.

Rather than beating themselves up for their mistakes, potential leaders learn from their mistakes because, as the late actress Rosalind Russell pointed out: "Flops are a part of life's menu." By learning from one's mistakes, rather than berating oneself, a person's errors become the raw material out of which future success is forged.

Consider Jim Burke, chairman of Johnson & Johnson, as an example. When he first became head of the division of new products at

Johnson & Johnson, he was responsible for developing a chest rub for children, which failed on the market and cost hundreds of thousands of dollars.

Burke expected to be fired over his failure, but when he was summoned by the chairman of the board, he received a surprising reception: "Are you the one who just cost us all that money?" asked Robert Wood Johnson. "Well, I just want to congratulate you. If you are making mistakes, that means you're taking risks, and we won't grow unless you take risks."

Jim Burke remembered the lesson, and years later, when he became chairman of the board, he reminded other junior executives of the importance of taking risks and learning from mistakes.

A follower is one who focuses on positive thoughts by filtering out negative ones on the trail of leadership. Helen Keller, who became blind and deaf shortly after birth, often counseled people to "keep your face to the sunshine and you cannot see the shadow." Similarly, President Dwight D. Eisenhower was fond of saying, "No pessimist ever won a battle."

But it was tennis player Billy Jean King who provided the most graphic example of positive thinking. Every time she made a bad swing with her racket, she followed it with the correct swing, even in a televised tournament. She was constantly correcting her mistakes as she made them and thus left the thought and feeling of the positive swing in her psyche.

Seeing, recognizing, and seizing an opportunity is a behavioral trait that stands out because it is rarely encountered. People who affect society and make great leaders are those who not only recognize an opportunity but also seize the moment. It is an important quality of leadership because, as author Dennis Waitley reminds us, "Opportunity rarely looks like an opportunity. Often opportunity arrives incognito, disguised as misfortune, defeat, and rejection." People who recognize an opportunity and seize the moment are worth looking for in the crowd.

Taken in isolation, these traits, while good in and of themselves, do not constitute a potential leader. When taken in the collective, however, the potential for a servant leader is clearly present. Conversely, a follower who wants to become a leader must learn to nurture these qualities.

In addition to the above qualities, a good follower must exhibit the following characteristics, *but none of them mindlessly*:[71]

1. **Loyalty**—This implies commitment not only to the leader and the leader's vision but also to the principles of sound leadership. Loyalty manifests itself in one's willingness to daily work with enthusiasm on behalf of one's leader. But, as Petra Kelly reminds us, "Loyalty toward the whole of life is far more important than any ideology."

2. **Understanding**—The ability to articulate and integrate into one's daily life the vision and principles espoused by one's leader.

3. **Candor**—The courage to speak one's mind clearly, succinctly, and authentically to one's leader and fellow followers, but gracefully and in private.

4. **Listening**—This demands attention and care and must be coupled with observing the subtle nuances of a leader's speech and behavior if maximum clarity of understanding is to be achieved.

5. **Predictability**—Being accountable for one's own behavior in such a way that one's leader knows who can be counted on when the need arises.

6. **Creativity**—Having a beginner's mind that allows one to discover or help discover novel solutions to the problems of leadership as they arise.

7. **Effectiveness**—Getting things done in a manner that helps accomplish the intent of the action.

8. **Efficiency**—Getting things done in the most expedient and cost-effective manner without compromising either the quality or principles of sound leadership.

9. **Insightfulness**—The ability to ask relevant, probing questions and foster innovative ways of seeing and thinking about ordinary things; the ability to advance new perspectives that set the tenor of the success that follows.

10. **Honesty**—Allows a leader to know a person can be trusted to accurately represent the leader's vision and/or principles with the highest standards of integrity.

11. **Persistence**—The tenacity to attack a problem with gusto and stay with it until it is either solved or all conceivable possibilities have been exhausted.

12. **Practicality**—Being grounded enough to face a problem head on and come up with thoughtful, positive suggestions about how to solve it, even when the possibility of success seems bleak.

13. **Communicative**—The personal commitment to keep one's leader abreast of important developments before they come as surprising news from others who might put the leader in the awkward position of having to play catch-up from a position of disadvantage.
14. **Helpfulness**—The constant willingness to lend a hand to further the leader's vision and/or to uphold the leader's principles.
15. **Complementary**—The willingness to lend a hand in such a way that one's thoughts and actions complement—rather than compete with—those of one's leader in achieving a particular end.
16. **Cheerfulness**—The choice and determination to maintain an even-tempered disposition come what may; hence the ability to smile in the face of adversity and make things a little brighter for everyone.

The foregoing characteristics are also those of a servant leader because a servant leader must at times be a follower.

Servant Leader

As auto manufacturer Henry Ford once said, "Coming together is a beginning; keeping together is progress; working together is success." In the end, it is the collective heart of the people that counts; without people, there is no need for leaders. Chinese philosopher Lao-tzu thought a good leader was one who, "when his work is done, his aim fulfilled, they will all say, 'We did this ourselves.'" Such is servant leadership.

A good servant leader is a person with a fine balance between the masculine and feminine aspects of his or her personality. Such balance is critical because servant leadership often means putting relationships ahead of immediate achievement and knowing when each is important.

A servant leader intuitively knows that service is an attitude, not a function. Hence, such a leader does what is right from moral conviction, usually expressed as enthusiasm, which causes people to want to follow with action.

A leader is one who values people and helps them transcend their fears so they might be able to act in a manner other than they were capable of on their own. This is the essence, the first rule, of true leadership. As such, it calls to mind a scene from the movie *Karate Kid*

II, in which Miyagi, a Japanese man who is the central character, is translating the rules of karate displayed on the walls of the Miyagi family dojo in Okinawa: "Rule number one: karate is for defense only. Rule number two: first learn rule number one."

One might translate this to leadership as follows: *Rule number one: Leadership is service to others based on inner strength of character. Rule number two: first learn rule number one.*

Leadership has to do with authority, which is control, or the right or power to command, enforce laws, exact obedience, determine, or judge. Two kinds of authority are embodied in this definition: that of a person and that of a position.

The authority of a person begins as an inner spiritual phenomenon. It comes from one's belief in one's higher consciousness, which acts as a guide in life when one listens to it. As James Allen noted: "As a man thinketh in his heart, so is he."

Thus, a person who has only the authority of position may have a socially accepted seat of power over other people, but such power can exist only if people agree to submit their obedience to the authority. A person who holds a position of authority yet does not live from the spiritual authority within can only manage or rule—through coercion and fear—but cannot lead, because, as American mathematician Norbert Wiener observed, "A conscience which has been bought once will be bought twice," to which Lord Acton might have added, "Power corrupts, and absolute power corrupts absolutely."

A leader's power to inspire followership comes from a sense of authenticity, because the individual has a vision that is other-centered rather than self-centered. Such a vision springs from strength, those Universal Principles that govern all life with justice and equity, as opposed to the relatively weak foundation of selfish desire. It is the authenticity that people respond to, and in responding, they validate their leader's authority.

Managerialship, on the other hand, is of the intellect and pays minute attention to detail, to the letter of the law, and to doing the thing "right" even if it is not the "right" thing to do. A manager relies on the external, intellectual promise of new techniques to solve problems and is concerned that all the procedural pieces are both in place and properly accounted for; hence the epithet "bean counter."

Good managers are thus placed at a disadvantage when put in positions of leadership, because all such people can do is rise to their level of incompetence and remain there, in which case an ounce of image is worth a pound of performance. Similarly, a leader placed in the position of managerialship is equally inept because the two positions require vastly different skills.

Only an effective leader can guide the process of sustainable community development; an effective manager is the one who keeps it running smoothly. By way of example, think of driving a herd composed of a hundred head of cattle.

There are three basic positions in driving cattle, with two basic functions: point (= leader) and flank and drag (= managers). The person riding point is the leader, the one out front guiding the herd. The flankers, or people riding along the sides of the herd, manage the herd by keeping it moving in the desired direction while preventing individuals from leaving the herd. Riding drag means bringing up the rear or keeping the cattle moving at a given speed while preventing individuals from dropping out of the herd, which is part of good managerialship. Together, leader and manager are responsible for moving the whole herd safely from one place to another.

A leader must be the servant of the parties involved. Servant leadership offers a unique mix of idealism and pragmatism.

The idealism comes from having chosen to serve one another and some Higher purpose, appealing to a deeply held belief in the dignity of all people and the democratic principle that a leader's power flows from commitment to the well-being of the people. Leaders do not inflict pain, although they often must help their followers to bear it in uncomfortable circumstances, such as compromise. Such leadership is also practical, however, because it has been proven over and over that the only leader whom soldiers will reliably follow when risking their lives in battle is the one who they feel is both competent and committed to their safety.

A leader's first responsibility, therefore, is to help the participants examine their senses of reality and his or her last responsibility is to say "thank you." In between, one not only must provide and maintain momentum but also must be effective.

But beware! Most people confuse effectiveness with efficiency. Effectiveness is doing the right thing, whereas efficiency is doing the thing right, although at times it may not be the right thing to do.

When the difference between effectiveness and efficiency is understood, it is clear that efficiency can be delegated but effectiveness cannot. In terms of leadership toward sustainable community development, effectiveness is enabling others to reach toward their personal potential through participation in the process. In so doing, a leader leaves behind a legacy of assets invested in other people.

A leader is also responsible for developing, expressing, and defending the follower's civility and values. Paramount in the process of sustainable community development are good manners, respect for one another, and an appreciation of the way in which we serve one another. In this sense, civility has to do with identifying values as opposed to following some predisposed process formula.

For a participant to lose sight of hope, opportunity, the right to feel needed, and the beauty and novelty of ideas is to die a little each day. For a leader to ignore the dignity of the interpersonal relationships, the elegance of simplicity and truth, and the essential responsibility of serving one another is also to die a little each day. In a day when so much energy seems to be spent on mindless conflict, to be a leader is to enjoy the special privileges of complexity, ambiguity, diversity, and the challenge of including others in a meaningful way.

Shared Leadership

Shared or revolving leadership comes about in two ways: first, when "subordinates" break custom and become leaders, and second, when someone's particular expertise is needed and he or she takes over the leadership during that time. Revolving leaders are indispensable in our lives because they take charge in varying degrees as they are needed.

Such leadership relies on three things: (1) inclusivity, which presumes that lasting solutions require the participation of all affected parties; (2) mutual accountability, which presumes that sustainable solutions depend on all sides taking responsibility for answers (which means mutual blaming is not enough); and (3) cultivating the skills of democracy, which presumes that we are not born knowing how to be effective within a democratic system of government and must be taught the art of participation—from active listening to negotiation and evaluation. When we view government as distinct from civil society, we exempt it from practicing inclusive, participatory approaches to interpersonal relationships.[72]

Revolving leadership is the basis of day-to-day expression in the participative democratic process required in sustainable community development. Such participation is both one's opportunity and responsibility to have a say in the future of one's community through the example and accountability of one's personal behavior, by influencing its government through participation in the democratic process and by extending one's willingness to accept ownership in the resolution of its problems.

Because no one person can be an expert in everything, the person in the official position of overall leadership must have the good sense and grace to support and follow the lead of a person whose expertise is momentarily in demand. It is difficult for many people to be open enough to recognize what is best for their community and to step aside when necessary in favor of issue-oriented or problem-oriented leadership.

In the last analysis, leadership must be shared (but neither given away nor sold) because a time will arise when we must count on someone else's special competence. If we think about the people with whom we share our community, it becomes apparent that we must be able to count on one another if our community is to meet our needs while protecting our deepest values. By ourselves, we are severely limited, but together we can be something truly awesome.

According to Max DePree, CEO of Herman Miller, Inc., a furniture manufacturing company, "The condition of our hearts, the openness of our attitudes, the quality of our competence, the fidelity of our experience—these give vitality to the work experience and meaning of life." Freely and openly shared revolving leadership is one of the vehicles we can use to help ourselves and one another reach our potential as both human beings and citizens of our respective communities.

"But," you might say, "I'm only one person. What can I do? My actions account for so very little." Because so many people feel this way, it might be instructive to consider snowflakes.

When snowflakes begin falling, those coming down first land on the warm soil and melt, entering the ground without a trace. One after another, they come into view out of the sky, fall past our faces, and land on the ground, only to disappear as rapidly as they appeared—or so it seems at least.

But each snowflake does something as it touches the soil. Its coolness dissipates the soil's heat. As flake after snowflake touches the ground and melts, the collective coolness of their beings creates a cumulative effect by which the soil is eventually cooled enough that falling snowflakes melt progressively more slowly until some don't melt at all. Now snow begins gradually to accumulate until the land is covered in a blanket of white.

Is one snowflake more important than another? Is the one you see sparkling in the sun more important than the one that melted upon landing? Neither is more or less important than the other. Without those that melted and cooled the soil, the ones that ultimately formed the blanket of white would not have survived to do so. Therefore, just as every snowflake (individually and as part of the collective) is important to the whole of winter, so is each person (individually and as part of the collective) important to the whole of a community.

Just as no two snowflakes are exactly alike, no two people are identical. Thus, each individual has a unique gift to offer, a special talent that in the collective of a community is complementary rather than competitive. Each person's belief, being a little different from all the others', helps a community to see itself when that person's voice is raised in expressing his or her particular point of view.

Willingness to Delegate Authority

Delegating authority and responsibility is a vital dynamic of leadership because when people share the work, more than one person shares the satisfaction of a job well done, a victory well earned.[73] Delegating will challenge one's skill as a leader to communicate, listen, plan, make decisions, and solve problems. It teaches a leader to expand her or his rapport and builds productive relationships with both those who are destined to follow and those who are destined to lead. Delegating has at least six basic steps.

1. Choose people who are willing to get the job done and then support them with incentives and motivation. When searching for people to whom to delegate work, it is wise to remember that a person's motivation and dependability are more important than his or her level of skill, which can be learned on the job if necessary.

The way in which you present a task to someone can bolster his or her willingness not only to participate but also to follow through, especially when he or she is infused with your vision and enthusiasm for the work ahead. It is important for the person to know how this participation will meet his or her values and psychological needs. For example, saying "We want you to join us" appeals to a person's need for belonging. "Your unique gift of skills and talents is critical to the completion of the project" appeals to a person's self-esteem. "If you are willing, I can help you expand your comfort zone by stretching your abilities into areas you may never have thought you could master" appeals to personal self-mastery.

Self-actualization, as psychologist Abraham Maslow pointed out, is the highest form of human need. When people are self-actualized, they are capable of maximizing their potential, which enhances their self-concept. One's self-concept, in turn, is based on one's sense of one's core values. To motivate a person toward the level of self-actualization, it is crucial to appeal to his or her highest personal values.

Because each person's values are unique, one must consciously get to know another person by asking her or him about herself or himself and then actively listening to what she or he has to say. A person's answers will inevitably reveal her or his values if one but listens.

2. Match a particular person to a particular task. This is important because people enjoy using their expertise, especially if they feel the cause is worthwhile, but first the leader must get to know the person to ensure a proper match. When possible, a good way to help people expand on their skills is by asking them about their education, training, profession, family, interests, and/or hobbies.

If one is organizing a team or committee, it is critical to match people not only to tasks but also to one another because a team or committee must work as an individual entity in order to be effective and of value to the participants. For instance, some people require little or no supervision, whereas others want nothing less than a recipe. Some people are technicians and like details; others are dreamers and thrive on creativity and global concepts. Some excel in the limelight, while others are more comfortable in the shadows. Some are good with numbers, others with words. It is therefore important for a leader to structure a team or committee in such a way that the diversity of personalities, talents, and skills is in a harmonious working balance.

3. Define the task and communicate it concisely. Clearly communicate the purpose of the project to each member of the committee or team and spell out his or her responsibilities and the project schedule. Specify exactly what the final outcome is to be, and, if necessary, rewrite unclear and/or complicated instructions in the form of an outline or diagram.

Explain how each task dovetails with, supports, or is contingent on the completion of other tasks in order to integrate them into a creative whole. Then either provide the delegatees access to relevant reference materials or tell them how to obtain such materials should they need to. Ask questions to ensure they understand what is expected of them. Finally, give every member your phone number(s) and be available throughout the project to answer questions and provide additional guidance and/or clarification, in addition to moral support when things get overwhelming, as they often do.

4. Monitor progress. It is important for a leader to keep tabs on the progress of all those who are working on a given project because without such monitoring, it is easy to build inadvertent mistakes into the work itself through lack of understanding instructions or simple human error. A leader must always remember to be positive in the way she or he states things. To wit: "I like the way you have done part A of the task. Do you think it would work to do part B this way? Could that bring it in line with the quality of part A?"

If work is behind schedule or is found to be flawed, it is critical for the leader to remain open and positive. Blame only shuts people down by putting them on the defensive. One must therefore call the team or committee together, discuss the problem, and look for solutions, such as further clarification of instructions, additional reference materials, restructuring work assignments, or getting more people involved. If it turns out that a particular individual is poorly suited to a task, a mentor can be assigned to work with that person or that person could be reassigned to a task more in line with her or his capabilities.

If a person must resign because of illness or conflicting priorities and/or responsibilities, empathize with the problem, thank the person for the work completed thus far, and allow her or him to bow out gracefully. There may be another day or another project on which that person might be willing to serve if today she or he is treated with kindness.

5. Encourage creativity and allow for different styles of working. A leader must remain focused on the outcome, the final result, not on the detail of how the job gets done. Encouraging creativity not only vitalizes a project with interest but also highlights an observation by Albert Einstein: "In the middle of every difficulty lies opportunity," which creativity helps one to find.

With respect to styles of working, people feel a sense of ownership of their work when they are allowed to work in their preferred ways. For example, some people work piecemeal and start with any part of a project, whereas others start at the beginning and complete the whole project with continual effort. Some are dramatic and add a flare to their work; others can't be bothered. It is probable that few people will work as you expect them to, but if you selected them for the quality of their skills and those skills are aptly applied, however creatively, the way in which the work gets done is immaterial as long as it gets done on time, is done well, and the people had a good time doing it and found personal value in the experience.

6. Always reward effort. A good and sensitive leader always—always—shows appreciation for and recognition of work well done! Such a leader might send a thank-you note as a token of appreciation, hold a party for all those involved, or write a letter of gratitude for inclusion in the person's personnel file, should that be appropriate.

An emotionally mature leader always shares the credit and lets people know how valuable their work is. If one treats people well, they are more likely to be available the next time their help is needed, which in turn may allow them to give of their talents and skills in such a way that they find the inner satisfaction of continued personal growth in whatever capacity they choose. Helping others to become good followers is one way a leader can begin to encourage them to develop their potential skills of leadership.

Encourage Leadership in Others

Every leader needs to encourage others to find within themselves their own budding tendencies toward leadership and to help them develop, because to succeed in sustainable community development, a community must become, to the greatest extent possible, a community of leaders. All it takes for a leader to encourage leadership in others is to keep eyes and ears open and paper and pencil ready.[74]

One of the most important tasks of a community leader is to continually expand the opportunities for leadership and to support those with the courage to step forward. "I already do that," you might think, "that is, when I can think of something worthwhile to say." I suggest writing an evaluation in a similar way every time you observe someone assuming the role of leader. What do you have to offer? Your point of view.

Each person's point of view is unique and important. The same is true of his or her thoughtful comments. Why? Because each person reacts differently to a given leader, in addition to which professionals who take surveys know that feedback on a questionnaire reveals more about the evaluator (in this case you) than the person being evaluated. This means that even as you help others through your gift of unique feedback, you help yourself (the evaluator) to find things you can use to enhance your own learning and performance.

Further, sustainable community development, which depends for its survival on information, is based on a leadership in relation to a followership. And because the meeting of any given committee can be a microcosm of the community "out there," leaders need feedback from as many people as they can get. Once that feedback is available, the leaders will have a better idea of how they are affecting the community as a whole. So, what do you do?

First, nurture and counsel to encourage the leader. "That's a fine notion," you might say, "but I don't always have a comment. Besides, that feels like criticism and I don't like being criticized, so if I do it to someone else, they might do it back to me." Perhaps you are thinking of the Yugoslavian proverb: Speak the truth, but leave immediately after.

To alleviate your anxiety, I suggest a particular format from the field of learning theory. Begin by finding something the leader did well.

Second, be specific. Learning theory suggests that improvement happens most quickly when we can distinguish specific behaviors that are successful. Pointing out specific behaviors also adds credibility to your comments, which can be thought of as catching someone doing something right and pointing it out to them.

By way of example, I was facilitating a visioning process some time back. During the course of explaining how a vision to which people are committed determines what happens to their community, I paused several times and asked: "Am I making sense to you?" After the visioning process was over, a gentleman remarked: "I really liked your asking us if you were making sense. It not only told me that you really care about us as people and a community but also gave me permission to respond honestly without worrying too much about putting you on the defensive."

One way to find specific behaviors about which to comment is to ask yourself the following questions: What one thing in this person's style of leadership works best? What one thing distracts the most?

Third, suggest an improvement. The last step is to identify a specific behavior that could be improved. Although this may seem difficult, there are several ways to gently suggest improvements. One way is to ask a question, such as "Would it work better to make eye contact with the whole audience instead of focusing on one person?" Or begin your comment with "You might try...." Another way to soften your comment is by turning it into a positive: "Your ability to talk *to* people rather than at them is a real gift; it is particularly important that you use this gift during the committee's deliberations on the vision statement."

Identifying something specific is critical because it both depersonalizes and neutralizes the observation. You could say, for example, "If you speak from your heart, what you really feel, your authenticity will come across," instead of saying, "You need to be more authentic."

Comments must always include a word of encouragement for a specific behavior that is positive and a suggestion for improvement for a specific behavior as needed. Remember, the duty of a true leader is to lead by example, which means keeping your eyes and ears open and your pencil ready for the benefit of other leaders. Now the question becomes how one copes with the demands of leadership.

COPING WITH THE RESPONSIBILITIES AND PRESSURES OF LEADERSHIP

7

This chapter is based on circumstances described by Corey[64] for psychotherapists and my own experiences in leading workshops on sustainable community development, vision statements, and the resolution of environmental conflicts. As I said in the preface, I believe the circumstances faced by psychotherapists and leaders have much in common, a thought affirmed by author Caroline Myss: "So much of the way we respond to the external challenges is determined by how we respond to ourselves. In addition to all the relationships we have with people, we must also form a healthy and loving relationship with ourselves...."

I have also found in leadership that which Corey has found in psychotherapy, namely, that leaders soon realize, despite their study and training, that all they really have to work with is themselves—their own life experiences, values, and humanity. It is therefore armed only with themselves that they must face the vagaries of circumstances to which they are exposed as leaders.

CIRCUMSTANCES FACED BY LEADERS

A circumstance is a condition or factor that accompanies an event and has some bearing on it. As such, one must consider the circumstance in determining one's course of action so one may effect a desired outcome. Although no one can directly control a circumstance, each one of us can control how we respond to a circumstance and thereby de facto control the circumstance by controlling ourselves. Self-knowledge and thus self-control are perhaps the greatest challenges of leadership.

I therefore caution aspiring leaders not to be seduced into mimicking or consciously copying another's style. There is no "right" way to lead, only ethical principles to follow. Although the principles remain the same, there are as many ways to lead as there are people to become leaders, which represents a wide variation of effective approaches to the art of leadership. In fact, one leader cannot reach all people because not all people respond equally to the personality of any given leader.

While an aspiring leader may accept the influence of a person's individual style, the aspirant must chose carefully and be sure to keep clear those boundaries (discussed later in this chapter) that both protect and nurture the gift of his or her *own unique* developing style of leadership. If the aspirant allows his or her personal boundaries to blur, he or she will at best be a carbon copy and at worst a poor imitation of someone else's style, which means not only that his or her gift is lost but also that he or she will be accepting the other person's limitations in addition to his or her own.

Although I neither have nor know of a formula for leadership, I do know beyond a doubt that to lead well one must work diligently on resolving one's own emotional and psychological issues, because one can only take people as far along the path as one has personally traveled. With this in mind, I advocate selecting the highest, other-centered principles to follow and then adhering tenaciously to them, regardless of the boundless temptations to take the easier, more traveled, self-centered road.

Beyond that, I recommend finding that place of quiet within, where one can hear the message of one's own heart, because the message (intuition) of one's heart is the knowing beyond knowledge, the personal truth of one's being. It is from this still place within that a true leader leads into the uncertainty of time's distant horizon. And it is from this still place within that a leader must seek the succor of dispassion if she or he is going to unfold as a leader and deal effectively with the myriad circumstances which she or he will inevitably encounter, beginning with anxiety.

Dealing with Anxiety

Most budding leaders, and even some seasoned ones, still tremble inwardly with anxiety, which can be called "stage fright" or "performance anxiety," when they anticipate standing in front of an audience. They ask themselves: What will I say? How will I say it? Will the people believe me? Will I make a fool of myself? If I do, how will I ever face them again? Will they accept me or trust me if I make a mistake?

Such anxiety usually comes from a lack of experience as a leader and/or a deep sense of uncertainty about one's future with those one would lead. After all, the approbation of the public at large is normally portrayed to be exceedingly fickle. What, therefore, is one to expect over time? Clearly, one must continually prove oneself as a leader if one is to lead successfully, which requires the ability to assert oneself.[74]

Asserting oneself effectively is perhaps one of the most challenging skills of leadership and communication. If you have the wrong attitude and poor verbal skills, you will likely do more harm than good.

Paradoxically, the first step in effectively asserting yourself is the realization that the problem you are experiencing is your own. It is you who are annoyed by the behavior of someone else. Therefore, instead of blaming, judging, or attacking the other person and putting that person on the defensive while you express your feelings, try the following approach:

- State the problem, situation, or behavior that is bothering you.
- State your feelings by explaining to the other party how the problem affects you.
- Specify a solution by explaining what you would like to happen.
- Describe the consequences of your request being fulfilled.

Beyond this, your efforts at assertiveness will be most effective if you follow a few simple rules:

- Speak up immediately rather than waiting hours, days, or weeks before approaching the other party with your problem. It will be less stressful and more productive if you deal with the problem immediately rather than letting your fear inflate it to gigantic proportions, which it most certainly will do.
- Be direct in telling the other person what your problem is. Beating around the bush usually leads to an imprecise under-

standing of the problem by the other party and fosters unnecessary confusion over an initially simple issue.

- Be pleasant. A smile and friendly tone of voice will accomplish more of what you want than any kind of aggression ever will.
- Be calm and maintain your composure, which can only help to retain your credibility and to elicit empathy from the other party. If, on the other hand, you act outraged and in so doing offend the other person, he or she is not likely to help you by complying with your wishes.

Be that as it may, because leadership is a most serious business, some anxiety is probably normal, but too much can torpedo one's confidence and literally incapacitate a person. One may also compare oneself either with peers or with famous leaders of great stature, but one always loses when making such comparisons. Remember, each person is unique in the world and each person's talents are therefore also unique. No one else has the gift you personally have to offer and vice versa.

The willingness to accept and deal with your anxieties, as opposed to denying them through pretenses, is a mark of courage. Although your self-doubts seem normal, how you deal with them is what counts. If you lead from the heart and intuition *as well as* the intellect, you will find over time that self-doubt gradually disappears until, for the most part, it is no more. As self-doubt fades, your sense of authentic inner personal power will grow.

Use of Power

"From the time we are young," writes Caroline Myss, "we test ourselves and our capacity to learn what and who has power, to attract power, and to use power." If we decide that we cannot attract power, says Myss, we begin living in a type of "power debt" and imagine ourselves living off the energies of other people—but not our own. "For all of us," continues Myss, "the challenge is not to become 'power celibate' but to achieve sufficient internal strength to interact comfortably with physical power without negotiating away our spirits."

"Power breeds isolation," wrote George Reedy, press secretary and special assistant to President Lyndon B. Johnson. Reedy went on to say: "Isolation leads to the capricious use of power. In turn, the capricious use of power breaks down the normal channels of communication between the leader and the people whom he [or she] leads. This ultimately means the deterioration of power and with it the capacity to sustain unity in our society. This is the problem we face today."

Power, or the ability to control oneself and others, is a quality every effective leader possesses. A vital component of effective leadership is that citizens can empower themselves as a result of sharing in the power of a good leader.

There are two struggles with power: for power and against power. The struggle for power carries with it a grave danger for the weakling who would lead, namely that absolute power corrupts absolutely. Of the converse, Milan Kundera wrote that the "struggle against power is the struggle of memory against forgetting."

A leader must be a good role model in the sharing of power, and one aspect of this model is for a leader to be a potent person in his or her own right, that is, to have clarity in an other-centered purpose that is vital to those who follow. Leaders who are genuinely powerful with inner authority have no need to dominate the lives of others and do not dwarf others so that they themselves can feel superior. They are, instead, able to appreciate potency in others and in themselves at the same time, which calls forth a thought by Ben Franklin: "Next to knowing when to seize an opportunity, the most important thing to know in life is when to forgo an advantage."

Clearly, the fact that power can and often is used against people is an ethical concern. Consider, for example, a leader's use of control to reduce a sense of personal threat and anxiety. A leader who fears losing control because of a personal need to retain control over his or her constituency may resort to all kinds of destructive strategies (both consciously and unconsciously), as witnessed every day in local, regional, national, and global newscasts. But leaders are also subject to such abuse by their constituencies through the ego-defense mechanism of projection, which is one's attribution of both one's unacceptable and most worthy traits to others. For example, one sees others as deceitful, kindly, or generous only if one has those qualities within oneself.

Criticism in the Form of Projection

Criticism is really projection, which is casting forward or outward something one perceives to be within oneself as a means of coping with one's personal discomfort in life. It means the externalization of an inner thought or motive and its subsequent behavior, which is then attributed to someone else. As such, projection (in the form of negative criticism) as a mechanism of absolving oneself from personal responsibility has been around for many centuries and has a long-recognized history:

> ...and Aaron shall lay both his hands upon the head of the live goat, and confess over him all the iniquities of the people of Israel, and all their transgressions, and all their sins; and he shall put them upon the head of the goat, and send him away into the wilderness....The goat shall bear all their iniquities upon him to a solitary land; and he shall let the goat go in the wilderness.[75]

In biblical times, on Yom Kippur (the Jewish day of atonement), all the transgressions of the Jewish people were heaped (projected) onto the back of a "scapegoat," which was then driven away into the wilderness, "taking" all the people's transgressions with it.

Projection as a Means of Avoiding Personal Responsibility

A movie projector can only cast light when there is no film inside it. The Christian ideal of making no judgment against another human being is, in essence, to become like an empty projector. Achieving this ideal seems a virtual impossibility in life because our every thought becomes the film within our own projector, which we cannot help but cast outward, project, onto the screen composed of human beings other than ourselves. In other words, one can project onto other people only what one thinks about oneself, because without thought, there is nothing to project. One thus sees in others, both consciously and unconsciously, what one sees in oneself—nothing more, nothing less.

As such, judgment, the projection of that which one sees in oneself, is the projectile one casts outward in the word "should" (You should do this; you should do that). "You should" is thus a common attitude of the opposing sides in a conflict.

In reality, however, "should" is the stuff of someone else's standard of operation, of someone else's concept of right and wrong, of what one should or should not be or do. Someone else's "should" is only one's own if one chooses to accept it. On the other hand, one can choose to ignore another person's "should," and then it has no effect.

Leaders have probably always been the subject to such projections as criticism, especially by those who would rather blame out of fear than take responsibility for their own actions, as noted by President Theodore Roosevelt:

> It's not the critic who counts, not the…[person] who points out how the strong…[person] stumbled or where the doer of deeds could have done them better. The credit belongs to the…[person] who is actually in the arena; whose face is marred by dust and sweat and blood; who strives valiantly; who errs and comes up short again and again; who knows the great enthusiasms, the great devotions and spends himself [or herself] in a worthy cause; who at the best knows in the end the triumph of high achievement; and who at the worst, if he [or she] fails, at least fails while daring greatly so that his [or her] place shall never be met with those cold and timid souls who know neither defeat nor victory.

In effect, a person who serves the people as a leader must pass the tests described in the eulogy that Senator William Pitt Fessenden of Maine delivered on the death of Senator Foot of Vermont in 1866:

> When, Mr. President, a man becomes a member of this body he cannot even dream of the ordeal to which he cannot fail to be exposed;
> of how much courage he must possess to resist the temptations which daily beset him;
> of that sensitive shrinking from undeserved censure which he must learn to control;
> of the ever-recurring contest between a natural desire for public approbation and a sense of public duty;
> of the load of injustice he must be content to bear, even from those who should be his friends; the imputations of his motives; the sneers and sarcasms of ignorance and malice; all the manifold injuries which partisan or private malignity, disappointed of its objects, may shower upon his unprotected head.
> All this, Mr. President, if he would retain his integrity, he must learn to bear unmoved, and walk steadily onward in the path of duty, sustained only by the reflection that time may do him justice, or if not, that after all his individual hopes and aspirations, and even his name among men, should be of little

account to him when weighed in the balance against the welfare of a people of whose destiny he is a constituted guardian and defender.[76]

Two years after Senator Fessenden delivered this eulogy, his vote to acquit Andrew Johnson brought about the fulfillment of his own prophecy. This is the test of leadership: to stand firmly by one's inner convictions even when they are the cause of one's being cast out of office because it was morally necessary to tell the people what they needed to know, rather than what they wanted to hear.

Projection Can Be Either Negative or Positive

The negative fears people harbor represent the human shadow into which we shove all the unwanted nefarious qualities we think we possess. These are eagerly projected onto our public servants, albeit they deserve none of them.

There is another kind of projection, however, called hero worship, which represents the positive part of ourselves that we choose to disown. Hero worship means that people project onto another person the positive qualities (the glow) they themselves possess but are afraid to make manifest in their own lives.

Such projections place an incredible burden of unknown responsibility on a leader because he or she not only is seen as larger than life but also is expected to be perfect by those who project onto others their own positive qualities for safekeeping. Consider, for example, the often impossible expectations of human perfection that we project onto clergy, teachers, and elected officials. The illusions we create are dangerous people because we see in them no flaws.

But what happens when one of our flawless illusions turns out to be an imperfect human after all? Are we filled with mercy, compassion, and understanding? No! He or she is dashed to the ground, like a sculptor might in anger cast down a flawed statue, because there has been found in him or her a weakness that calls forth the fickle-heartedness of those who projected their positive qualities onto others rather than take personal responsibility for their own development.

These are the things a leader must be prepared to bare, the things a leader must learn not to take personally. A leader, to be effective, must learn to remain grounded in his or her own spiritual center while all about rage the storms of fear in the material world, which means one must learn to handle projection in the form of criticism.

Criticism and Your Image

In order to make the following discussion as concrete as possible, I shall speak directly to you, the reader.[74,77] How you personally handle criticism is related to the way in which you perceive yourself and how you want others to perceive you.

The way in which you perceive yourself is your "self-image," which consists of the beliefs you hold about yourself and the values based on those beliefs. Your self-image, as is mine and every one else's, is bestowed on you by your parents, siblings, and family, as well as your teachers, peers, and friends. If you are fortunate enough to be treated well by these people, you develop a positive, healthy self-esteem, which translates into a positive sense of self-worth and a corresponding self-image. Unfortunately, the converse is also true.

The way in which you would like others to perceive you is your "public image" or "persona," which you, as well as almost everyone else, try to make as favorable as possible. You may, for example, want others to see you as authentic, knowledgeable, patient, funny, and so on. To achieve your desired public image, you make your actions reflect these characteristics to the very best of your ability.

The problem arises when people criticize you because they are making judgments (projections) about either your self-image or your public image or both, and such judgments most likely conflict with your own perception of your self-image and/or public image. Being called a liar, for example, may cause you to become defensive because you see yourself as honest, especially if you were raised to be so. If, therefore, some truth exists in the accusation, you become even more defensive in trying to reinstate your favorable public and/or self-image.

Responding to Negative Criticism

Verbal criticism that is perceived as negative can be responded to in at least six ways: by (1) withdrawing, (2) denying, (3) ignoring, (4) rationalizing, (5) counterattacking, and (6) responding nondefensively.

Withdrawing is when you opt to accept criticism silently by simply leaving the room without a response. Although the conflict may not escalate, you may feel that you lost your self-respect as well as self-esteem because you chose not to defend yourself.

Denying is a form of defense against criticism in that you flatly deny the accusation of your critic. Such denial is rampant in our federal, state, and local governments these days and thus offers many examples of the dynamic.

Ignoring criticism is not the same as withdrawing from it. You can only ignore criticism when you are truly not bothered by it, when you recognize it for what it is, consider the source, and let it pass without taking ownership. Although you can retain your self-respect and self-esteem, you forgo the chance to correct your critic's misperception.

Rationalizing as a strategy of defense is to admit the merit of the criticism, then quickly follow with an explanation of why you did whatever you did. Unfortunately, by the time you conclude your rationalization, the other person has usually had ample time to find all the holes in it.

Counterattacking to divert the negative attention from yourself to the criticizer and her or his faults only escalates the conflict and avoids the real issue.

Responding nondefensively means that you listen calmly and nonjudgmentally to your attacker, who clearly feels a need to communicate something to you for whatever reason. By listening calmly and nonjudgmentally, you not only learn what the perceived problem is but also begin disarming your protagonist. This obviously is the most productive and rewarding way of dealing with criticism, but it demands the greatest maturity and effort on your part.

The following steps are useful in responding to criticism nondefensively: listen, acknowledge, ask questions, paraphrase, and agree with the truth.

Listen. Although we tend to take criticism at face value, automatically *assuming* that we are somehow in error, there may be a lot of buried feelings beneath the spoken words (such as fear of a new idea, unwanted change, or any number of other things). It is thus critical to listen, really listen with an open mind (which means without forming any kind of mental rebuttal), to what is being said, after which it is appropriate to ask questions. If you are concerned about clarification of certain points as you try to find out what feelings are hidden by the angry words, quietly write the points down to remember them, but do not interrupt the speaker. Once these feelings have been ferreted out and addressed, it is much easier to determine the real issue and resolve the conflict.

Acknowledge. In the name of human decency, indicate to your protagonist that you recognize the criticism. Acknowledging the criticism does not mean that you either agree with or accept its content; it only means that you recognize the other party's right to have opinions and feelings that merit consideration, which allows your criticizer to feel heard and reduces the level of his or her anger.

Be careful about your tone of voice and your body language (such as your facial expressions and gestures) when acknowledging criticism because any hint of sarcasm or patronization may only serve to put you on the defense and make your protagonist angrier. If, however, you are truly sincere about resolving the conflict, then your words will have the ring of authenticity and signal that it is acceptable to discuss the other party's feelings.

Elevate the level of the discussion. Shift the focus from the points of conflict toward the fundamental principles underlying your perception of the issue. Once both parties can agree on the principles, the conflict is usually much easier to resolve. You can do this most easily if you anticipate areas in which you might be questioned or challenged.

Always tell the truth. Remember, there is only truth and untruth; there is no such thing as a "half-truth." If you try to bend the truth, you will almost always be caught. Be totally honest, even if your position is momentarily weakened. In the spirit of truth, learn to say "I don't know" when you really do not, and follow it with "but I will find out for you if you wish."

Be friendly. When the questioner is hostile, it is critical that you respond as if she or he were a friend who is frightened and asking for help. Any attempt to defame the questioner with sarcasm will not only immediately draw the audience's sympathy to the questioner but also will put you in a position of becoming that which you are against. The more in error you feel your opponent to be, the more incumbent it is on you to act with principle and dignity.

Show your opponent a new way of viewing the issue. Consensus on the fundamental principles may be reached by discussing the issue from your opponent's point of view. Then point out that there may in fact be more agreement between your opponent's point of view and yours than he or she thought.

In other words, change his or her view of the situation from black or white to gray, but do so in a helpful, informative manner. Never become argumentative. If you seem to be denigrating the opposition, whoever is listening will argue back mentally, and hostility may well return.

Ally yourself with positive symbols. Along with your presentation of the underlying principles, be sure to include the emotional aspect of the discussion because this is most likely where your opponent's fear lies. Controversial issues inevitably involve symbols, and the side most effectively associated with positive symbols (such as law, human dignity, freedom of choice, and so on) is more likely to prevail.

Tactfully refute the opposition. If you are in a public meeting, you will need to counter the criticism that may already have convinced the audience that your opponent is correct, but this must be done in a nonthreatening manner. Avoid any statement that might be misconstrued as a personal attack on your opposition, your listeners, or their associations.

Listen carefully to all questions and repeat them aloud. Begin by making sure you understand the question correctly and that the audience not only understands the question (as much as possible) but also knows to which question you are responding.

Clear up any vagueness. If you did not clearly hear all of the question or if some part of it was obscure, clarify it before wasting everyone's time by responding to something that was not asked. Define any vague terms or acronyms at this point to avoid confusion and unnecessary misunderstandings.

Ask questions. It is virtually impossible to uncover another person's true feelings without asking questions. Most people will initially tell you what sounds good, but it is rarely the real reason. To ferret this out, you must ask questions, and your interest must be sincere. If, however, you are facing a hostile audience, be sure to both ask and receive questions from all parts of the audience, and do not allow one questioner to monopolize the available time.

Paraphrase. Repeat in your own words what you think the other person has said as a means of coming as close as possible to understanding what the other person really meant. This is critical because it is common for one party to say something and the other party to hear or understand something completely different. Paraphrasing ensures, as much as is humanly possible, that this kind of misunderstanding is avoided by giving your protagonist the chance not only to clarify his or her own thoughts and feelings but also to correct your interpretation of what you heard.

Agree with the truth. If the criticism has merit, say so. While denying the "facts" is futile, agreeing with the facts does not mean that your protagonist has interpreted them correctly. Remember that a "fact" is still the interpretation of an event as seen through the eyes of the beholder. By the time this final step is reached, it is likely that the real issue will be on the table and you will be able to discuss possible solutions with the other party.

The following are some tips that may help you:

- Remain calm because a true nondefensive response means that you have an equipoise of character while you are being criticized.
- Criticism is not personal, so do not take it as such. Criticism is usually based on personal fear of some kind and is most often leveled by people who are afraid to take a personal risk themselves.
- Smile, lean forward, nod, or otherwise acknowledge that you are listening, and maintain eye contact. In this way, the speaker will know that she or he is being heard, which is paramount if she or he is to be able to move beyond her or his attack.
- Show your opponent respect even if he or she is yelling or cursing you. Acknowledge the anger and frustration by saying, "It is clear that you are really upset by this. I'm open to talking about it if you are."

Answer directly. Always give simple answers to simple questions. If the question demands a lengthy reply, either ask permission to answer the question now or agree to discuss it later with anyone interested.

Although clearly one is not always being criticized, the very notion of criticism raises questions about how one must act and how much of oneself to disclose.

Being and Disclosing Yourself

One of the greatest gifts a leader can give his or her constituency is to be authentically oneself. This means putting one's theories and academic learning in the background and following one's intuition—complementing one's intellect with one's inner spiritual core. To fully understand what I mean, I recommend that you watch the movie *It's a Wonderful Life*.

In the small town of Bedford Falls, as the story goes, lives a young man named George Bailey, who cannot wait to leave his hometown to see and conquer the world. But for one reason or another, he never leaves. Being altruistic in his outlook on life, he is other-centered and keeps passing up his chances to go to college and beyond.

Finally, however, facing bankruptcy just before Christmas, through no fault of his own, George decides that he is worth more to his family dead than alive because of his life insurance policy. He therefore tries to kill himself by jumping off a bridge into the river, but an angel, Clarence Oddbody, is sent to save him. Clarence, however, cannot convince George that his life has any value. Adamant that his life is worthless, George wishes he had never been born, and Clarence grants his wish.

To the townspeople, George never existed, so while he knows everyone, no one knows him. He sees how the town would have developed and how the people would have fared had he never been born. George finally sees and understands just how many lives the ripples of his actions have affected by his just being who he is—a simple man who never left his hometown, who never conquered the world. He was perfectly himself because of and despite all his personal foibles, and that was all God asked of him—just to act as himself and to give what he could to the best of his ability, one day at a time.

It takes a great deal of courage to simply be oneself, and not everyone has such courage. Some people become so encrusted in a professional or political role that one cannot tell where the role ends and the real person begins.

The other extreme is one who labors hard to demonstrate his or her humanness and in so doing overreacts and blurs any distinction between the one who leads and the one who follows. If as leader one inappropriately discloses too much about oneself, one is stealing attention from one's constituency in an act of self-fulfillment. "Well then," you might ask, "when is self-disclosure appropriate?"

Disclosing persistent feelings that are directly related to the present transaction can be useful, even dutiful. For example, it would be both appropriate and dutiful to express one's feeling that the townspeople do not have a clear sense of what they want a particular city park to be like and to help them clarify their vision of the desired outcome. But regardless of the circumstances, it is wise to always ask why one is revealing oneself, what purpose it will serve, and to what degree it is appropriate, remembering, of course, that one is not flawless in the sense of perfection.

The Zen of Perfection

A leader must learn early on that she or he need not and cannot afford to burden herself or himself with thinking she or he must be flawless in the sense of perfection. Perfection and being perfect are two different things. Perfect, as it is meant in the Judeo–Christian tradition, means to be whole (not flawless, but rather emotionally and spiritually healed despite the flaws), while perfection means to be flawless. As previously discussed, it is the duty of a good leader to struggle constantly toward wholeness, even knowing one may not attain it.

Consider the following story: As autumn arrived in a distant monastery, a Zen master told his disciples to sweep the path because it was being covered with falling leaves. The disciples obeyed and swept clean the path. The Zen master came at eventide and, inspecting the leafless path, told his disciples to sweep it again the next day because they had not done a perfect job. Again they swept the path, and again he told them to do it over because they had failed to do a perfect job.

Finally, after the third try, one of the disciples asked the Zen master what was wrong with their job of sweeping. He reached up and gently shook a branch. Five leaves fell onto the path, whereupon the master looked at his disciples and said, "Now the path is perfect."

A leader driven by the need for perfection is so afraid of criticism that he or she is loath to admit errors, which then become demons in the form of secrets that must be hidden and guarded, all the while increasingly ensnaring the person in the web of denial. Only when one is willing, openly and forthrightly, to admit one's mistakes can one learn from them and in the process create and maintain interpersonal relationships built on trust that both allows and accounts for human frailty and human error.

When the need for perfection rears its ugly head, there is an alternative to accepting its tyranny. One can always build a little conscious imperfection into one's endeavors and thus free oneself from the tyrant.

A lovely Persian story illustrates this point well: Persian rug weavers of old, although capable of weaving a perfect rug, always inserted a single flaw because to create the perfect rug would be blasphemous since "only Allah is perfect." In this way, they honored their Higher Power and kept their "right size," which is to say that they confirmed their humanity and protected themselves against the neurosis of perfectionism. This is a good practice for a leader to follow because death of the tyrant of perfectionism allows one to be more honest with one's followers.

Honesty with Followers

A fear of many leaders is facing their limitations because they think they will lose the respect of their followership if they say "I really don't know where to go with this situation" or "I can't see any solution to this problem." However, an honest leader not only has the best chance of retaining his or her following but also has the best chance of winning their respect by frankly admitting his or her limitations.

From the perspective of a follower, on the other hand, the evidence is overwhelmingly in favor of direct honesty as opposed to an attempt to fake competence. Nevertheless, leaders—especially those young in experience—often burden themselves with what they perceive to be the expectation of their followers, namely, that they should be all-knowing and skillful in their leadership, even without experience. But even if they were "all-knowing" and possessed vast experience, it would not be enough in every situation. Ignorance would still at times reign supreme, probably more often than they would like.

Although ignorance is thought of as the lack of knowledge, there is more to it than that. Our sense of the world and our place in it is couched in terms of what we are sure we know and what we think we know. Our universities and laboratories are filled with searching minds, and our libraries are bulging with the fruits of our exploding knowledge, yet where is there an accounting of our ignorance?

Ignorance is not okay in our fast-moving world. We are chastised from the time we are infants until we die for not knowing an answer that someone else thinks we "should" know. If we do not know the correct answer, we can even be labeled as stupid, which is not the same as being ignorant about something. Being stupid is usually thought of as being mentally slow to grasp an idea, but being ignorant is simply not knowing the acceptable answer to a particular question.

When a leader can answer a follower's question with a purposeful "I don't know," that leader is *allowed* not only to freely admit his or her limitation but also to affirm that he or she neither is nor must be in charge of the Universe. Secreted in one's ignorance is the incredible freedom to accept the frailty of what it means to be human, to be simply what one is.

Society's preoccupation with building a shining tower of knowledge blinds us to the ever-present dull luster of ignorance that underlies the foundation of the tower from which all questions must arise and over which the tower of knowledge must stand. Each new brick in the tower of knowledge is born of a question that simultaneously originates in and illuminates our ignorance. Yet ignorance, which often is seen as negative, is but a point along the continuum of consciousness, as are knowledge and the intuitive knowing beyond.

The quest for knowledge in the material world is a never-ending pursuit, but the quest does not mean that a thoroughly schooled person is an educated person or an educated person is a wise person. I say this because leaders, in common with all of us, are too often blinded by their ignorance of their ignorance, and the only thing worse than not knowing is not knowing you don't know. Therefore, one's pursuit of knowledge is no guarantee of wisdom. Hence, a leader is prone to becoming the blind leading the blind when her or his overemphasis on competition in nearly everything makes looking good more important than being good. The resultant fear of looking bad is one of the greatest enemies of a leader who sincerely wants to be wise enough to learn.

Although our ignorance is undeniably vast, it is from the vastness of this selfsame ignorance that our sense of wonder grows. But when we do not know we are ignorant, we do not know enough to even question, let alone investigate, our ignorance.

A leader cannot, however, teach anyone anything. All a leader can do for someone else is to facilitate learning by helping that person discover the wonder of his or her own ignorance. By asking an appropriate question in an appropriate way, a wise leader may be able to help a person become aware of his or her ignorance in a given area without stealing his or her dignity.

A teacher is but a "midwife," as the Greek philosopher Socrates said, because once a person realizes his or her ignorance and begins in earnest to search for understanding, that person slowly comes to see that such understanding can only be drawn out from within. Understanding, after all, is the unique perspective of each and every person, and that includes understanding silence.

Understanding Silence

Most people, including many leaders, are profoundly uncomfortable with silence and feel compelled to speak. It is not uncommon for a leader to become so threatened by silence that he or she does something counterproductive to break the silence and thus relieve his or her anxiety, especially when addressing a small group of people or in a one-on-one conversation. Silence, when allowed to flow unimpeded through indeterminate seconds and minutes, draws people out, causing them to engage both uncomfortable circumstances and one another.

Silence, in addition to drawing people out, can have many meanings. Some of the possible meanings include the following: (1) agreement; (2) quietly considering things just discussed or evaluating some insight just acquired; (3) waiting for another person to break the silence; (4) boredom, distraction, preoccupation, or just not having anything to say at the moment; (5) hostility; (6) hidden or unexpressed disagreement; (7) communication without words, where perhaps words are inadequate or the silence is refreshing; and (8) communication on a superficial level with some fear or hesitancy to reveal real concerns.

A leader would do well to explore the meaning of silence when it occurs. He or she can be the first to acknowledge the silence, tell the other person(s) how he or she feels about it, and then pursue the meaning of the silence rather than pretending that it does not exist by making useless small talk to regain one's lost sense of comfort. In pursuing the meaning of silence, however, one must listen, really listen, to what is being said because we all need to feel we have been heard.

Understanding the Need to Be Heard

Although one may not think of it as such, listening is the other half of communication. Communication is a gift of ideas; therefore, another person can give you a gift of ideas through speaking only if you accept the gift through listening. The spoken word that falls on consciously "deaf ears" is like a drop of rain that evaporates before it reaches the Earth. "Intolerance of another's ideas belies one's faith in one's cause," as Gandhi once said.

The watchword of listening is empathy, which means imaginative identification with, as opposed to judgment of, a person's thoughts, feelings, life situation, and so on. The more a leader can empathize with a person, the more that person feels heard, the greater the bond of trust, and the better the leader understands the situation. This means, however, actively, consciously listening with a quiet, open mind, without forming a rebuttal while the other person is speaking. Such listening is an act of love, and anything short of it is an act of passive violence.

For example, the intent of a television program some years ago was to discuss the issue of ancient forests in the Pacific Northwest. An elderly lady on the program tried in vain to be heard, but the moderator consistently ignored her. Even after the program was off the air, she tried again to tell the moderator how she was feeling, but he continued to ignore her. In the end, just to be heard, perhaps only by herself, she spoke out loud to no one; she spoke into space. She may as well have been alone in the world.

Not listening is an act of violence because it is a purposeful way of invalidating the feelings—the very existence—of another person. Each of us needs to be heard and validated as a human being because sharing is the bond of relationship that makes us "real" to ourselves, nurtures trust, and gives us meaning in the greater context of our respective communities, society, and the Universe at large. We simply cannot find meaning out of relationship with one another. Therefore, only when a person has first been validated through listening as an act of love can that person really hear what a leader is saying. Only then can a leader share another's truth. Only then can a leader's gift of ideas touch receptive ears.

A leader cannot give his or her gift of leadership, however, if there is no one to receive it, if there is no one to hear. Therefore, if a leader listens—really listens—and validates the other person's feelings, even if that leader does not agree, he or she can begin to resolve differences among his or her constituency before they become disputes, and one's role as leader will be much easier, especially if one establishes clear boundaries.

Establishing Your Boundaries

Boundaries are those lines of silent language that allow a person to communicate with others while simultaneously protecting the integrity of his or her own personal space as well as the personal space of those with whom he or she interacts.

The language of boundaries transcends individual space to include familial space, cultural space, and even national space. Understanding personal boundaries among individuals of the same culture is difficult enough, but expanding that concept into a fluid working ability among different cultures is most difficult to accomplish. This is especially true in situations where work may be done through a translator in a language a leader can neither understand nor speak.

A simple way of looking at boundaries is the adage "good fences make good neighbors." As an example, consider cliff swallows, which attach their mud nests to such surfaces as the faces of cliffs, the sides of buildings, and under bridges. These enclosed, globular nests share common walls, which not only strengthen the nests but also keep the peace by preventing the inhabitants from peeking into each other's abodes. If, however, a hole is made in the common wall and the swallows can see each other, they bicker and squabble until the hole is repaired, which immediately restores tranquillity.

A more complicated way of dealing with physical boundaries is to compare them to the home ranges and territories of animals. A home range is that area of an animal's habitat in which it ranges freely throughout the course of its normal activity and in which it is free to mingle with others of its own kind. A territory, in contrast, is that part of an animal's home range that it defends, for whatever reason, against others of its own kind. This defensive behavior is most exaggerated and noticeable during an animal's breeding season.

How does this concept apply to us? Suppose it is Saturday morning, and you leave your home to take care of a few errands. You simply go about your business without paying much attention to what is going on around you or to the people you pass, unless you happen to meet someone you know. In general, you are simply engrossed in what you are doing. When you have finished your errands, you start home.

The closer you get to your neighborhood, the more alert you unconsciously become to changes around you, such as the new people moving in two blocks away. This "protective feeling" becomes even more acute as you approach the area of your own home and notice a car with an out-of-state license plate parked in your neighbor's driveway. You get out of your car and immediately notice, perhaps with some irritation, that the neighbor's dog has visited your lawn while you were gone. If your neighbor's dog had anointed someone else's yard with its leavings, you probably would have paid scant attention.

The same general pattern extends to your home. Inside your home, how well you know someone and how comfortable you feel around that person determine the freedom with which he or she may interact with you and your family and use your house. You are the most particular about your ultimate private space, your physical being.

For example, an unwanted salesperson may not be allowed inside your home. A casual acquaintance, on the other hand, may be allowed in the living room and use of the guest bathroom, but he or she is not allowed to wander about the house without permission. If one of your child's friends comes over, he or she may be allowed in the living room, kitchen, family room, guest bathroom, and your child's bedroom (but only with both your and your child's permission), but is not allowed in your room or your bathroom. At times, even your children may not be allowed in your bedroom without your permission, or perhaps you in theirs.

As you return home after a Saturday morning of errands, the closer you get to your home, the more you notice what is going on and the more observant and protective you become. Inside your home, the closer you get to your own room, and beyond that to your physical person, which represents your ultimate territory, the more clearly and carefully you define your boundaries. The reverse is in effect, however, as you leave your room and go into the rest of your house or your neighborhood, which represents your home range.

Although the above dynamic may function in a "normal" manner for strangers, it often becomes so blurred among the members of a dysfunctional family that personal boundaries, including the physical body itself, are violated. In some families, appropriate personal boundaries are all but absent. This dysfunctional trait is too often carried over into the arena of leadership.

Leaders, particularly those young in experience, are often puzzled about how to deal with the overly demanding follower or constituent. Because caring leaders typically feel they *should* extend themselves in being helpful, they often burden themselves with the unrealistic standard of giving unselfishly, regardless of how great the demands placed on them.

These demands can manifest themselves in a variety of ways. To give you, the reader, a better sense of the trespass of boundaries, this paragraph and part of the next are written using the personal pronoun "you." Suppose a person calls you frequently at home and expects to talk at length over the telephone, demands to see you more often and for a longer period than is necessary or you can accommodate, wants to see you socially, wants you to take care of them and assume their responsibilities, expects you to "pull strings" in their favor, demands that you make them "special" in your life by paying continual attention to them, or demands that you make their decisions for them. This is the reason a leader must draw clear boundaries.

It is useful for a leader to review her or his encounters with overly demanding constituents and see how she or he feels about these interactions. How were the demands placed on you, and how did you handle those situations? Can you say no when it is necessary or desirable? Do you value yourself enough to protect yourself from unreasonable demands? Do you allow yourself to be manipulated because you are afraid of losing your constituents or because of your need to feel needed?

The demanding constituent can feed the ego of an inexperienced leader, and for the unaware leader, there can be a personal, if unconscious, payoff. An unaware leader can delude himself or herself into an exaggerated sense of self-importance by thinking that he or she must at all times be available to those who are in need. What would my followers do without me?

There are two imperatives in dealing with demanding constituents. First, one must be aware of the nature of the demands and one's reactions to them. Second, one must have the courage to confront the person with one's perceptions of the person's behavior and one's own needs.

It is therefore a leader's task to set the behavioral boundaries as the rules of conduct that are acceptable to him or her. This is critical not only because the rules of conduct are the infrastructure of society but also because the rules of conduct make true leadership possible. Understanding and respecting boundaries helps to build and maintain trust, which is important because interpersonal boundaries are an absolute social necessity of communication.

Let's look at a few concrete examples. The most important interpersonal boundary for a leader to maintain is that of a servant at all times (but *not* a slave), because one serves as leader at the behest of one's constituency. By staying within "servant boundaries," one is nonthreatening and can create and maintain a safe environment within which one's followers feel freer to communicate. This means that a leader must never crack a joke or allow anyone else to do so if that joke is at the expense of someone, which can only be insulting, such as jokes about race, religion, or gender.

One of the more important behavioral contracts that a leader must make with each person who speaks to him or her is to listen without interrupting. This is imperative because waiting one's turn is part and parcel of civility and equality, both of which are prerequisites for true leadership and the safe environment in public debate that such leadership inspires. Listening empathically can also sway the uncommitted constituent.

Dealing with the Uncommitted

The uncommitted constituent is the flip side of the overly demanding one. The uncommitted person generally lacks motivation and has little investment in the democratic system of government. This lack of motivation may be evidenced by a stated indifference or an unwillingness to assume any personal responsibility in the democratic process.

It is easy for an inexperienced leader to be drawn into unproductive games with an uncommitted constituent or group. In such games, the uncommitted person(s) receives an unprecedented amount of attention as the leader tries to convince him or her of the value of getting involved in the democratic process, the validity of the leader's point of view, or both. As with the aforementioned overly demanding constituent, a leader must draw clear boundaries with the uncommitted constituent or risk wasting a tremendous amount of irreplaceable time.

Too often, however, an inexperienced leader continues in these games without confronting the person(s) for fear of either "losing" her or him as a potential supporter or losing face as a leader. An effective leader must learn not only to risk confronting those people who straddle the middle of the fence but also that some people are simply not interested and nothing is likely to change their minds. One must let the disinterested go and pay attention to those who are interested. Even then, measurable results may be slow in coming.

Accepting Slow or Delayed Results

No leader should expect instant results, although they may occasionally arise in a most unexpected manner. From my experience, a leader must remember at least two related things about people: (1) whatever the current situation people find themselves in, they did not get there overnight, and hence the situation will not be changed overnight, and (2) the situation will not change overnight because the best way to engage people's resistance to nearly anything is to ask them to change from a known situation (almost regardless of how bad it seems) to an unknown future, even if it can be demonstrated to be significantly better than the situation at the moment. In other words, people prefer the devil they know to the devil they don't.

A lack of visible signs of what the leader thinks of as positive forward motion may cause him or her to question his or her abilities as a leader and to doubt those abilities. Here it is important to learn that one must accept the ambiguities of not knowing what effect one is having, because for leadership to be authentic, it must be an unconditional gift that inspires those who choose to follow. A true leader is, after all, a servant to those whom she or he would lead.

People in a group, even a political group, often act like clients in psychotherapy in that they seem to get worse before they get better when confronted by change. After they decide to work toward accepting the change, they must deal with a greater self-honesty whereby they must drop their defenses and facades in an act of personal transformation.

Having thus made the decision to accept change, people can be expected to experience an increase in personal pain or anxiety and its accompanying disorganization, which may lead to depression or a panic reaction. When looking change squarely in the face, people often say, "Maybe the old way wasn't so bad after all. At least I knew what to expect. I feel so vulnerable now not knowing what's ahead. I may have been better off before. Maybe there's still time to back out of my commitment before it's too late."

A leader, especially an inexperienced leader, must learn patience when dealing with outcomes because they are rarely predictable. One must also learn to trust oneself enough to allow the outcome to manifest itself as it will, without trying to control it, if one is truly a servant of the people. To give an unconditional gift as a servant leader, one must learn to be dispassionate.

Albeit one may be sensitive and feel acutely the effects of the words and actions that frightened people aim at leaders when confronted by the necessity of change, particularly that thrust upon them by circumstances, a leader must learn to take the often-disparaging comments wisely and dispassionately.[78] It is of the utmost importance that a leader develop inner strength and poise. He or she must learn to become dispassionate about the words and actions of frightened people and turn his or her thoughts outward toward the well-being of those same people instead of brooding over feelings of self-doubt, helplessness, impotence, uncertainty, and even ambivalence about leading that unkind words and actions can stimulate. Above all, turn not inward to brood on imagined wrongs.

Many leaders waste too much time on such introspection. This is a weakness of leadership that must be overcome. Although everyone makes mistakes, a wise person learns from them rather than brooding over them. It is what a leader is thinking, what he or she contributes in love, compassion, and truth by example to his or her constituents and humanity at large, that is all-important. Leading by example means that one must deal honestly with one's limitations.

Learning Your Limits

Although a leader cannot realistically expect to succeed all the time, he or she can, as Hubert Humphrey counseled, "...live your life so that even when you lose, you end up ahead." Having said this, it is still necessary to remember that even an experienced leader can become glum and begin to doubt his or her value as a leader when forced to admit that there are people, sometimes whole audiences, whom he or she cannot touch in a significant way. A leader must have the self-honesty to admit that he or she cannot work successfully with everyone.

As a leader, there is a delicate balance between learning your realistic limits and challenging what you sometimes perceive as "limits." You may, for example, tell yourself that you could never work with a certain type of person or group because you differ so much in your thinking that you could not "identify with them," so they would never trust you or you them.

To find out how real your perceived handicap is, however, it might be a good idea to test what you perceive as your limitations and open yourself to the person or group. If you dare to risk feeling uncomfortable for a while, you may find there are more grounds for identifying with the person or group than you thought. Thus, before deciding that you do not have the necessary life experiences, philosophical compatibility, or personal qualities to work successfully with a particular group of people, you might expand your leadership abilities by finding mentors in this selfsame group of people and develop the habit of asking for, receiving, and using ideas and counsel from the people around you.[79]

Cultivate an appreciation of information from people who can help you improve your leadership abilities and give you ideas for helping others. Develop a comfortable habit of systematically asking for, receiving, and using ideas, impressions, and counsel from those around you.

Listen carefully when you ask for counsel. Learn to ask the right questions for a maximum return, and, when possible, let people know how you have used what they told you. If you do not customarily ask for feedback, spend some time learning how.

You might, for example, say to someone you respect: "I think of you as a mentor and would appreciate hearing any ideas you might have that could help me improve my leadership skills." You might also ask, "How did you feel about my speech today? Can you suggest ways in which I can improve the next one?"

With colleagues, you would be wise to establish a continual flow of helpful feedback by asking questions or restating information to make sure you understand the counsel they are giving you: "Did I understand you when you said...?" or "Let me get this clear..." or perhaps "If I understood you correctly, I thought I heard you say...." Again, let them know when and how you use their counsel.

Remember, choose your counselors carefully. If you ask for counsel from a position of strength and authentic desire to improve, you will find that most people are willing to help you.

When you are fortunate enough to receive good information, accept it at face value in a defenseless demeanor. If is feels overly critical, accept it gracefully nonetheless. Assess it fairly from a point of personal detachment. Remember, you asked for it, and it is given as a helping gesture.

It is also important to show genuine behavioral change. People feel gratified when they see their counsel put to good, honest use, and they are more likely to continue to act like your mirror as you improve your abilities to lead.

You might even find your own self-evaluation useful. Ask yourself some questions after important meetings. Formally debrief yourself by asking: Did I open the session well? Did I say the right things and ask the right questions? Did I speak from my heart? Did I get the desired outcome for the good of the whole?

You might also debrief yourself at the end of each day, or at least at the end of days with important events: What did I do today? What did I need to do that I left undone? How can I do it better tomorrow? Follow up in a similar manner at the end of each week, month, and year.

Despite all this, you will have difficult times, which any mentor will tell you are times of personal growth. Appraise your own efforts when you encounter such difficulty, and determine what you have learned from the experience because every difficulty has hidden within a lesson you need to learn. Good judgment, after all, is often based on one or more bad experiences. You might also ask friends and colleagues how they handled the same problem or circumstance when they encountered it.

When confronted by a problem, imagine all the likely scenarios you could use to resolve it. This might include developing a flowchart of the options open to you. As your skills of simulation deepen, you will gradually become adept at predicting solutions to problems before they occur, which brings to mind a building contractor I met some years ago on an airplane.

I asked him how he built a house. "Well," he replied, "I build each house at least a hundred times in my mind before I purchase the first nail or board. That way, I see the problems before they arise and have figured out how to fix them with the least cost and loss of time. I'm the only person who really 'knows' the house. I know it better than the owners ever will, even if they live in it for 50 years!"

Another thing you might do as you happen upon important principles or conclusions about your leadership is record them in your personal "lesson" book. Although it may take years, your book will fill in with time and will become a powerful source of information, as well as a record of your personal growth and accomplishments.

However much you may think you require help in expanding your own perceived limitations of leadership, you undoubtedly have talents and skill that you can offer to someone else. Do it. Act as a mentor to a less experienced peer, and you will find that you are also helping yourself by sharpening your own skills of human relationships, which will in turn motivate you to learn and excel in your own ability to lead while helping to avoid self-deception.

Avoiding Self-Deception

Self-deception is not necessarily lying consciously to oneself; it can be subtle and unconscious. A leader's motivation for deception is the need to make the relationship with followers both worthwhile and productive. One's need to see change in the form of forward movement may blur reality and cause one to be less discerning than is wise because one's role as a leader carries with it an investment of succeeding as a leader.

What would happen if one had the sense that one was a flop as a leader? A leader's need to feel instrumental in assisting others to lead fuller lives is partly based on one's own need to feel that one is making a significant difference in the world, a need that can and does lead to self-deception.

At such times, a leader may look for evidence of progress, however slim, and rationalize away any elements of failure. In so doing, one gives oneself credit for the apparent progress when it may be largely due to another variable, something unrelated to one's leadership. When a leader understands that success or failure is not the event in and of itself, but rather one's interpretation of the event, one can be more honest with oneself and consciously explore the phenomenon of self-deception and thus lessen the chance of its occurrence, which in turn lessens the likelihood of becoming overinvested in one's constituency.

Overinvestment in Followers

A mistake an inexperienced leader is prone to making is worrying too much about his or her constituents. One can identify so closely with people that one loses one's own identity and takes on theirs. Empathy with one's constituents thus becomes distorted and counterproductive.

The most leadership-oriented thing a person can do is to be present (really present in the here and now) with the people, feeling with them and experiencing their struggles with them, but *without* assuming their responsibility for living their own lives responsibly. A leader who becomes lost in the struggle and confusion of his or her constituency cannot hope to lead the people out of their darkness. Thus, a leader who assumes the responsibility of his or her followers does them a great disservice by stealing their struggle, hence their experience of their struggle, hence their ability to grow and master themselves through the gift of insight that inner struggle offers.

Another mistake leaders, seasoned leaders, make is trying to derive personal fulfillment for their own needs or unfinished psychological business by becoming inappropriately enmeshed with individuals in their own constituency. The following are a few illustrations of such enmeshment:

- The personal need to be liked, appreciated, and approved of
- The fear of challenging followers lest they think poorly of the leader and abandon the cause
- Sexual feelings and sexually inappropriate behavior on the part of the leader toward an individual(s) in his or her constituency, to the extent that the leader is preoccupied with sexual fantasies or deliberately focuses the individual's attention on sexual feelings toward the leader
- Extreme reactions to certain individuals who evoke old feelings in the leader, such as followers who are perceived by the leader as being judgmental, domineering, controlling, and so on

- A leader's need to alleviate an individual's pain or struggle because her or his experience is awakening old wounds or unrecognized inner conflicts in the leader
- Compulsively giving advice, where the leader is always in the superior position of "teacher" and thus continually dictating how the individual should think, act, choose, and live

Because it is not acceptable for a leader to use his or her followers to resolve his or her own feelings toward them and the emotions they evoke, it is all the more important that the leader work diligently on his or her own unresolved psychological problems in an appropriate professional setting. Although recognizing how one's personal needs can intrude into one's leadership is a first step, one needs to willingly, consciously explore one's inner self or be in danger of losing oneself in one's constituents and using them, individually or collectively, to accommodate one's unfilled needs. In this circumstance, it helps to develop a sense of humor.

The Value of Humor

Leadership, although a serious responsibility, need not be deadly dull. A cause can be enriched, even enhanced, when a leader and the people can laugh together, but most particularly when one can laugh at oneself in front of others.

It is important that a leader recognize that genuine humor and laughter can help to accomplish the end rather than hinder it. There are times, of course, when laughter is used to cover up discomfort and to escape from the experience of facing a threat, such as the need to change. It is the leader's task to distinguish between humor that is used as a crutch and therefore distracts and humor that unites people and thus enriches their experience of life, such as dealing with a difficult situation or person.

Coping with Someone You Dislike

Have you ever encountered a person whose behavior was personally offensive, a person you wished would simply go away so you would not have the urge to chew the inside of your cheeks raw every time he or she spoke?[79] A common failing of leadership is to split one's energy among blaming, berating, and bemoaning someone else's behavior, which often causes one to lose sight of the vision toward which one is supposed to be leading. All is not lost, however; there are things you can do to "save your sanity," as it were.

1. Identify those specific behaviors that trigger your own emotions. Identifying your behavioral triggers is important because we each respond uniquely to those around us and the world at large. Each time we react strongly to another person, either positively or negatively, it says more about us than it does about the other person. It is important, in this sense, to accept personal responsibility for your own thoughts and feelings because what drives you to distraction may bother no one else or may actually be enjoyable to others.

2. Talk to the individual privately, and use the "sandwich technique." Once you have identified the specific behaviors that you find so annoying, share them with the person involved, but sandwich your comments between positive statements. Everyone has at least some positive attributes, although at times (depending on your state of mind) it may seem like you have to dig pretty deeply to find them.

Once you have ferreted out the person's positive attributes, visit with him or her, but be *assertive* rather than passive, passive–aggressive (indirect passively expressed aggression), or aggressive. Use "I" statements and address the specific behavior(s) that annoys you, as opposed to generalized "you" statements. For example, say "I felt uncomfortable when you told that sexist joke," rather than "You are sexist."

3. Timing is critical. Choose a time when you are calm and can stick to the issue at hand, which is your response to the person's specific behavior(s). Plan to meet in a relaxed neutral setting, perhaps for a cup of coffee. Make sure there is enough time for a friendly visit, and be prepared not only to express yourself directly and kindly but also to listen empathically.

4. Remember your role as leader. A leader must be willing to hear and bear the fears of his or her followers if a mutually supportive environment is to be forthcoming within the community. There are neither exceptions nor addenda to leadership that excuse a leader from dealing with someone he or she does not like.

A tremendous leadership challenge is to make inclusive democracy come alive when faced with someone who is self-centered, critical, and generally obnoxious in a way that strips others of their own self-confidence. Well-documented circumstances can be a powerful tool when coupled with well-communicated feedback. When such feedback is handled with quiet dignity, it has the potential to benefit not only the group as a whole but also the person to whom you, as leader, have been reacting with alarm, annoyance, or anger.

5. A leader does not quit when things get tough. Although it is not always necessary, a brief "time out" may help, provided someone is capable of taking over for a while. There are times when the most able leader is just too close to a situation to see it clearly. One must take a deep breath, stand back, refocus, and when focused once again assume leadership.

6. If nothing else works, find a facilitator. It is critical that the facilitator be transformative and free of personal investment in the outcome. (See *Resolving Environmental Conflict* for a thorough discussion of transformative facilitation.[80])

The ideal outcome of having to deal with someone you do not like is that your nemesis becomes your teacher. Although you may not be alleviated of your annoyance in the way you might wish, you can always change yourself for the better in response to the problems posed by your opponent. An unmistakable sign of a true leader is the ability to change oneself in such a way that one's protagonist becomes one's teacher and—perhaps—one's friend, because, in the end, as Goethe said, "Kindness is the golden chain by which society is bound together." When that kindness takes over, you can, for a moment, see yourself through the eyes of another person.

Imagine Yourself as Different People

Being a good leader requires one to be aware of many different things happening simultaneously, such as the various ways different people respond to any given circumstance, especially when fear of loss or change is involved. Although conflict often arises where fear resides, a person who can imagine himself or herself in the shoes of another can often tap into what the other person may be feeling and why. To do this, one must ask: "How would I feel in that person's situation? Why would I feel that way?"

A few people assume this role naturally and automatically; others can learn to do so consciously. A person with this ability can often defuse conflict, either before it starts or before it gets out of hand and requires special resolution. Such a person can also anticipate where events are going and thus help people to have compassion and understanding for and patience with one another along the way. In addition, a person who can put himself or herself in another's shoes can often help people to put their talents together in a complementary (instead of competitive) way that actually inspires people to perform better than they thought possible.

Inspiring Performance

Excellent performance can produce excellent results, which may lead to strong participation. But here a major point to remember is that as a group, listeners as individuals may not understand their own feelings, let alone the feelings of others in the group. It is thus important for the leader to help the group understand that it is human nature to achieve, to build, and to want success.

The secret to success is the willingness to do the things that people who consider themselves failures do not like to do. Success is greatly aided by enthusiasm. The person with enthusiasm generally prevails to the end, whereas the person who lacks enthusiasm is easily discouraged. Generating enthusiasm can eliminate negative attitudes. With this in mind, a meeting that is well organized and flows easily provides a meaningful, if not enjoyable, time for all and is impressive to visitors who join in future activities.[74, 81]

Behind all of this, as one soon learns, is the hard work of a few people dedicated to the proposition of a shared vision of sustainable community development. A large part of the success of these endeavors is the insistence among those few that they all share in the work. Clear guidelines of acceptable conduct and firm enforcement of those standards will go a long way to ensure equal and meaningful experiences as people strive toward the creation of a shared vision for a sustainable community within the context of a sustainable landscape.

To foster the kind of participation and responsibility necessary to create a shared vision for a successful sustainable community, it is advisable to take seriously the installation of members into positions of leadership within a committee. Elevate the leaders into these positions of prominence and responsibility, and make sure all duties are clear and concise. Although this is especially important for first-time performers, seasoned leaders need reminders too, because negligence is often a matter of not knowing what to expect and what is expected.

If a problem develops, work to increase the person's level of commitment, but first do your homework. People usually do not perform well for one of the following reasons:

- **Poor training**—No one either told them or showed them how to do the work properly—and showing (which provides a concrete example) is a lot more effective than simply telling (which all too often is a poorly understood abstraction).
- **Inadequate equipment**—They lack the proper materials or equipment.
- **Time**—They lack the time necessary to work properly.
- **Motivation**—They are not motivated to perform because they feel overworked and underappreciated or are unhappy with the job, co-workers, management, or some other aspect of their lives.

Your immediate task as leader is to determine which of the above reasons applies to the situation you are facing. Asking yourself the following questions may help you figure out which reason applies and thus what your next step is:

- Does the person know what is supposed to be done and when? (If not, you will need to inform, preferably show, him or her what to do and how.)
- What is the specific difference between the present level of performance and the desired level of performance? (The person must know what he or she is required to do to perform satisfactorily.)
- Does the person even know that his or her work is unsatisfactory? (If not, you must express your concern about the area of the job in which the person's performance needs improvement.)
- Does the person have the necessary skills to perform the job satisfactorily? (If not, he or she will require the appropriate training.)
- Is the expected standard of performance realistic? (If it is not, no one may be able to meet the expectations of the job.)
- What effect does poor performance have on others? (The person needs to know how others are affected by his or her performance.)
- Does the person have the necessary resources to do the job? (If not, provide them.)
- Are there obstacles affecting the person's performance that are beyond his or her control? (If so, remove them.)

- Does a person's positive performance yield commensurate rewards? (If the person is performing well but receives an undesirable reward, such as twice as much work to do in the same amount of time, then his or her incentive to perform will likely decrease.)
- Could the person do the job satisfactorily if she or he wanted to? (If not, there is little you can do.)

Once you have analyzed the situation and decided the person can perform satisfactorily if she or he really wants to, you are ready to begin working with the person to improve her or his performance.

You might begin by praising work currently being accomplished and encourage greater excellence through sensitivity to small contributions so they may grow into bigger ones. An example might be: "Jim is doing a fine job as committee chair for participation by local government despite his busy schedule. (Applause.) Once he gets his agenda better established, it should be easier to meet with government officials."

At times, one must inquire subtly about work not being completed, but in a way that brings up the problem without criticizing. (No one needs criticism. We all need help.) Remember: *Praise in public, discuss shortcomings in private.* If necessary, have someone check with the delinquent leader before the meeting to see if the work is done. A sincere offer to help as a pretext for the call will avoid humiliation by: (1) keeping feedback related to behavior in a way that avoids judgments by describing rather than evaluating behavior; (2) using "I" statements, rather than "you" statements, to reduce defensiveness; and (3) speaking calmly with unemotional language, tone, and gestures.

If, however, work is still not being done, a more direct approach may be necessary. Call a meeting of the committee leaders prior to or just after the regular meeting, with the individual present. Discuss some normal business and insert a brief discussion about the person's performance toward the end of the meeting—but neither first nor last on the agenda, lest it come across as the main purpose of the meeting.

Because the goal is to call attention to the problem and promote discussion, briefly cite two or three examples of work not being done and express concern for the project as a whole. Allow the person in question to explain his or her difficulties, and honor the explanation no matter what it is. Keep in mind that this is a sensitive situation because it is difficult for people to admit they have not fulfilled their agreed-to duty.

Rather than initially asking the person to step down, offer help from a prearranged assistant, who may also be a replacement if the person resigns unexpectedly. One can also provide for an assistant to take over the duties on a temporary basis until the person can find more time. But be sure to get a firm commitment from the individual concerning his or her performance in the future.

If, after all of this, the work is still not getting done and the person is adamant about retaining his or her position, prepare for a replacement, but this must be the last resort. The person must be approached in private by the committee chair and one other officer. State the problem gently yet firmly and ask that a replacement be allowed to assume the duties, which will give the person an opportunity to voluntarily pass forward his or her duties while still retaining as much control as possible of his or her dignity.

If the person refuses to step down, express your concern for his or her feelings, but also express your concern for the feelings of the other members of the committee. It is now appropriate to again ask for the successor to take over, while encouraging the person to try again when his or her circumstances have improved, which continues to allow the person control of the decision and to retain dignity.

If the person insists on continuing, grant one final opportunity by allowing him or her a specific period within which to fulfill the stated duties of the position. If the position is important enough to the person to want to continue, a final chance may be in order, but make it clear that if conditions do not improve, replacement is inevitable.

At this point, the person is no longer in control. If he or she succeeds, the immediate problem is solved; if not, the replacement takes over and the immediate problem is solved. If a replacement must take over, have the incumbent make a brief checklist to familiarize the new person with the duties and to allow private discussion.

There is another kind of performance that also relies on inspiration. It is called creativity.

Nurturing Creativity

Although a leader's ability to lead can be greatly enhanced by a creative followership, it requires a sensitive and personally secure leader to nurture another's creativity because the outcome of such creativity must be openly shared. An effective leader understands that creativity requires the freedom of one's imagination as well as time to relax and read, have discussions with colleagues, and experiment. After all, the greatest creativity often comes in the quietude of an unguarded moment, often when it is least expected. One cannot, therefore, be creative on command or under the pressure of deadlines.

Creativity among one's followership can also be encouraged by appropriate recognition, such as praise before one's peers. Such recognition can also be in the form of a public explanation of how the idea is going to be implemented, which demonstrates a leader's sincerity in listening to an idea, grasping its essence, giving credit where credit is truly due, and acting.

Effective leaders also understand that creativity requires that the creator be allowed—even encouraged—to risk making mistakes and failing because of them. One must be willing to think of creativity as having a rate of failure that is at least twice the rate of success. This is but saying that if you are right more than half the time, you are ahead of the game.

Insecure leaders cannot handle such open-ended risk and usually kill creativity among their followers in one or more ways. One way is to encourage people to be creative, and when they are to sit on their ideas without extending the slightest feedback to those who offer them. Months later, this kind of leader wonders where all the ideas are.

Another way leaders kill creativity is by humiliating a person (often before his or her peers) who puts forth an idea: "This idea won't work; it's too 'pie in the sky.' Come on, get real; be practical. I want something for today's world, not something for fantasy land."

And then there are the leaders who act like mental parasites. They think that just because they asked for the ideas, they should get all the credit. They take someone else's wonderful idea and sell it as their own. If the idea is greeted with applause, they might mumble that they don't deserve all the credit, but they are at the same time very secretive when it comes to sharing any of it. On the other hand, should the idea bomb, they are very quick to give credit where credit is due. Such people can use a lesson from Zen cooking.

Making Do with What You Have

Making do with what you have brings to mind a lesson in Zen cooking.[82] Zen masters refer to a life lived fully and completely, with nothing held in reserve, as the "supreme meal." And a person who lives such a life is called a Zen cook because that person knows how to plan, cook, appreciate, serve, and offer the supreme meal of life.

Cooking, like leadership, is about transformation. "When we cook," says Buddhist teacher Bernard Glassman, "we work directly with the elemental forces of fire and heat, water, metal, and clay." When cooking or baking food, something almost magical happens as the heat transforms the ingredients, through chemical interactions, into a culinary delight. Although this kind of transformation, as does leadership, requires faith, a Zen cook follows the middle road in having faith that the food is coming along but also checking now and then to see how it is doing.

An accomplished Zen cook or leader is something of an alchemist in that he or she can transform poisons into virtues, not by adding a secret ingredient but by leaving something out—attachment to the self. Anger, for example, is considered a poison when motivated by self-centered interest and the need to control, but through detachment of the self, the same irrational emotion becomes a clearly focused, fiery energy of determination, which transforms a negative force into one that is positive. Take self-centeredness out of greed, for example, and it is transformed into a desire to help. Drop self-indulgence from ignorance and it is transformed into a state of sacred unknowing in which new things are allowed to arise.

"This is all well and good," you may say, "but how does a Zen cook or a leader find the necessary ingredients with which to prepare the meal?" One simply opens one's eyes, looks around, and does the best one can with the materials at hand in each and every moment. Consider the following story:

A father sees a map of the world in a magazine, cuts it out, cuts it into pieces, then gives the pieces to his son to put back together. To the father's astonishment, the boy hands him the assembled map within ten minutes.

"How did you put the world together so fast?" asks the father.

"On the other side of the world was the picture of a person," replied the boy. "I put the person together, and the world came together."

Our thoughts, emotions, actions, insights, and relationships are all ingredients for our meal, but we must be open to them. Instead of openness of mind, however, we usually create our own boundaries, our own tiny view beyond which we refuse to look. With practice, however, we can each expand our view until everything becomes a potential ingredient for our meal.

Here a story from Africa might be instructive: A little boy wanted to give his teacher a gift, but he was very poor. So he walked two miles to the beach and picked up a handful of sand. He then walked two miles back. The next day he gave the sand to his teacher.

She thanked him for the beautiful sand, then said, "But you walked so far."

"The journey," he replied, "is part of the gift."

As we learn to see ourselves as part of at one with the world, we become attuned to the unity of all life, and the whole of the world becomes available. Then the Zen cook or leader knows that every aspect of life offers itself as an ingredient for the supreme meal.

Our natural tendency in cooking is not to use an ingredient and in leadership not to avail ourselves of a person we think will ruin our meal. In so doing, we all too often deny their existence or discard them through dismissal as of no value for our meal. But as Dogen, the 13th century founder of the Japanese Soto Zen tradition, instructs us, we must take the very ingredients we think will ruin our meal and figure out how to use them to improve it because they will be there whether we like it or not.

"No matter who we are," observes Glassman, "we tend to reject someone or something." Some Zen students found it incongruous to cook a gourmet meal and then learn to set a table properly for rich people because to the students it did not constitute traditional *samu,* or work practice, like chopping wood, carrying water, or weeding a monastery garden. Many of the students asked, "How can you serve the rich? What kind of a thing is that for a Zen center to do?"

Rejection takes many forms. A Zen student who rejects a person because he or she is rich has the same problem as a rich person who rejects a Zen student because he or she is poor. If you can learn to work with that which you would reject, it turns out that you are working with yourself, with those shadow parts of yourself, both good and bad, that you reject. In other words, if you can learn to work comfortably with a rich person whom you have rejected, then you can begin to accept and work with the richness rather than the poverty in yourself, which merits a brief discussion of the "shadow."

Many years ago, Dr. Carl Jung, the Swiss psychoanalyst, defined the dark side of our psyche as the "shadow." The shadow is a handy dumping ground for all the characteristics of our personality we choose to disown, that part of us we fail to see or know, that which has not adequately entered into our everyday waking consciousness.[83]

The shadow may be thought of as the despised quarter of our being and is paired with being wrong, bad, or evil. But also held within the shadow of our psyche is the pure gold, the noble, creative aspects of our personality of which we are afraid.

The root of this whole shadow-making process within us begins as we enter into culture and cultural ideals. We divide our lives and separate things into good and evil, acceptable and unacceptable because culture insists—literally demands—that we behave in a particular manner.

The bad news is that these refused, unaccepted, bury-in-the-deep-dark-basement parts of ourselves don't go away, for all our characteristics must appear somewhere in our personal inventories. Nothing may be left out. That which we try to omit simply collects in the corners of our personalities and, when hidden long enough, takes on a life of its own, such as sudden "unexplainable" outbursts of anger, often with an energy potential nearly as great as that of our egos, which are those parts of ourselves we know about and consciously accept.

When the energy of the shadow builds up too much, it can erupt as a black mood, anger, rage, harsh words spewed out of our mouths, some indiscretion slipping past us, depression, accidents, or even psychosomatic illness. Conversely, ignoring the golden qualities within ourselves can be every bit as damaging as hiding our dark sides. It may even be necessary to suffer a severe shock or illness before a person learns to let out the magnificent inner gold.

The good news is the imagined mirror in front of us, and the work is to own every aspect of ourselves, rather than to disown those parts we do not want and thus project them outward onto someone or something else. The latter would be like the scapegoat driven once a year from a community with all the people's shadow elements heaped firmly onto its back.

Instead of heaping all our unwanted psychological parts onto a scapegoat, our task is to restore ourselves to wholeness by putting these fractured, alienated parts together again. If each of us can learn to truly love our inner enemies, then we can also begin in like measure to redeem and love our so-called outer enemies.

Many personal and collective benefits will result if we each see ourselves in totality. For example, we would fall in and out of love a lot less frequently because we would not be initially projecting the golden parts of ourselves onto another and then, as love grows thin, replacing the gold by projecting instead those parts of ourselves that are annoying, distasteful, and even downright intolerable.

If we saw ourselves in totality, relationships in general would be truer and more enduring than they currently are. Hero-worship in its varying degrees would cease because we would each accept our finest qualities and be responsible for them. We would stop making others the bad guy and look first within to assess what about ourselves we refuse to see, know, and accept.

The shadow is the cause of war on all levels, both within and without. In addition, the process of owning our inner heaven and hell is the highest form of creativity. A great deal of energy is released and begins to flow as we reach a place of inner wholeness. This place where light and dark touch is where miracles arise, where personal and collective peace is possible.

If you do not think you have a shadow, ask yourself: How many times a day do I employ compulsive substitutes (such as food, caffeine, alcohol, cigarettes, television, and so on) for emotions? How many times do I run away from facing my emotions through the use of distractions?

You cannot run away from something that is negative; it will only grow larger and stronger each time you try. You must steadfastly confront your fears by moving through them toward something that is positive.

Dogen taught that every meal has to include a harmony of the six flavors—bitter, sour, sweet, spicy, salty, and plain—just as every leader must deal with the various kinds of personalities—exasperater, relater, fatalist, and appraiser. None of them is better or more important than the other. As each ingredient has a different flavor and a different reason for being part of the meal, so each personality type has a different strength and a different reason for being part of the team. They are all important to the Zen of cooking and of leadership. In addition to the above, if a leader is truly interested in helping his or her followers use their creative ability to fashion what they need from that which is at hand, he or she must be careful to establish realistic objectives.

Establishing Realistic Objectives

Realistic objectives are essential for a viable relationship between a leader and his or her constituency. If the objectives are too ambitious to be accomplished, the people soon become discouraged and flee what they consider a sinking ship. On the other hand, if the objectives are realistic and most of them are achievable and achieved, people will likely forgive the few that may go unmet. A leader is therefore wise in doing the necessary homework to assure, as much as possible, that the objectives he or she selects not only are attainable as stated but also clearly further the cause as a whole while fostering a sense of urgency.

The Need for Urgency

Creating and maintaining a genuine sense of urgency to accomplish a task deemed important is a sign of an effective leader. I say this because, in my experience, people seldom act singly, much less collectively, in the absence of a feeling of real urgency.

Consider, for example, that most people steadfastly refuse to deal with making out a will, let alone prearranging their own funeral (even for the benefit of their children), until it is absolutely necessary. And then they balk because of the sense of finality, which brings with it a foreboding.

Part of the reason for the palpable finality and foreboding is that until now—this instant—dealing with one's will and funeral arrangements were abstractions somewhere in the future. Suddenly, they are not only in the present—in the here and now—but also concrete in one's experience, which to most people is frightening; hence their avoidance.

Therefore, one of the daunting tasks, should a leader seriously want to accomplish something for the benefit of the people (such as crafting and implementing a vision for a sustainable future), is to create and maintain a sense of urgency about that which is important—even for the immediate public good. Without a sense of urgency, most people languish because it is easier to deal with a mediocre but known (concrete) present than it is to work toward an excellent but unknown (abstract) future. And for the sake of the future, one must know how to give and receive good counsel.

Give Counsel, Not Advice

One must lead by example, as Francis Bacon noted when he said: "He that gives good advice, builds with one hand; he that gives good counsel and example, builds with both." To this, George Eliot might add: "Blessed is the...[person] who, having nothing to say, abstains from giving wordy evidence of the fact."

A mistaken notion of those who are naïve about the nature of leadership is to equate giving advice with giving good counsel. Counseling must not be confused with dispensing information or advice. The role of a leader as counselor is to help another person (or group of people) discover, usually through questions, his or her own solutions and direction and to recognize his or her own freedom to act. A leader's task is to ask questions in such a way that a person can most easily make wise choices and find sufficient courage to act for the benefit of the people at large and willingly accept the consequences of his or her decisions.

It is not a leader's task to direct a person's thinking by giving advice and thereby limiting her or his ability to act freely from her or his own conscience. After all, a person is responsible for the outcome of her or his decisions.

Unfortunately, too many leaders who are inexperienced in counseling yet who are called upon for counsel fall into the trap of believing they are leading only when being prescriptive and imparting advice to their constituents—even other leaders. It is therefore critical to understand the power of the questions we ask.

The Questions We Ask

Each question is a key that opens a door to a room filled with mirrors, each one a facet of the answer. Only one answer, however, is reflected in all the mirrors in the room. If we want a new answer, we must ask a new question—open a new room with a new key.

We keep asking the same old questions—opening the same old door and looking at the same old reflections in the same old mirrors. We may polish the old mirrors and hope thereby to find new and different meanings out of the old answers to the same old questions. Or we might think we can pick a lock and steal a mirror from a new and different room with the hope of stumbling onto new and workable answers to the same old questions.

The old questions and the old answers have led us into the social/ environmental mess we are in today and are leading us toward the even greater mess we will be in tomorrow. We must therefore look long and hard at where we are headed with respect to the quality of the world we help shape as a legacy. Only when we are willing to risk asking really new questions can we find really new answers.

The answer to a problem is only as good as the question and the means used to derive the answer. There is, however, no single reality, but rather a multiplicity of realities, the representation of which depends on one's position in the process of negotiating an acceptable social/environmental view of reality.

If, therefore, we are going to ask intelligent questions about the future of the Earth and our place in the scheme of things, we must be free of scientific opinions based on "acceptable" interpretations of scientific knowledge. In addition, we would be wise to consider the gift of Zen and approach life with a beginner's mind—a mind simply open to the wonders and mysteries of the Universe.

A beginner sees only what the answers might be and knows not what they *should* be. If, on the other hand, one becomes an expert, one thinks one knows what the answers should be and can no longer see what they might be.

The beginner is thus free to explore and to discover a multiplicity of realities, while the expert grows rigid in a self-created prison of a single pet reality, which often turns into an obsession to be protected at any cost—an all too common fate of leaders. Hence, the beginner understands the question better than the expert does. It is therefore a wise and effective leader who keeps a beginner's mind open to a multiplicity of realities, each of which has secreted within its possibilities a heretofore untapped opportunity.

We must keep a beginner's mind if we are going to ask intelligent questions and be open to multiple hypotheses, realities, and explanations, and we must be willing to accept a challenge to our ideas in the spirit of learning, rather than as an invitation to combat. The greatest triumphs of leadership are not, after all, triumphs of facts but rather triumphs of new ways of seeing, of thinking, of perceiving, and of asking questions.

Such triumphs of vision and thought come not only through knowing which questions to ask but also through a willingness to risk what most people think of as failure. The avoidance of risk, says university president Harold Shapiro, is, in the end, "an acceptance of mediocrity and an abdication of leadership." We must beware of giving in and "raising the flag of failure" too soon, because if we don't immediately achieve our stated objective, society is quick to judge something as a failure.

But true success or failure is a personal view and lies not in an event itself but rather in the interpretation of the event. When, for example, Thomas Edison's 10,000 experiments with a storage battery failed to produce results—and society would surely have deemed that a failure—he said, "I have not failed. I've just found 10,000 ways that won't work." This same line of reasoning is implicit in Winston Churchill's famous commencement speech: "Never, never give up! Never, never give up!"

Before we can get fundamentally new answers, we must be willing to risk asking fundamentally new questions. This means that we must look long and hard at where we are headed with respect to the quality of our environment and the legacy we are leaving our children. Remember, old questions and the old answers not only have gotten us where we are today but also are guiding us to where we will be tomorrow.

Heretofore we have been more concerned with getting politically right answers than asking morally right questions. Politically right answers validate our preconceived economic/political desires. Morally right questions would lead us toward a future in which environmental options are left open so that generations to come may define their own ideas of a "quality environment" from an array of possibilities.

A good question, one that may be valid for a century or more, is a bridge of continuity among generations. We may develop a different answer every decade, but the answer does the only thing an answer can do: it brings a greater understanding of the question. An answer cannot exist without a question, so the answer depends not on the information we derive from the illusion of having answered the question but on the question we asked in the first place.

In the final analysis, the questions we ask guide the evolution of humanity and its society, and it is the questions we ask, not the answers we derive, that determine the options we bequeath to the future. Answers are fleeting, here today and gone tomorrow, but questions may be valid for a century or more. Questions are flexible and open-ended, whereas answers are rigid, illusory cul-de-sacs. The future, therefore, is a question to be defined by questions asked by those who dare to lead by the authenticity of personal example, each in her or his own style. To do so, however, one must first "stay alive" as a leader.

Burnout

It is Corey's thesis in psychotherapy[64] and mine in leadership that the single most important instrument we have to work with is ourselves, what we are and what we progressively become as we grow. The most powerful technique we have at our disposal is our ability to model aliveness, authenticity, compassion, and dispassion. And because leadership is about helping others to fulfill their potentialities, it is our responsibility to take care of ourselves so we are able to continue functioning as servant leaders from our own aliveness. To accomplish this, we must consciously work to deal with those factors that threaten to drain our life's essence from us and render us helpless. One of these lethal factors is "burnout."

People who suffer from burnout feel tired, drained, and without enthusiasm, where once they were idealistic and going to make their mark by changing the world for the better. Now, they no longer care; their ideals appear to have lost their meaning. They feel like slaves instead of leaders because what they have to offer seems neither wanted nor accepted, which leaves them feeling unappreciated, unrecognized, and unimportant. They therefore go through the motions of their jobs with all the aliveness and zest of a robot.

Burnout steals one's sense of being grounded in the everyday world, where one can see some measure of concreteness in the results of one's efforts. People often begin to feel oppressed and thus begin to fight as an enemy the very "system" they were going to change for the better. But the more they actively resist the system, the more the system resists their changing it, which, in their minds, stifles any sense of personal initiative.

Because a person at this point in the cycle of burnout has lost sight of both his or her vision toward which to build and of dispassion, burnout begins to feed off itself. When this happens, the person suffering from burnout feels increasingly isolated and in despair, the latter of which further increases the sense of isolation, and so on in a seemingly never-ending self-reinforcing feedback loop. Such a downward spiral effectively prevents an individual from reaching out to others for help and support.

Because burnout can rob a leader of the vitality he or she needs personally and professionally, it is critical to examine some of its causes, possible remedies, and ways of prevention. Here again, I acknowledge Corey[64] for his excellent and concise listing of some of the causes, remedies, and preventions of burnout, which I have adapted and added to.

Causes of Burnout

Recognizing the causes of burnout can in itself be a step in its remedy. A few of the causes of burnout among leaders are:

- Caring for the cause and being invested in it more than the other people, so that one has a continual sense of needing to pull the other people along as opposed to simply guiding them
- Giving a great deal of personal time, ideas, and energy and getting little or nothing in return by way of appreciation or other positive and meaningful responses
- Always trying to stop things from happening, such as cutting forests, grazing public lands with livestock, building a particular bridge or road, tearing down a historic building, and so on
- Being under constant pressure to produce, perform, and meet deadlines, many of which are both personally meaningless and unrealistic
- Working with a difficult population, such as those who resist any kind of change, personally or otherwise, unless it is somehow seen as self-serving, and those who are involuntary participants in changing times within their own community, state, or nation and therefore change at glacial speed, even in the face of a crisis, environmental or other
- Disillusionment when one's ideals of service come up against greed, apathy, or even corruption
- Inability to deal with the calumny and criticism that inevitably come with leadership
- Unresolved personal conflicts beyond the responsibility of leadership, such as marital problems, chronic health problems, financial problems, and so on

Remedies for Burnout

Learning ways in which to care for ourselves beyond recognizing burnout as an initial problem is critical for leaders who truly want to serve. My own experience, in concurrence with that of Corey,[64] leads me to think that accepting *personal responsibility* for one's thought, motives, and actions is one of the most critical factors is remedying burnout.

The remedy for burnout is within, not without. It is examining the self-centeredness or other-centeredness of one's own agenda: "Do I really want to serve as an unconditional way of extending love, or am I really trading my service for approbation as a way to find personal fulfillment?"

To reverse the negative cycle of burnout (which is projecting blame for one's sense of failure and the feelings it engenders onto whatever seems handy and/or sounds good outside of oneself), one must turn the searchlight inward. One must examine, with direct honesty, the root causes of one's negative feelings and accept that they come from within, not without. Therefore, the cure must also be within.

Until one understands and accepts that both the cause and the cure are within, one is not only surrendering personal power to forces outside of oneself but also acting out the role of a helpless victim, the behavioral gateway to cynicism. Although there are obstacles to leadership that make if difficult to function as one might wish, there are ways of learning to keep one's own counsel and to act out of personal integrity and meaning.

To do this, however, one must not blame the external system for the dysfunction internal to oneself. And where there are things within the external system that need fixing, one can begin working on them one at a time with diligence and persistence, along with a healthy dose of patience and dispassion.

Preventing Burnout

Learning to look within ourselves to determine what choices we have, what choices we are making or not making to keep ourselves alive, and why we are or are not making them can go a long way in preventing burnout. There are also other ways to prevent burnout, most of which include assuming the responsibility of consciously, actively nourishing ourselves:

- Making sure one has a clear, exciting, believable, attainable vision toward which to lead
- Taking responsibility for one's own motives, thoughts, and actions and leaving to others the responsibility for theirs
- Finding interests in addition to the role of leader
- Taking initiative
- Attending to one's own health through adequate sleep, relaxation, an exercise program, proper diet, and time for reflection or meditation
- Cultivating nourishing relationships with people with whom one can find mutual sharing of love, support, ideas, humor, and so on
- Learning how to ask for what one wants, though not expecting to always get it, and learning how to accept not getting what one asked for

- Learning how to grow inside so that one is clearly focused, other-centered, and well grounded spiritually as a leader while being both dispassionate and detached from the outcome of one's leadership, which renders external recognition unimportant to the validation of one's accomplishments
- Learning to play and honor the child within by freely giving expression to it
- Learning to be honestly in touch with one's emotions, including pain and tears when necessary
- Evaluating whether the project one is working on is still worth one's time and commitment or whether it is necessary in terms of personal growth to move on to other challenges
- Taking the initiative to form a support group with colleagues to openly share feelings and find better ways of approaching difficult situations that inevitably arise as a condition of leadership
- Finding a mentor with whom to debrief and from whom to glean counsel

The above list is not meant to be exhaustive but rather only to provide some insight into keeping oneself alive and healthy while allowing one to accept the trials and enjoy the fruits of leadership by exclusively keeping a personal scorecard about one's own success or failure. If one remains true to one's ideals and retains a healthy zest for living, one will continue to grow and change and in so doing find life to be exciting and ever-new.

To remain personally and professionally alive, therefore, one must periodically evaluate the direction in which one finds oneself traveling and determine if one is in fact living in the way one really wants—true to one's beliefs. If, perchance, one is not living according to one's true beliefs, then one must decide what changes are necessary to fulfill truth in one's life and find the courage to risk acting, rather than simply waiting for circumstances to force one's hand.

By being well grounded spiritually and in tune with oneself, one finds the experience of life to be one of harmony, where one has the unmistakable feeling of personal power, which is the power of self-control and self-mastery. This personal power allows one to integrate the experiences of life, including one's feelings and spirituality, with one's experiences as a leader in such a way that one has empathy and compassion for one's constituency without being captured by them. Such a personal synthesis provides a solid, insightful foundation for true servant leadership, something sorely needed in today's governments the world over. Having said this, let's examine some ways in which a government (any government) can foster exemplary leadership from within.

LEADERSHIP WITHIN ORGANIZATIONS

Organizations, including governments and corporations, cannot empower people, but they can give them the proper tools and the capacity to work actively in achieving the outcomes they want. For instance, incentives for good trusteeship of a local community's natural resources by the community itself can replace tax breaks used to recruit multinational corporations with little or no stake in either the ecological sustainability of a community's natural resources or the high-quality jobs needed to sustain a community's cultural well-being.

In addition, organizations for economic development can provide expertise and financial backing, rather than merely ladling out grants, so that local community partnerships can learn how to create their own vision and plan strategically how to achieve their goals. Such support would include assistance in strategic planning for businesses, including marketing, to help communities retain those small businesses deemed critical to their social sustainability.

Local leadership can also employ measures of performance for agencies and their staffs to reward those actions that help the growth and sustainability of community partnerships. In this spirit, a governor, mayor, or city council can require the use of cross-agency or cross-departmental decision making and can combine funding for programs in order to increase the efficient and effective access of local communities to resources at the agency's or department's disposal. And greater devolution of decision-making authority to the local level can make participation in community partnerships more effective, which creates the opportunity for community self-empowerment.

A prerequisite for sustainable development in a local community is that it must be inclusive, relating all relevant disciplines and special professions from all walks of life. Setting a good example is one of the most important functions of any local organization or government involved in implementing the principles and practices of sustainable community development. Leading by example—breaking down bureaucratic barriers of turf through interdisciplinary crossing of departmental lines, recycling and buying recycled goods, providing day care, encouraging car pooling, and offering flexible working hours—increases not only the capacity of an organization to govern its own people but also its effectiveness *and* efficiency.

It is thus important for organizations to both identify departmental and community links concerning mutually interrelated issues and to bring all people affected to the table in an effort to collectively resolve shared problems, which means dealing with human diversity. Understanding and accepting diversity allows us to acknowledge that each of us has a need to be needed, to contribute in some way. It also enables us to begin admitting that we do not and cannot know or do everything and that we must rely on the strengths of others with complete trust.

Diversity of thought, culture, expertise, and economic status thus allows all persons to contribute to the development process in a special way, making their unique gifts a part of the effort necessary to create a sustainable local community. Accepting diversity helps us to understand the need each person has for equality, identity, and opportunity in the process. Recognizing diversity gives us all a chance to provide meaning, fulfillment, purpose, and a gift of our talents to our community and future generations. Conversely, just as simplifying an ecosystem or complicating a mechanical system increases its vulnerability to destruction, so, too, will segregating diverse elements within a community lead to its social, moral, and economic decay, which may then spread throughout society, one community at a time.

Assuming people accept the notion of diversity, what is it they most want from the development process? People want the most effective, productive, and rewarding way of working together to achieve a common end. They want the process and the relationships forged therein to meet their personal needs for belonging, meaningful contribution, the opportunity to make a commitment to a special place—their community, the opportunity for personal growth, and the ability to exert reasonable control over their own destinies.

Control over personal destinies and thus the destiny of a community can be increased if federal agencies will focus on a community's goals for social/environmental sustainability. Having said this, however, it must be recognized that federal agencies (*not* the local community per se) have jurisdiction over *public* lands and thus are ultimately responsible and accountable for the ecological sustainability of those lands as a national legacy for the generations to come.

It is also possible to create organization-to-community trusteeship contracts—including the government, local and otherwise—that recognize that it is the results that count, not necessarily how many rules were followed. Such action can devolve authority closer to the citizens of a community and simultaneously allow employees at all levels of government to empower themselves to achieve quality results, which may well improve citizen participation in the process of crafting a collective vision of sustainable community development.

AFTERWORD

Having finished writing this book, I am saddened by an article in *The New York Times*, from which I quote:

> During a fiery debate on financing education [in Rockford Illinois, on December 9, 1997], the president of the school board...chose a rather dramatic way to express his disagreement with a fellow board member. He grabbed him by the throat.
>
> The throat-grabbing incident is only the latest example of incivility in American civic life, as the work of town councils, county assemblies, and school boards becomes increasingly nettled by behavior that is boorish, menacing, even violent. The National League of Cities...has made the problem of unruliness at local meetings its top focus during the past year, while Governing Magazine, a publication for state and local officials, recently fretted about a nationwide "epidemic of incivility."[84]

The kind of behavior addressed in the above article all but precludes the crafting of a shared vision, let alone becoming a Planetary Citizen with enough psychological maturity to implement any aspect of *The Prime Directive*, for a sustainable future within a community and the world. It also exemplifies the abysmal psychological immaturity of many of those currently in positions of leadership to whom we look for guidance, which raises a question: What are we teaching our children by example?

"History," wrote French historian Fernand Braudel, "may be divided into three movements: what moves rapidly, what moves slowly, and what appears not to move at all." This statement contains the fear of almost everyone—those for whom change comes too fast, those for whom change comes too slowly, and those for whom the world seems to stand still no matter how hard they try to change it. In each case, those who want things to be different feel they have no control, which is universally frightening and thus isolating to most people.

This pervading sense of isolation is precisely why we as human beings must always remember that we are creatures for whom sharing is an *absolute necessity* of life if we are to know we exist and to find value in living. As Mother Teresa often said, the worst kind of poverty is not being wanted.

One cannot share in life's experiences, cannot offer the gift of one's own experience and talent if there is no one to accept it because one is shunned by fellow human beings. Being unwanted and ignored is to shrivel inwardly like a dying leaf in a hot wind and, once soul-dead, to blow listlessly about without purpose or hope. Never have I found loneliness more completely than being unwanted while in the midst of a crowd of connected people.

As I travel around the world, I find over and over again that all we have of value, real value, as human beings is one another—someone with whom to share the experience of being human, with all its frailties, uncertainties, and magnificence. We *need* one another to be whole and healthy. To be an island is to have the spirit of our humanity die within, while our physical bodies turn into fleshy robots, which act more and more like unconscious sociopaths.

If we, as adults, do nothing else, we can and must find the moral courage to lead by example in how we treat one another and thereby help teach our children *the absolute social necessity of common civility.* After all, our future and theirs increasingly depend on it.

ENDNOTES

1. Editorial. 1997. Remembrance, commemoration. *Corvallis Gazette-Times* (Corvallis, OR) May 26.
2. The information listed is from Heather Dewar. 1997. Survival depends on resource management. *Corvallis Gazette-Times* (Corvallis, OR) July 27; Steve Newman. 1997. Earthweek: a diary of the planet. *Corvallis Gazette-Times* (Corvallis, OR) December 7; Robert S. Boyd. 1997. Arctic temp hikes preview global warming. *Corvallis Gazette-Times* (Corvallis, OR) November 14; Charles J. Hanley. 1997. Islanders appeal for help with encroaching seas. *Corvallis Gazette-Times* (Corvallis, OR) June 25.
3. Charles J. Hanley, Thomas Wagner, Bryan Brumley, Joe McDonald, and Rohan Sullivan. 1997. World seeks global response to climate. *Corvallis Gazette-Times* (Corvallis, OR) November 24.
4. Charles J. Hanley. 1997. Climate talks near agreement. *Corvallis Gazette-Times* (Corvallis, OR) December 10.
5. Stephen Arroyo. 1996. *Exploring Jupiter.* CRCS Publications, Sebastopol, CA.
6. The next three paragraphs are based on the writing of Brian Swimme and Thomas Berry. 1992. *The Universe Story: From the Primordial Flaring Forth to the Ecozoic Era—A Celebration of the Unfolding of the Cosmos.* HarperCollins, San Francisco.
7. Ed Mayo and Edward Hill. 1996. Shared vision. *Resurgence* 177:12–14.
8. The Associated Press. 1997. Water weed taking over Tahoe marinas. *Corvallis Gazette-Times* (Corvallis, OR) June 15.
9. Robert D. Kaplan. 1996. Fort Leavenworth and the eclipse of nationhood. *The Atlantic Monthly* 278(3):75–78, 80–82, 85–86, 88–90.
10. Georg Feuerstein, Subhash Kak, and David Frawley. 1995. The Vedas and perennial wisdom. *The Quest* 8(4):32–39, 80–81.
11. The following discussion of architecture and history is based on James Howard Kunstler. 1996. Home from nowhere. *The Atlantic Monthly* 278(3):43–66.

12. James Swan and Roberta Swan. 1996. *Dialogues with the Living Earth*. Quest Books, Wheaton, IL.

13. Sarah van Gelder. 1997. Beyond greed & scarcity. *YES! A Journal of Positive Futures* Spring:34–39.

14. The following discussion of the difference between money and wealth is based on an article by David C. Korten. 1997. Money versus wealth. *YES! A Journal of Positive Futures* Spring:14–18.

15. The following discussion on the health of living in a community is based on an article by Mark Harris. 1997. The ties that bind are the ties that heal. *Vegetarian Times* August:63–67.

16. Wendell Berry. 1993. *Sex, Economy, Freedom, and Community*. Pantheon Books, New York.

17. Marc Luyckx. 1997. The re-enchantment of politics. *YES! A Journal of Positive Futures* Winter:16–17.

18. The following discussion is based in part on the Advanced Communication and Leadership Program of Toastmasters International. 1994. Interpersonal Communication. Toastmasters International, Mission Viejo, CA.

19. Calvin S. Hall, Gardner Lindzey, John C. Loehlin, and Martin Manosevitz. 1985. *Introduction to Theories of Personality*. John Wiley & Sons, New York.

20. Ronald L. Warren. 1972. *The Community in America* (2nd ed.). Rand McNally College Publishing, Chicago.

21. Joanne Jacobs. 1996. Americans' civic involvement still strong, but changing. *Corvallis Gazette-Times* (Corvallis, OR) July 25.

22. Abraham Maslow. 1985. *The Farther Reaches of Human Nature*. Penguin Books, New York.

23. Robert A. Johnson. 1994. *Lying with the Heavenly Woman*. Harper, San Francisco.

24. Austine Roberts. 1977. *Centered on Christ: An Introduction to Monastic Profession*. St. Bede's Publications, Still Rive, MA.

25. Brother David Steindl-Rast. 1984. *Gratefulness and the Heart of Prayer: An Approach to Life in Fullness*. Paulist Press, Ransey, NJ.

26. The following discussion of time is based on Jay Walljasper. 1997. The speed trap. *Utne Reader* March–April:41–47; Stephan Rechtschaffen. 1997. The rhythm method. *Utne Reader* March–April:49–51, 96; Dick Dahl. 1997. The tick-tock syndrome. *Utne Reader* March–April:50–51; Jon Spayde. 1997. Slow like me. *Utne Reader* March–April:52–53.

27. This paragraph and the next three are based on an article by M. Boyd Wilcox. 1996. Residents should have right to cap population growth. *Corvallis Gazette-Times* (Corvallis, OR) September 10.

28. The following discussion about the growing chaos in the world is based on an excellent article by Robert D. Kaplan. 1994. The coming anarchy. *The Atlantic Monthly* 276(2):44–46, 48–49, 52, 54, 58–60, 62–66, 68–70, 72–76.

29. Denis D. Gray. 1997. Taming the Mekong. *Corvallis Gazette-Times* (Corvallis, OR) May 11.
30. The next ten paragraphs are based on the excellent ideas presented by Sarah van Gelder. 1997. Out of chaos: finding possibility in complexity. *YES! A Journal of Positive Futures* Winter:27.
31. D.T. Suzuki. 1959. *Zen and Japanese Culture.* Princeton University Press, Princeton, NJ.
32. Lin Yutang. 1938. *Wisdom of Confucius.* Random House, New York.
33. The discussions of values and aspects of vision follows Laurence G. Boldt. 1993. *Zen and the Art of Making a Living.* Penguin/Arkana, New York.
34. The Associated Press. 1997. Ah-choo, Arizona no longer haven for allergy sufferers. *Corvallis Gazette-Times* (Corvallis, OR) March 25.
35. Fred Matser. 1997. Nature is my God. *Resurgence* 184:14–15.
36. Kevin Preister. 1996. Community assessment. *Community Ecology, A Newsletter of the Rogue Institute for Ecology and Economy* 2:1, 5.
37. The following discussion is based in part on the Advanced Communication and Leadership Program of Toastmasters International. 1978. Public Relations. Toastmasters International, Mission Viejo, CA.
38. The following discussion on communicating with children is based on an article by Patricia L. Fry. 1997. Speaking to kids. *The Toastmaster* 63(5): 24–27.
39. Chris Maser, Russ Beaton, and Kevin Smith. 1998. *Setting the Stage for Sustainability: A Citizen's Handbook.* Lewis Publishers, Boca Raton, FL.
40. The following story about Ray Anderson is from a piece written by Donella Meadows. 1997. Managing for life. *YES! A Journal of Positive Futures* Spring:44–45.
41. Daniel J. Boorstin. 1983. *The Discoverers: A History of Man's Search to Know His World and Himself.* Vintage Books, New York.
42. Lewis Carroll. 1933. *Alice's Adventures in Wonderland.* Doubleday, Doran, & Co., New York.
43. *The World Book Encyclopedia.* 1985. World Book, Inc., Chicago.
44. Coldstream, Scotland. 1996. Stone of Scone returned. *Corvallis Gazette-Times* (Corvallis, OR) November 16.
45. The following discussion of coho salmon is based on an article by Scott Stouder. 1997. Coho need more than volunteers. *Corvallis Gazette-Times* (Corvallis, OR) March 27 and an article by Scott Sonner. 1997. Salmon get biggest day in court yet. *Corvallis Gazette-Times* (Corvallis, OR) March 31.
46. Carl D. Holcombe. 1997. 1996 rainfall crushes old record. *Corvallis Gazette-Times* (Corvallis, OR) January 1.
47. The Associated Press. 1997. Wheat variety offers hope of good yields in dry conditions. *Corvallis Gazette-Times* (Corvallis, OR) January 2.
48. The discussion about California is based on the following articles: John Howard. 1997. Crews struggle to save California levees. *Corvallis Gazette-Times* (Corvallis, OR) January 7; Matthew Yi. 1997. Brimming reservoirs

keep California flood threats alive. *Corvallis Gazette-Times* (Corvallis, OR) January 10; John Howard. 1997. Receding floodwaters reveal fields of dead cows, horses. *Corvallis Gazette-Times* (Corvallis, OR) January 10; The Associated Press. 1997. Levy failure causes new floods in California. *Corvallis Gazette-Times* (Corvallis, OR) January 11; Scott Faber. 1997. Get people off of nation's floodplains. *Corvallis Gazette-Times* (Corvallis, OR) January 21.

49. Steven C. Ames (Ed.). 1993. *A Guide to Community Visioning: Hands-on Information for Local Communities.* Oregon Visions Project, Oregon Chapter, American Planning Association, 35 pp; *FUTURE FOCUS 2010: A Vision Statement about Corvallis* [Oregon]. 1989. Corvallis Planning Division, City of Corvallis, 8 pp.

50. Roberta Ulrich. 1991. Growth fuels coastal-protection laws. *The Oregonian* (Portland, OR) June 16.

51. Daniel B. Wood. 1991. Report details decline of Hawaiian paradise. *The Oregonian* (Portland, OR) November 7, 1991.

52. Tracy Loew. 1997. Survey: housing is the county's no. 1 problem. *Corvallis Gazette-Times* (Corvallis, OR) January 10.

53. Aaron Corvin. 1997. West Hills plan worries neighbors. *Corvallis Gazette-Times* (Corvallis, OR) February 18.

54. Edward Donnally. 1997. Public should get say if plans change after land is annexed. *Corvallis Gazette-Times* (Corvallis, OR) March 2.

55. Ed Klophenstein. 1996. New land-use law may limit public comment. *Corvallis Gazette-Times* (Corvallis, OR) March 26.

56. Landon Hall. 1997. Builders battle to add land. *Corvallis Gazette-Times* (Corvallis, OR) February 22.

57. Larry Williams. 1997. Report: suburbs eating up prime U.S. farmland. *Corvallis Gazette-Times* (Corvallis, OR) March 23.

58. George Monbiot. 1997. Land reform in Britain. *Resurgence* 181:4–8.

59. Rebecca Adamson. 1997. People who are indigenous to the Earth. *YES! A Journal of Positive Futures* Winter:26–27.

60. W.H. Moir and W.M. Block. in press. *Why Adaptive Management Fails.*

61. Garrett Hardin. 1986. *Filters Against Folly: How to Survive Despite Economists, Ecologists, and the Merely Eloquent.* Penguin Books, New York.

62. Aaron Corvin. 1997. N. Corvallis development goes to council. *Corvallis Gazette-Times* (Corvallis, OR) January 16.

63. The New Zealand Values Party Manifesto. 1975. Wellington, New Zealand.

64. I have, with gratitude, drawn freely throughout the rest of this section from the excellent book by Gerald Corey. 1986. *Theory and Practice of Counseling and Psychotherapy* (3rd ed.). Brooks/Cole, Monterey, CA.

65. Thomas Fleming. 1997. General Washington's journey to freedom. *Guideposts* July:24–27.

66. Leonard Pitts, Jr. 1997. Few public figures show real remorse. *Corvallis Gazette-Times* (Corvallis, OR) November 23.

67. This discussion is based on the following: Nesha Starcevic. 1997. Serbian protests bring unexpected return of civility. *Corvallis Gazette-Times* (Corvallis, OR) February 10; *Chicago Tribune*. February 5, 1997. *Corvallis Gazette-Times* (Corvallis, OR) February 11; Julijana Mojsilovic. 1997. Victory doesn't stop Belgrade protests. *Corvallis Gazette-Times* (Corvallis, OR) February 13.

68. The discussion of the balance between the masculine and feminine characteristics in a leader is drawn in part from Susan St. John. 1997. Making the emotional connection. *The Toastmaster* 63(8):16–18.

69. Elizabeth Sherrill. 1997. Meeting Mr. Truman. *Guideposts* February:7.

70. The discussion in this section is based in part on Victor M. Parachin. 1997. Mastering your universe—five simple steps for success. *The Toastmaster* 63(1):8–10.

71. Richard G. Ensman, Jr. 1997. How to be a great follower. *The Toastmaster* 63(7):19.

72. Frances Moore Lappé and Paul Du Bois. 1997. A place for democracy. *YES! A Journal of Positive Futures* Winter:37–38.

73. The discussion in this section is based on Judith E. Pearson. 1997. Dare to delegate. *The Toastmaster* 63(7):8–11.

74. The discussion in this section is based on Jean Marsh. 1997. Keep your eyes & ears open and your pen ready! *The Toastmaster* 63(1):20–21.

75. *The Holy Bible, Authorized King James Version,* World Bible Publishers, Iowa Falls, IA, Leviticus 16:21–22.

76. John F. Kennedy. 1961. *Profiles in Courage.* Harper & Row, New York.

77. White Eagle. 1988. *Spiritual Unfoldment 4: The Path to the Light.* The White Eagle Publishing Trust, New Lands, England.

78. The following discussion about expanding one's limitations is based on Fred Pryor. 1997. Do you have an appetite for input? *The Toastmaster* 63(2):11; Richard G. Ensman, Jr. 1997. Become your own mentor. *The Toastmaster* 63(2):14–15.

79. The discussion in this section is based on Luann Lee Brown. 1997. Coping with a disliked member. *The Toastmaster* 63(1):6–7.

80. Chris Maser. 1996. *Resolving Environmental Conflict: Towards Sustainable Community Development.* St. Lucie Press, Boca Raton, FL.

81. The discussion in this section is based in part on Wade Chabassol. 1996. Inspiring officer performance. *The Toastmaster* 62(8):13–14.

82. This section is based on an article by Bernard Glassman. 1997. The sacred act of cooking. *Delicious!* November:32–34.

83. The discussion of the "shadow" is based largely on the book by Robert A. Johnson. 1991. *Owning Your Own Shadow.* Harper, San Francisco, 118 pp.

84. Dirk Johnson. 1997. Civility in politics: going, going, gone. *The New York Times* December 10.